The Snake Dance of
Asian American Activism

The Snake Dance of Asian American Activism

Community, Vision, and Power

Michael Liu, Kim Geron, and Tracy Lai

LEXINGTON BOOKS

A division of
ROWMAN & LITTLEFIELD PUBLISHERS, INC.
Lanham • Boulder • New York • Toronto • Plymouth, UK

LEXINGTON BOOKS

A division of Rowman & Littlefield Publishers, Inc.
A wholly owned subsidary of The Rowman & Littlefield Publishing Group, Inc.
4501 Forbes Boulevard, Suite 200
Lanham, MD 20706

Estover Road
Plymouth PL6 7PY
United Kingdom

British Library Cataloguing in Publication Information Available

Library of Congress Cataloging-in-Publication Data

Liu, Michael, 1948–
  The snake dance of Asian American activism : community, vision, and power in the
struggle for social justice, 1945–2000 / Michael Liu, Kim Geron, and Tracy Lai.
    p. cm.
  Includes bibliographical references and index.
  ISBN-13: 978-0-7391-2719-3 (cloth: alk. paper)
  ISBN-10: 0-7391-2719-5 (cloth: alk. paper)
  ISBN-13: 978-0-7391-2720-9 (pbk.: alk. paper)
  ISBN-10: 0-7391-2720-9 (pbk.: alk. paper)
  eISBN-13: 978-0-7391-3019-3
  eISBN-10: 0-7391-3019-6
  1. Asian Americans—Politics and government—20th century. 2. Asian Americans—
Social conditions—20th century. 3. Political activists—United States—History—20th
century. 4. Civil rights movements—United States—History—20th century. 5. Social
movements—United States—History—20th century. 6. Community life—United
States—History—20th century. 7. Social justice—United States—History—20th
century. 8. Power (Social sciences)—United States—History—20th century. 9. United
States—Race relations—History—20th century. 10. United States—Social conditions—
20th century. I. Geron, Kim, 1951– II. Lai, Tracy, 1951– III. Title.
  E184.A75L58 2008
  305.895'0730904—dc22

2008024245

Printed in the United States of America

∞™ The paper used in this publication meets the minimum requirements of American
National Standard for Information Sciences—Permanence of Paper for Printed Library
Materials, ANSI/NISO Z39.48–1992.

This book is dedicated to . . .

Andrew Ngon Sim and Louise Ching Woon Liu and to my heartbeats, May Louie and Mark Liu.

Stan, our activism together define(d/s) our lives, and to Misa and Kiyoshi, may our book shed light on the journey forward. None of this would be possible without the support and encouragement from my parents, William and Ruby.

My parents, Al and Kiyo; my family—Elizabeth, Viviana and Isaac, Armando, Danny, Tomio, and Mark Anthony, thank you for all your patience and understanding; my many colleagues, friends, and comrades, thank you individually and collectively for your keen insights and contributions to this project.

Contents

Acknowledgments

Completing our book always seemed just around the next bend, but like a snake dance, once we reached it, there was always another turn. And like the pioneers who came before us, venturing to imagined, embellished places, if we'd known more about the journey, we might have been too intimidated to embark on it. What has sustained us through these seven years is that those who lived or heard about the Movement wanted to see its story told. All the tea poured in Chinatown, *Nihonmachi* and other "Asiatown" small family restaurants couldn't wash away that responsibility to describe what had crossed over such tables for the past decades.

What was a collective enterprise was buoyed and realized by collective contributions. The three of us started the journey but could not have finished it without the help of many others.

May Louie, Francis Wong, and Eddie Wong contributed and shared insights into areas of the Movement where we were blind, particularly around art and culture and electoral politics. Ken Yamada's dedication in maintaining an archive of images and eye for visualizing the necessary images made illustration of the periods possible. With the Movement's thousands of artifacts scattered in haphazard places, we couldn't do without community archivists like Richard Siu, whose diligence and organization in preserving slices of this history provided primary sources of Movement activity and life.

We also want to thank the generosity of members of the Nikkei for Civil Rights and Redress, particularly Kathy and Mark Masaoka, for facilitating trips to the Los Angeles area, one of the vital centers of the AAM but one that was far from home. Likewise Jean and Lyle Wing and Sadie and Irwin Lum provided insight and support in the Bay Area

We also want to thank our interviewees, young and old, who, as activists, took time from issues and personal responsibilities to share core parts of their lives with us, even if we were strangers or casual acquaintances knocking at their doors.

Finally, each of us owes a debt to our families and Michael Liu particularly owes the Institute for Asian American Studies, which provided moral and institutional support, for an effort that undoubtedly tried their patience.

Acronyms

AAA	Asian Americans for Action
AAFEE	Asian Americans for Equal Employment (later AAFE: Asian Americans for Equality)
AAM	Asian American Movement
AAPA	Asian American Political Alliance
AARW	Asian American Resource Workshop
ACJ	American Citizens for Justice
ACWA	Alaskan Cannery Workers' Association
AIWA	Asian Immigrant Workers Association
APA	Asian Pacific American
APALA	Asian Pacific American Labor Alliance
API	Asian Pacific Islanders
APSU	Asian Pacific Student Union
ASU	Asian Student Union
BAACAW	Bay Area Asian Coalition Against the War
BLM	Black Liberation or Black Power Movement
CAAAV	Committee Against Anti-Asian Violence (later CAAAV: Organizing Asian Communities)
CCBA	Chinese Consolidated Benevolent Association
CDC	Community Development Corporation
CPA	Chinese Progressive Association
CPUSA	Communist Party, United States of America
CSWA	Chinese Staff and Workers' Association
CWMAA	Chinese Workers' Mutual Aid Association
CWRIC	Commission on Wartime Relocation and Internment of Civilians

ECASU	East Coast Asian Student Union
FFP	Friends of the Filipino People
HERE	Hotel Employees and Restaurant Employees Union
ID	International District (Seattle)
ILGWU	International Ladies' Garment Workers' Union
ILWU	International Longshoremen's and Warehousemen's Union
IWK	I Wor Kuen
JACL	Japanese American Citizens League
JACS-AI	Japanese American Community Service – Asian Involvement
JFC	Japan Food Corporation
KDP	Katipunan ng mga Demokratikong Pilipino (Union of Democratic Filipinos)
LRS	League of Revolutionary Struggle
LTPRO	Little Tokyo People's Rights Organization
NAACP	National Association for the Advancement of Colored People
NCRR	National Coalition for Redress and Reparations (later Nikkei for Civil Rights and Redress)
PKO	Protect Kaho'olawe Ohana
SAYA!	South Asian Youth Action
SIPA	Search to Involve Pilipino Americans
UC	University of California
UCLA	University of California–Los Angeles
UFW	United Farm Workers
WTO	World Trade Organization
YKU	Young Koreans United

Introduction

On a hazy, sunny June afternoon in 1974, immediately following the close of the Boston Public Schools' academic year, Federal District Court Justice Arthur Garrity passed down a judgment for the plaintiff in Morgan v. Hennigan,[1] ordering mandatory busing as a remedy for segregation in the city's school system. In this prelude to decades of violent tumult, the Court created plans to bus Black students to overwhelmingly white schools and White students to facilities with primarily Black enrollment. As the local leadership prepared a permanent plan for school busing, those whom the ruling and local judicial, educational, and political institutions overlooked were the system's many Latino and Asian American students. While the Boston Public Schools hired bus monitors to shield buses full of Black children rolling off to face mobs of stone-throwing residents in White neighborhoods (and buses empty of white students that arrived at Black schools), no one had thought about what to do with Asian American, primarily Chinese, and Latino, students. Schools where Chinese students were bused had neither Chinese teachers nor aides on staff nor representation on parents' councils nor the ability to communicate with the students or their parents.

In response, Asian American Movement activists, led by Suzanne Lee, one of the few Chinese American teachers in the Boston public school system, organized Chinese parents into an association. Defying warnings and hostility from the community's traditional leadership, the parents called for protest politics to call attention to their issues. They announced that "The Boston Chinese Parents Association today unanimously agreed to boycott the opening days of school. . . . Chinese parents are united in boycotting all schools because we felt that school and court officials, by not taking concrete actions on our demands, have demonstrated an overall disregard for the rights of all

Chinese parents and students. It must be realized that we boycott in order to affirm the right of all minorities to equal quality education." Through knocking on neighborhood doors, word of mouth, and patrolling the bus stops, garment workers and activists organized a boycott that was 90 percent effective, despite Federal Department of Justice pressure. They would successfully organize and hold their boycott of the schools for three days until the decision-makers agreed to eight of the parents' nine demands. Those demands included provisions for the safety of Asian American children, better communication with the parents, and the hiring of more Chinese bus monitors and staff.[2]

We highlight this signal campaign as an example of "excluded history," an absence that animated the writing of this text. Our notion of excluded history applies on two levels. On one level, it is a history of those excluded from the consideration of social institutions, as Asian American communities have often been. Except in notable antagonistic episodes, public policy and social sciences typically overlooked their interests, voices, and concerns. The definitive recounting of the Boston busing crisis, Anthony Lukas's otherwise meticulously researched book *Common Ground*, did not acknowledge the presence of Asian American families in the system, not to speak of their successful boycott in the busing drama.

Extending our inquiry to the Asian American community itself, we see another level of excluded history. In Asian Americans' own contemporary narratives of the development of our communities, how Asian American activism for social justice shaped them is another instance of excluded history. As academics who actively participated in the Asian American Movement's (AAM) passage and continue to work in its values, we have long been struck by the dissonance between our experience in and conclusions about Asian American activism and the narrative within the canon of Asian American studies. From our differing geographies and experiences, we wanted to treat that activism with the seriousness that stirred and shaped it. It has been too easy to simply conclude, as one noted Asian Americanist has, that the AAM bifurcated into radicals and reformers and that only the reformers left anything of lasting value—community agencies.[3] In contrast to this view, having had multiple perspectives from being participant observers and then having been some steps and time removed, we can perceive the myriad ways that the process of activism beginning in the late 1960s mediated frameworks of thought, methods of work, institutions, alliances, rights and privileges, and yes, identities of Asian Americans today.

The Chinese Parents Association's activism in Boston, in challenging the traditional leadership, led to an eventual decentralization of power in the local Chinese enclave and a reevaluation of Asian Americans by urban elites. Similar strains of resistance and collective effort, this text argues, influenced many aspects of contemporary Asian American political and community life. Asian American agency—activism and organizing—helped bring about, among other effects, greater community democracy, academic recognition of Asian Americans, participation in the larger society, alliances with "communities of color," legitimization of working class and enclave redevelopment issues, a pan-Asian identity, and an Asian American aesthetic.

We reinterpret a period of the Asian American experience, the Asian American Movement, as an effort that persisted until the late 1980s. We trace the history of the AAM from its roots in the 1930s and ground the Asian American communities' contemporary activism in that legacy, while distinguishing its unique characteristics. We direct this alternative narrative primarily to the many students grappling with the development of the modern Asian American communities as well as to Asian American scholars who, we hope, will give serious thought to our argument to recast the role of the AAM. We also direct this to past and contemporary Asian American activists in the community to encourage them to reenvison their work in a lengthier and broader context.

The main aspects of our argument are:

1. The Asian American Movement's length, breadth, and effects were of a significantly greater magnitude than generally understood. During its tenure, it spanned a diversity of political viewpoints and reached into most aspects of community life. The AAM became increasingly sophisticated and effective even after the height of mass protests in the mid-seventies. As the political environment became more difficult after 1975, Asian Americans, we argue, continued to be active in and provide leadership to significant social movements. Asian Americans played unique roles in neighborhood redevelopment, labor, campus, and civil rights struggles. In the ensuing period until 1990, they helped to build the anti-nuclear power movement, the Asian American labor movement, the Jesse Jackson presidential campaigns, democracy in Asian countries, and credible pan-Asian organizations. Asian American activists also helped lead the struggle to win redress and reparations for Japanese Americans in the 1980s. The AAM was the vehicle that brought the Asian American communities into the mainstream of civic life by demanding access, equity, and equality in all facets of society. The participants in the Asian American Movement became community leaders who provided a new type of leadership that gained access to institutional power, achieved selective reforms, altered perceptions about Asian Americans and won significant positions in government. Along with the post-1965 immigration, the AAM was the other

most influential current that shaped the contemporary Asian American communities.

2. The AAM was grounded in a vision for structural change and was not primarily an assertion for identity. From its inception, both the reform and revolutionary poles of the AAM saw a need to restructure society to serve universalistic principles of peace, social justice, and equality to Asians in America. Politically, the AAM challenged the U.S. social and power structure. Where a need for services and programs existed, it was fought for and extracted from institutions or established through voluntarily provided "serve the people" type projects. Building upon the institutional funding, non-profit agencies, which members of the AAM helped develop, grew into community institutions and a new community infrastructure. The AAM was also a search for an alternative social system to improve the lives of Asian Americans. This striving contributed to the creation of new alliances, social forces, and social norms in the United States. The AAM's structural grounding does not negate the importance of the quest for identity. Part of the strengthening of the AAM was reimagining itself in a pan-Asian context and as part of a cross-race struggle to throw off a history of oppression. However, a new identity was never the primary goal.

3. A social movement lens better assesses the AAM's significance and analyzes its development than do current narratives. Social movement theory is used widely to analyze various groups' efforts to mobilize people to pursue a common cause. We argue that the AAM constituted a distinct, identifiable, and relatively stable social movement that organized for social change and dramatically impacted the direction of Asian American politics and political actors. By examining the factors of grievances, resources, framing, methods of contention, and political opportunities, we can better explain the AAM's rapid rise and growth and the causes for its ultimate ebb. This lens also situates it in the continuum of resistance in the Asian American communities' development. The AAM followed collective actions for labor rights in fields and factories, efforts to end discrimination through the legal system, and support for homeland issues. A social movement lens also allows a preliminary evaluation of what the AAM contributes to future struggles around its uncompleted agenda and those universalistic principles that inspired the AAM. Part of the AAM's legacy is its role in informing new activists and new forms of organizing in a more transnational and informational-based world. This text looks at the political economic context and changing community dynamics that led to the Movement's growth. It situates the AAM's emergence as part of a general transition from traditional immigrant leadership to native-born and newer community activism

and from a more homogenous Asian American working class community to a rapidly evolving, ethnically and class diverse population.

As scholars and teachers, using the lens of social movement theory, we wanted to provide a more comprehensive and coherent interpretation of the AAM's rise and ebb, something we felt was sorely absent. One issue that we faced was getting our arms around the diverse scope, components, and geographies of the Movement. Despite the difficulty of multiple authors coalescing on one coherent interpretation, there were important reasons to collaborate. They included, most critically, a capacity to develop a more inclusive narrative and capture the social range of the AAM. While coming from both the West and East Coasts presented opportunities to represent various viewpoints, we acknowledge that, in a Movement as diverse and far-flung as the AAM was, we may not have fully captured the intergenerational experiences of Asian American community activists. Due to space and time limitations, many struggles could not be included. This text focuses on the developments in the labor, student, women's rights, community, grassroots electoral, and art and culture areas. A lot of travel, conversations, and interviews were necessary to satisfactorily characterize the AAM's work even in this limited set of areas. Even so, we solicited contributions from those more fluent than we in the AAM's electoral and art and cultural work. We thank May Louie, Frances Wong, and Eddie Wong for their work in these areas. For those areas not acknowledged in this text, we hope that it will be evident how they can be placed within our geographic, social, and political timeline. For the many who contributed to this fledging and then persistent movement, we hope that this text testifies to their work and sacrifices so that they would be acknowledged within the collective memory of the Asian American community and the wider society.

We also wanted this manuscript to be useful for the many who are today addressing the continuing but evolving issues of peace, justice, equality, and a more progressive society. We decided to address the AAM's connection to the present state of the community and features of current activism by bringing the text's scope up to the present day, particularly given the changes in antihegemonic organizing after the Seattle World Trade Organization protests and the 9/11 terror attacks. Being of particular older generations, we faced the challenge of reflecting the different world and frames of reference of contemporary activists. To be useful we needed to accurately reflect their voices. Many interviews with current activists partially addressed this issue. We have also closely followed and documented the activities and viewpoints of their associated activism for a number of years. Finally, our perspectives have also been informed by a number of collective efforts to analyze activism and conditions to serve particular areas of work such as community and labor organizing.

The text proceeds from a fresh look at primary sources, interviews with participants, and the existing literature on the subject. For the first time, social movement theory is used to fully explore the rise, decline, and aftermath of the Asian American Movement and document the long march of activism and grassroots organizing efforts that culminated in 1990. We also explore some underexamined areas of activism such as Asian American student organizing that peaked in the 1980s decade and, particularly, Asian American labor, an area of immense activity by the community but largely ignored in recounting of the recent Asian American experience.

We hope scholars in social movement theory, ethnic studies, political science, and sociology will find this work of interest. Participants in AAM, from the 1960s to the present, will want to examine how accurately the book captures their experiences. Many younger activists are also looking to the history of Asian American grassroots activism to better understand what role the AAM has played in shaping the contemporary state of Asian Pacific Islanders (APIs) in the United States.[4] They want to understand the meaning and content of an API identity and why a movement based on racial and ethnic identity is still needed in the twenty-first century. This book explores the answers to these and other questions.

DESIGN OF THE BOOK

Organized into eight chapters, this book moves chronologically through AAM mobilization in diverse areas. It follows the AAM's roots in the pre-1960s decades, its rise in the seventies, increasing complexity and sophistication in the eighties, ebb in the nineties, and influence in the present. Each chapter describes and analyzes the conditions, changes, and activities of Asian American activists during a defined period. Because of the many converging influences operating in any given time, we included narratives of important campaigns that capture the character of the activism in each of those periods.

In chapter 1, we explore social movement theory and its application to the Asian American Movement. Chapter 2 reviews the community in the era before the AAM and its barriers and contributions to formation of a social movement. Chapters 3 and 4 explore the 1968 to 1975 period, the conditions and influences that nurtured the creation of a new movement, and the AAM's vision and work to create new methods of mobilization, a new community infrastructure, and a unique identity for Asian Americans. Chapter 5 analyzes the period between 1976 and 1982 when the AAM, facing more challenging conditions, developed and became a more organized, sophisticated movement. This is a period where activism has been often discounted but where, we argue, activism continued to grow in influence. In chapter 6, we assess the period between 1983 and 1990. Within an increasingly difficult environment, AAM activists carried out some of the most complex work at a nationwide level, including a shift toward electoral work. Chapter 7 examines the effects of the end of the AAM, the localization of focus, and how Asian American activism has evolved with growing diversity and a new globalized, connected world. We end with a short conclusion.

NOTES

1. Morgan v. Hennigan, 379 F. Supp. 410 (1974 U.S. Dist.).

2. *Pacific/Asian American Coalition—New England* 1:5 (October 1975), Pacific/Asian American Coalition—New England, Boston (please see bibliographic citation under Asian American Resource Workshop); *Sampan* (Boston), September 1975, 1–4; Suzanne Lee, conversation with Michael Liu, Brookline, MA, 10 May 2006.

3. Sucheng Chan, *Asian Americans: An Interpretive History* (New York: Twayne Publishers 1991), 174–75.

4. We have attempted to use the prevalent contemporary terms for the relevant population. Thus, the Asian American Movement and community, when the term originated, intended to include the Asian and Hawai'ian population. Today, Asian Pacific Islander or Asian Pacific Americans is more typically used and includes other Pacific Islander populations. We're aware of the problems in using or applying any of these terms, but have adopted these conventions for convenience.

Chapter One

Exploring the Asian American Movement Using Social Movement Theory

The contemporary Asian American Movement (AAM) began nearly simultaneously in numerous campuses and communities across the country. Galvanized by issues that directly affected them, young Chinese, Japanese, Korean, and Filipino Americans took collective action as part of pan-Asian efforts to achieve their goals of building Asian American studies programs on college campuses, establishing badly needed social services in their communities, and ending an unjust war in Vietnam. The efforts of Asian American students were part of a broad movement of students of color to construct programs of study relevant to their needs. During the formation of the Asian American Movement in the late 1960s, many Asians were already involved in campaigns and struggles in their communities and workplaces and around national and international issues. However, these efforts involved small numbers working individually or as ethnic groupings acting as part of larger societal mass movements. As the idea of building Asian American unity was popularized on college campuses, many community youth and students soon spread the idea of building a movement of Asian Americans in their own urban and rural neighborhoods.[1]

The new generation of Asian Americans became active in support of the emerging Black, Brown, and Red power movements in this country, unionization drives of Mexican and Filipino farm workers, opposition to the Vietnam War, support of Native American land struggles, and efforts to address long neglected inequalities and poverty rampant in Asian ethnic enclaves. Through the organizing and mobilizing efforts of community and labor activists and the post–World War II generation of Asian Americans, a new social movement was forged in the United States—the Asian American Movement.

1

This chapter will present first a definition of a social movement; second, a brief review of how other scholars have viewed the AAM; third, an exploration of social movement theory and the theoretical approaches to movement formation and growth; and fourth, a description of some of the unique factors that influenced the emergence of the AAM. A large body of scholarship known as social movement theory informs this study. To interpret collective experiences and determine whether they represent more than individual acts of defiance and rise to the level of a social movement, it is necessary to apply theory to analyze group experiences and behavior. The framework of social movement theory is used to analyze the grass roots efforts to construct an Asian American Movement.

WHAT IS A SOCIAL MOVEMENT?

Since the late 1960s, the organized activities of thousands of Asian Americans were self-identified and labeled as the Asian American Movement. What is a social movement? Among the many definitions that of Mary Darnovsky, Barbara Epstein, and Richard Flacks[2] seems clearest. "Social movements are collective efforts by socially and politically subordinated people to challenge the conditions and assumptions of their lives. These efforts are a distinctive sort of social activity: collective action becomes a movement when participants refuse to accept the boundaries of established institutional rules and routinized roles. Single instances of such popular defiance don't make a movement; the term refers to persistent, patterned, and widely distributed collective challenges to the status quo."

THE LITERATURE ON THE ASIAN AMERICAN MOVEMENT

Scholars of 1960s and 1970s activism have ignored the contributions and actions of the AAM.[3] But with the 1989 publication of a special edition of *Amerasia Journal* that commemorated the birth of the Asian American Movement on the twentieth anniversary of the San Francisco State University strike for ethnic studies, the AAM was acknowledged as a distinct area of research. Asian American scholars and activists have used a variety of approaches to explore the Asian American Movement experience. Most contemporary scholars view the AAM as a quest for identity. William Wei conducted an extensive study and labeled the AAM a social movement. His work, however, lacked a discussion of social movement theory and did not develop the argument of how the AAM constituted a movement. Wei emphasized rather the social history of the movement and "the evaluation of the Movement's effort to develop a unique but cohesive ethnic identity."[4]

Similarly, Yen Li Espiritu discussed how diverse national origin groups came together to create a new, enlarged pan-ethnic grouping. The formation of a pan-Asian ethnicity by the children of immigrants was a strategy to unite Asians. As Espiritu noted, "Although broader social struggles and internal demographic changes provided the impetus of the Asian American movement, it was the group's politics—confrontational and explicitly pan-Asian—that shaped the movement's content."[5] Espiritu's thesis was that the main thrust of the AAM was identity formation, but other constituencies appropriated and transformed the concept: "Although originally conceived by young Asian American activists, the pan-Asian concept was subsequently institutionalized by professionals and community groups."[6]

Espiritu's concept of constructed identity was based on the theory of racial formation by Michael Omi and Howard Winant, who argued that race is not fixed. Rather it is "an unstable and 'decentered' complex of social meanings constantly being transformed by political struggle."[7] Their notion is that race is socially constructed and can be transformed into different racial meanings based on government actions and social consciousness. While Omi and Winant did not specifically analyze the AAM, they did address the racial minority movements of the 1960s. The focus of their research didn't fully address how social movements are constructed and the organizational forms they take, issues integral to the establishment and maintenance of the Asian American Movement. They were concerned with the construction of racial identity. In their view, the movement of racial minorities splintered in the late 1960s into different tendencies of mainstream electoral politics, socialism, and nationalism: "By the late 1960s, the fragmentation within the racial minority movements was clearly visible and consolidated into discernible currents. New social movement politics had galvanized activists in their respective community, but the lack of theoretical clarity about racial dynamics splintered political action."[8]

Sucheng Chan briefly explored the AAM in the broad context of an interpretive history of Asian Americans. In general, she viewed young Asian American activists as a group of people disconnected from their ethnic communities. In an assessment that is similar to Wei's dichotomization of the movement into revolutionaries and reformers, Chan divided the AAM into two kinds of political activists—radicals and reformers. The radicals' efforts had little effect, according to Chan; however, the reformers created community agencies that still remain.[9]

This analysis unfortunately surveyed only the treetops and not the dramatic social and cultural changes that a nationwide upsurge of AAM activists brought to the surface. Moreover, AAM activists were not so neatly divided. Many activists worked together to bring badly needed services to Chinatowns and other ethnic enclaves. Some activists chose to focus on building community institutions while others moved on to build new forms of organizing including art and cultural, grassroots community, and overtly political groups. Others formed anti-imperialist organizations that combined disseminating political analysis with essential services to establish contact with their communities. Some who began with a more limited understanding of society and social change decided to become revolutionaries; others who gravitated toward working with revolutionaries later chose to focus on more immediate issues and problems. While debates swirled around the best path to address the problems confronting Asian Americans, these were fluid and evolved into differing trends over time. This early history of the AAM will be explored more carefully in chapters 3 and 4.

Activist scholar Glenn Omatsu moved beyond ethnic awakening and identity formation and reminded us that the Asian American Movement included the idea that Asian Americans should become active participants in the making of history: "Activists saw history as created by large numbers of people, not by elites," and that political power grows from grassroots organizing, from the bottom up, not top down. "Further, this new understanding challenged activists to build mass, democratic organizations, especially within unorganized sectors of the community. Through these new organizations, Asian Americans expanded democracy for all sectors of the community."[10] Omatsu captured the visionary ideals that the AAM explored and more importantly the motivation of its participants "to serve the people" and to expand democracy and community consciousness. According to Omatsu, the AAM also confronted fundamental questions of "power and domination in U.S. society" and the world. He argued that the AAM was about how activists sought to build a movement among the least well off segments of the pan-Asian community, in solidarity with other oppressed peoples internationally, and through creating new leadership and organization and was not solely about identity politics.

More recently, Linda Trinh Võ studied the mobilization efforts of Asian Americans in San Diego over two decades and found that networks of single ethnic groups and pan-Asian organizations served as the vehicle to build broader pan-Asian unity. Asian American organizations survived and thrived in this city by engaging in a "politics of resistance and a politics of accommodation."[11] As an outgrowth of the Asian American Movement, she pointed to large numbers of Asian American activists involved in daily struggles working for social change in communities away from New York, Los Angeles, and San Francisco employing different strategies of resistance. Võ argued that Asian American identity, activism, and social change engines are constantly in flux and this multi-dimensional community has continually adapted to changing global and domestic, factors and conditions.

Other recent studies have also focused on specific aspects of the AAM. For example, Diane Fujino's in-depth study of Japanese American revolutionary activist Yuri Kochiyama captured the dynamic role Kochiyama played in establishing and giving credibility to the Asian American Movement and her role in educating a new generation of young Asian American activists about the legacy of the struggle for Black liberation and freedom in the United States. The pivotal role of community activists such as Kochiyama has been downplayed by some scholars who limit the discussion of the AAM to simply a generational identity change rather than a political struggle of multiple generations for power and institutional change in the United States.

Another important study of the AAM was conducted by Laura Pulido, who studied "Third World Left organizations" in Los Angeles in the 1960s and 1970s. For Asian Americans, she studied East Wind, the area's major Marxist oriented organization of Asian American activists of this period. This study explores the ideology of East Wind, the influence of Chinese communist leader Mao Tse-Tung on the thinking and actions of this revolutionary collective of primarily Japanese Americans, and its belief in building Third World solidarity. While focused on one Asian American organization, this study provides insights into the motivations and actions of Asian American revolutionaries and is useful in placing the AAM as part of the larger movement of U.S.–Third World organizations.

Estella Habal's *San Francisco's International Hotel* is a significant case study of a seminal focal point for the Filipino American and Asian American Movements, a local anti-eviction campaign (1968–2005) that redefined Filipino American consciousness. It illuminates the evolution of Asian American activism, specifically a new generation of Filipino youths who, through organizing with the I-Hotel tenants, discovered the links between impoverished *Manongs* (first generation Filipino sojourners) and U.S. imperialism in the Philippines and sharpened their understanding of class struggle, multiracial coalitions, and city politics. In mobilizing thousands of supporters to win low-income housing and a community center, Filipino youth activists built a community base that affirmed the strength and possibility of mass organizing.

In addition to the 1989 *Amerasia Journal* issue, there were other book-length studies of the AAM. In the 1970s, University of California–Los Angeles (UCLA) published two anthologies of AAM perspectives including historical pieces, contemporary analyses, and poetry.[12] Both are excellent portrayals of contemporary values and ideas in the Movement. Both included a variety of perspectives, which reflected the diversity of views in the AAM. Also, more recently, two new anthologies captured individual accounts by AAM activists. One focuses on a variety of Movement activists from different perspectives who discuss their experiences and roles in the Movement.[13] Another anthology focuses on radical and revolutionary movement building among Asians in the U.S.[14] Together these works and many other articles, newspapers, journals, and magazines offered a varied picture about the AAM.

SOCIAL MOVEMENT THEORY AND THE AAM

With this brief review of contemporary analyses of the AAM, the next section will explore how social movement theory offers an explanation for the rise of Asian American pan-ethnic consciousness, the incorporation of its constituencies, the development of new organizational formations, and the causes for its ebb. As others have noted, in the past, social movement theorists focused on a single theory such as resource mobilization to explain their research.[15] Given the complexities of explaining why movements emerge, what issues they articulate, how movement activists build organization, and who participates, it is necessary to explore different theoretical approaches and specific factors. This book explores different approaches in social movement theory that help explain the emergence and growth of the AAM, including political opportunities, mobilizing structures, and framing processes. The specific relevant factors include group grievances, collective identity and group identification, framing of issues, microstructural network recruitment, and indigenous resource mobilization.

This book avoids the unnecessary and what these authors feel is unwise dichotomization of structure and culture. In the 1980s and 1990s, many social movement theorists have embraced cultural explanations for the rise of new social movements. However, this view limits the connections with structural forces. Aldon D. Morris noted, "Human action cannot be reduced to social structures and impersonal social forces. . . . But neither are they simply detached cultural actors, given that they are also embedded within structural context that shape their actions and limit their options. To understand human action, therefore, attention has to center on the intersection of culture and structure."[16]

In communities of color with a long tradition of oppression and resistance, community resources and social activism take indigenous forms. It is the task of scholars that study collective group experiences to explore and unearth the particular methods of struggle that were employed during specific periods based on the structure of the situation. For example, Morris discusses the necessity for an "indigenous" approach to explore the African American Civil

Rights Movement. Morris argues that the emergence of a sustained movement within a particular dominated community depends on whether that community possesses: "1) certain basic resources; 2) social activists with strong ties to mass-based indigenous institutions, and 3) tactics and strategies that can be effectively employed against a system of domination."[17]

Morris identifies two types of resources that enable a dominated group to engage in sustained protest. Well developed internal social institutions and organizations provide the community with encompassing communication networks, organized groups, experienced leaders, and social resources, including money, labor, and charisma, can be mobilized to attain collective goals. At the beginning phases of a movement, indigenous resources are important, as external support is sporadic.

The presence of indigenous resources within a dominated community does not ensure that a movement will emerge. Rather activists deliberately organize and develop movements by seizing and creating opportunities for protest. Social activists play creative roles in movements; they must skillfully direct and transform indigenous resources in such a manner that they can be used to develop and sustain social protest, such as the role Black activists played on historically Black college campuses and within the Black church during the Civil Rights Movement. Finally, to crystallize into a protest movement, a dominated group must also develop tactics and strategies that can be effectively used to confront a system of domination.

When these three elements are present, then a movement center can be established. "A local movement center is a distinctive form of social organization specifically developed by members of a dominated group to produce, organize, coordinate, finance and sustain social protest."[18] San Francisco's International Hotel, ringed with community organization storefronts, was a local movement center for the Asian American Movement in the 1960s and 1970s.

POLITICAL OPPORTUNITIES, MOBILIZING STRUCTURES, AND FRAMING

Assuming that grievances exist and that a population has certain "indigenous" factors, to comparatively study the emergence and development of social movements, most scholars have focused on three key factors: (1) the structure or context of political opportunities available to the movement; (2) the forms of organization and recruitment or mobilizing structures; (3) shared meanings that people bring into the movement or the framing processes.[19] The first factor to consider in understanding the development of a social movement is the importance of the broader political system in structuring the opportunities for collective action. Movement scholars aim to explain the emergence of a particular social movement on the basis of changes in a given national system's institutional structure. Social movements are shaped by the broader set of political constraints and opportunities unique to the national context in which they are embedded.

The 1960s era of mass upheavals and new social movements took place in the context of what Sidney Tarrow calls "political opportunities"—the consistent, but not necessarily formal, permanent, or national dimensions of the political struggle that encourage people to engage in contentious politics. During such periods, there are cycles of contention, and if many of the early actions are successful, these types of activities spread to ordinary people. As Tarrow explains, "During such a period, the opportunities created by early risers provide incentives for new movement organizations."[20]

Tarrow identifies four dimensions of political opportunities: (1) the degree of openness of the political system to influence and participation by insurgent groups; (2) the stability or instability of political alignments, with instabilities associated with increased opportunities for insurgent groups; (3) the presence or absence of influential allies available to support policy demands of insurgents; (4) the presence or absence of political splits or conflicts within elites. During the late 1960s, political elites were sharply divided on most social issues confronting the country, and the political system was undergoing major instability. For example, the Democratic Party's liberal wing was pressured by mass upheavals to support many of the movements of the period, and they opposed continued U.S. involvement in the Vietnam War.

All four of these elements were present during this period of the late 1960s. The external dynamics of the opportunities available in the political system, coupled with the long pent-up frustration and existing underground organizing networks, enabled numerous new social movements to emerge, including the environmental, women's, gay and lesbian, and people of color movements. Unfortunately, most scholars of the period have ignored the significant organizing efforts of the Chicano, Native American, and Asian American Movements.[21]

If the political system shapes the prospects for collective action, then what forms will social movements take? The political opportunities available are not independent of the various kinds of mobilizing structures that groups seek to organize. Mobilizing structures are the collective vehicles, informal as well as formal, through which people mobilize and engage in collective action. The theory of the impact of mobilizing processes and organizations is known as resource mobilization theory. Resource mobilization focuses on these processes and their formal manifestations—the social movement organizations.[22]

In resource mobilization theory, ideological orientation and motivations were taken for granted; instead, the variability of resources, both internal and external to the movement, becomes the most important factor in explaining the emergence and development of insurgency. Resource mobilization theory examines the variety of both tangible and intangible resources available to facilitate the success of social movements. However, judging movement success or failure based on external support resources limits crucial exploration of the emergence of ideas, identities, and values that motivate many movement participants. The young AAM had virtually no outside economic or political support, unlike the more mature African American Civil Rights Movement that received large amounts of material resources from liberal Whites.

The second trend in the mobilizing structures literature revolves around those who focus on the critical role of various grassroots settings—work and neighborhood. Morris and Douglas McAdam[23] both analyzed the critical role played by local Black institutions, Black churches, and colleges, in the emergence of the Civil Rights Movement. The AAM also differed from the Civil Rights Movement because the AAM had only marginal community institutional support. Resources available to the AAM were limited to a few churches, social service organizations, and public universities.[24] The AAM's insinuation of new movement structures onto the campuses and into the communities combined to facilitate and structure oppositional meanings and cultural expression. Without them, the AAM would have been unable to sustain itself and grow.

While the combination of political opportunities and mobilizing structures affords groups a certain structural potential for action, they still are insufficient to account for collective action. Mediating among opportunity, organization, and action are the shared meanings and definitions that people bring to their situations. At a minimum level, people need to feel aggrieved about some basic aspect of their lives and optimistic that by acting collectively they can redress the problem. Conditioning the presence or absence of these perspectives is social psychological dynamics—collective attribution and social construction known as the framing process. Steven M. Buechler states that "Framing means focusing attention on some bounded phenomenon by imparting meaning and significance to elements within the frame and setting them apart from what is outside the frame. In the context of social movements, framing refers to the interactive, collective ways movement actors assign meanings to their activities in the conduct of social movement activism."[25]

While the activation of framing is important, movements must also engage in additional frame alignments to increase their recruitment efforts. This frame alignment is the linking of individuals and social movement organizations to draw upon deeply held beliefs and attach those values and beliefs to movement issues. In this process, someone's preexisting values provide the fuel to recruit them into the movement. This third factor addresses the relationship of ideas and sentiments with frame transformation that leads to collective action. Movement entrepreneurs orient their movements' frames toward action in particular contexts. They must compete with mainstream media and the dominant culture's manipulation of framing for cultural supremacy. The ability of movement leadership to frame an issue as an injustice against a group of people and convey the importance and legitimacy of the movement spurs individuals into action.[26]

The AAM grew rapidly because its message that Asian Americans were victims of institutional racism challenged the media-hyped "model minority" myth that pitted Asian Americans against other people of color and resonated with young Asian Americans' experiences. Asian Americans, particularly young people who identified strongly with other oppressed groups and some veteran community activists opposed the model minority myth's divisive effects among America's minority groups. Yuri Kochiyama, a New York City community activist who worked closely with the Black Liberation Movement, worked tirelessly to link the struggles of Asians with Blacks and other oppressed groups.[27] Kochiyama, with other veteran community activists in New York City, Kazu Iijima and Minn Matsuda, were able to draw attention to the racial nature of the Vietnam conflict and how the Vietnamese people were portrayed in a negatively racist light.[28] This aroused strong emotions among many Asian Americans who viewed themselves as part of Asian peoples' liberation struggles.[29] Asian American women activists were also conscious of highlighting the leading roles played by Vietnamese women revolutionaries, inspiring many young Asian American women to become involved in activism in this country.[30]

SUMMARY

Much of the existing scholarship has dismissed the AAM as a phenomenon of a unique period of rebelliousness by young Americans. This view fails to capture the deep-rooted social forces that gave rise to the AAM and what was new, inventive, and authentic in its social construction. This book is an effort to capture the collective experiences of a social movement that constructed new identities, institutions, leadership, and forms of cultural expression. It scratches the surface of a generally neglected aspect of Asian Americans—the grassroots organizing efforts of community activists, students, and workers to build a sense of community and solidarity with others, seemingly different in class status, ethnicity, and gender, yet still sharing "a bright spirit of intercultural experience, of resistance, and of proud survival."[31]

While many have approached the AAM as primarily collective identity formation, we argue that it is more fruitful and revealing to analyze the AAM as a social movement with a strong group identification. Proceeding from the perspective of social conditions, social forces, and ideas that brought it to life, this text will examine its strengths and weaknesses, effects, and trajectory. Social movement theory will also allow us to look at what was "indigenous" to the AAM that distinguished this social movement from parallel social movements of the time and contextualize the construction of the Asian American identity, placing questions about identity into a larger discussion of the structural, political, and cultural dynamics that surround the Asian American experience.

Within the context of a rapidly changing global economy, there has been a new immigration of millions of Asians, many of whom are highly skilled professionals, and the entrance of large numbers of political refugees from Southeast Asia. The consequent demographic changes may, at first glance, make the discussion of the AAM no longer relevant to today's sensibilities and political contours. The power of globalization to draw seemingly distant elements together has brought Asian immigrants thousands of miles from their homelands to within one national border. The impact of this huge migratory flow is still unfolding, but it is likely that, given the racially polarized character and continued social injustices and inequities of U.S. society, the need for an ongoing movement of Asian Americans is still salient. In spite of the dissimilarities in languages, cultures, and orientation to U.S. politics, there is a need to understand why growing segments of the Asian American community recognize the need to organize to serve the needs and interests of Asian and Pacific Islanders.

NOTES

1. Nelson Nagai, "Yellow Seed," in *Gidra: The XXth Anniversary Edition*, ed. Gidra Staff (Los Angeles: Gidra, 1990), 7.

2. Marcy Darnovksy, Barbara Epstein, and Richard Flacks, eds., *Cultural Politics and Social Movements* (Philadelphia: Temple University Press, 1995), vii.

3. Todd Gitlin, *The Sixties: Years of Hope, Days of Rage* (New York: Bantam Books, 1987); Jo Freeman, ed. *Social Movements of the Sixties and Seventies* (New York: Longman Inc, 1982).

4. William Wei, *The Asian American Movement* (Philadelphia: Temple University Press, 1993), 9.

5. Yen Le Espiritu, *Asian American Panethnicity: Bridging Institutions and Identities* (Philadelphia: Temple University Press, 1992), 31.

6. Espiritu, *Panethnicity*, 52.

7. Michael Omi and Howard Winant, *Racial Formation in the United States: From the 1960s to the 1980s* (New York: Routledge Press, 1986), 55.

8. Omi and Winant, *Racial Formation*, 107.

9. Chan, *Asian Americans*, 175.

10. Glenn Omatsu, "The 'Four Prisons' and the Movements of Liberation: Asian American Activism from the 1960s to the 1990s," in *The State of Asian American Activism and Resistance in the 1990s*, ed. Karin Aguilar-San Juan (Boston: South End Press, 1994), 32.

11. Linda Trinh Võ, *Mobilizing an Asian American Community* (Philadelphia: Temple University Press, 2004), 230.

12. Amy Tachiki, Eddie Wong, and Franklin Odo, eds., *Roots: An Asian American Reader* (Los Angeles: UCLA Asian American Studies Center, 1971); Emma Gee, ed., *Counterpoint: Perspectives on Asian America* (Los Angeles: UCLA Asian American Studies Center, 1976).

13. Steve Louie and Glenn Omatsu, eds., *Asian Americans: The Movement and the Moment* (Los Angeles: UCLA Asian American Studies Center Press, 2001).

14. Fred Ho, ed., *Legacy to Liberation* (San Francisco: AK Press, 2000).

15. Verta Taylor, "Emotions and Identity in Women's Self-Help Movements," in *Self, Identity, and Social Movements,* eds. Sheldon Stryker, Timothy J. Owens, and Robert W. White (Minneapolis: University of Minnesota Press, 2000), 271–99.

16. Aldon D. Morris, "Political Consciousness and Collective Action," in *Frontiers in Social Movement Theory*, eds. Aldon D. Morris and Carol McClurg Mueller (New Haven: Yale University Press, 1992), 351–73.

17. Aldon D. Morris, *The Origins of the Civil Rights Movement: Black Communities Organizing for Change* (New York: The Free Press, 1984), 282.

18. Morris, *Origins*, 284.

19. Douglas McAdam, J. D. McCarthy, and M. N. Zald, "Introduction: Opportunities, Mobilizing Structures, and Framing Process—Toward A Synthetic, Comparative Perspective on Social Movements," in *Comparative Perspectives on Social Movements: Political Opportunities, Mobilizing Structures, and Cultural Framings,* eds. Douglas McAdam, J. D. McCarthy and M. N. Zald (Cambridge, England: Cambridge University Press, 1996), 2.

20. Sidney Tarrow, *The Power in Movement: Social Movements and Contentious Politics.* 2nd ed. (Cambridge, England: Cambridge University Press, 1998), 24.

21. Carlos Munoz, Jr., *Youth, Identity, Power: The Chicano Movement* (New York: Verso Press, 1989), 1–5.

22. Until the early 1970s, the dominant approach to the study of collective behavior and social movements explored a wide range of sources for rapid social and economic change including fads, large crowds, panic, riots, and sects. These societal strains were viewed as creating structural changes (Smelser 1962), or frustration and anger (Gurr 1969). These theories share the assumption that individual deprivations, breakdowns of the social order, and individualized psychological reactions to these breakdowns are important preconditions for the emergence of social movements. Non-institutional collective behavior is formed to meet the unstructured situations of a breakdown of social control.

Some of the limitations of the earlier collective behavior models became obvious in the 1960s when large mobilizations were created by the civil rights movement and other movements. These grass roots social movements caused a shift in theoretical assumptions. The mass character of these newly emerging movements contradicted the previous interpretation of deprivation and fear guiding irrational and deviant behavior. This observation is evident in the formation of the AAM. The beginnings of the AAM began on college campuses among middle class and working class students; these students were not the most deprived economically or emotionally as discussed by collective behavior scholars.

23. Aldon D. Morris, "Black Southern Student Sit-in Movement: An Analysis of Internal Organization," *American Sociological Review* 46 (December 1981): 755–67; Douglas McAdam, *The Political Process and the Development of Black Insurgency* (Chicago: University of Chicago Press, 1982). See also Morris, *Origins of the Civil Rights Movement*.

24. Paul Wong, "The Emergence of the Asian-American Movement," *Bridge* 2, no. 1 (1972): 33–39.

25. Steven M. Buechler, *Social Movements in Advanced Capitalism: The Political Economy and Cultural Construction of Social Activism* (New York: Oxford University Press, 1999), 41.

26. McAdam, *Political Process*, 132.

27. Diane C. Fujino, *Heartbeat of Struggle: The Revolutionary Life of Yuri Kochiyama* (Minneapolis: University of Minnesota Press, 2006).

28. Hsaio, "Hidden History of Asian American Activism," 29–30.

29. Wong, "The Emergence of the Asian-American Movement," 36.

30. Evelyn Yoshimura, "How I Became an Activist and What It Means to Me," *Amerasia Journal* 15, no. 1 (1989): 106–09.

31. Mari J. Matsuda, "Here on Planet Asian America." Speech delivered at the Asian Law Caucus annual celebration (San Francisco, March 31, 2000), reprinted in the *Asian Law Caucus Newsletter: The Reporter* 22, no. 1 (July 2000).

Chapter Two

Background to the Formation of the AAM

This chapter will explore the period before an Asian American Movement was forged in the late 1960s. The intent of this chapter is to provide a basic historical context to understand the challenges involved in organizing among Asian immigrants and within Asian ethnic communities in the United States; it is not a thorough social history; rather it highlights the complexities and challenges that confronted Asian immigrants in the midst of dramatic international, homeland, and domestic upheavals between the 1850s and 1960s. This chapter seeks to answer the following questions: What were the challenges confronting different Asian ethnic groups upon their arrival to the U.S.; what legacies aided the formation of the Asian American Movement; what were the grievances that eventually precipitated the emergence of a broad social movement of Asian Americans; and what international and domestic factors created the structure of political opportunities that gave birth to the AAM as well as numerous other forms of contentious politics?

The first section explores the pre–World War II period when immigrants from diverse nations arrived in the United States and were immediately marginalized, isolated, and forced into low wage jobs. Each of the immigrant groups faced similar forms of subjugation as workers and life without the rights of citizenship to fully participate in society. At times, the dominant majority lumped together these different groups, and at other times, they singled out an Asian ethnicity. Having little in common in terms of language, culture, and homeland politics, the first waves of immigrants sought to distinguish themselves from one another.

Each of the Asian immigrant groups organized to resist the attacks they confronted at the time and place of arrival. Chinese, Japanese, and Filipino workers successfully organized around specific campaigns to win better working conditions with other workers. Each group also resisted racial attacks directed at them by groups and governmental bodies.

In the nineteenth century, Chinese and later Japanese workers resisted on their own. In the twentieth century, they continued to resist efforts to exploit their labor, oftentimes in union with workers from other races, such as when Japanese and Mexican beet workers in Oxnard in 1906 banded together to win better working conditions and for unionization.[1]

Each group also resisted discriminatory laws that blocked their full participation in society. Chinese immigrants developed sophisticated legal challenges to the enforcement of exclusionary immigration laws and procedures. In the 1860s, representatives of six Chinese district associations sought assistance to alter laws that had been passed in California that excluded Chinese from testifying in court and required the payment of a foreign miner's tax. A lobbyist and attorneys were hired by Chinese district association leaders to oppose these and other discriminatory laws of the era.[2] Subsequently, Chinese successful challenged several laws designed to exclude them under the Chinese exclusion laws in federal court. Wong Kim Ark, an American born Chinese sued when he was denied re-entry into the U.S. after traveling to China. The Supreme Court ruled that as a person born in the United States, the Chinese, Exclusion Act did not apply.[3] "That they were able to challenge the discrimination for so long and with such success was largely the result of the organization and persistence of Chinese and their attorneys."[4]

In addition to domestic protests, the treatment of Chinese immigrants in the United States was also the subject of a China-based boycott in 1905. Chinese in Shanghai launched a boycott of American goods to protest the U.S. policies that overzealously restricted Chinese immigration to the U.S. They demanded reforms from United States immigration officials for persons who were exempt from the anti-Chinese labor exclusion laws. Chinese Americans in the United States actively supported the boycott and raised funds to send to boycott leaders in China.[5]

While there were significant grievances among all Asian immigrants and fairly elaborate community institutions, including banks, services, business associations, family and regional associations in the Chinese and Japanese communities, other essential elements to construct a social movement did not yet exist for Asians in America. Group solidarity, networking, collective resources and organizations with an ideology that challenged the status quo were very limited. Anti-racist forces in the Asian immigrant communities such as the Chinese Workers Mutual Aid Association in the 1930s, the Punjabi farmers who opposed the alien land laws of the early twentieth century, World War II Japanese American internees who challenged their forced incarceration, the striking Filipino farm workers in California's agricultural fields in the 1930s, and other resisters were disempowered immigrants, and the first generation of American born Asians in America engaged in sporadic organizing. They mobilized different segments of their community at different times. The legacies of these collective acts of resistance, nevertheless, while oftentimes defensive in nature, spontaneous, and divorced from longer range goals, were the well springs from which a new generation of activists would build a new pan-Asian social movement in the 1960s.

ANTI-ASIAN VIOLENCE, RACIAL LUMPING, AND DISIDENTIFICATION IN THE PRE–WORLD WAR II ERA

Drawn by the promise of work and the opportunity for wages that would help support families, more than one million people from China, Japan, Korea, the Philippines, and India emigrated to the United States and to Hawai'i in the decades of the late nineteenth and early twentieth centuries. During this era of large scale Asian labor migration, Asian workers were paid significantly less than and positioned against their White counterparts to depress wages for both groups. Their arrival would alleviate the nation's labor needs but sparked acts of racial exclusion, discrimination, and violence, including numerous anti-immigrant laws.

There were also periodic outbreaks of racial hostilities directed at Asian immigrants. Between 1849 and 1910, numerous attacks against Chinese, including the razing of several ethnic enclaves and work camps, occurred in the western states. Japanese immigrants were also driven out of various locations in the West. In 1905, Whites forced Japanese cannery workers in Blaine, Washington, from their jobs so that the former could replace them. A mob drove scores of Asian Indian farm workers out of their camp and burned it down outside of Chico, California. Koreans, although small in number, were also victimized. In one incident in Riverside County in California, several hundred unemployed White workers terrorized and forced out fifteen Korean fruit pickers at a work site. Filipino farm laborers were also subjected to harsh racialized violence in the late 1920s and 1930s. These attacks included race riots outside of Watsonville, California, and numerous other locations where they were driven out of farm communities on the west coast for union organizing activities and for "race mixing."[6]

Anti-Asian sentiments stemmed from more than economic frustration. There was opposition and hostility to the influx of a racial group with different customs, languages, and religions. The U.S. government racialized these differences to create and reproduce structures of racial domination.[7] Xenophobic office holders passed legislation preventing Chinese immigrants from testifying in court, limiting their ability to operate businesses, and barring land ownership. Antimiscegenation laws in the West, first used to ban inter-racial sex and marriage between Blacks and Whites, were extended to Asians.[8] Employers, craft unions, and the government participated in dis-tancing Asian immigrant workers from their U.S.-born and European immi-grants counterparts. Irish American immigrants were at the forefront of anti-Asian campaigns in the nineteenth century. The anti-Asian movement in California played an important role in passage of anti-Chinese legislation and insertion of anti-Chinese language into the state's constitution in the 1870s.

DISTINCTIONS AND DIVISIONS
AMONG ASIAN IMMIGRANTS

While the larger U.S. society made few socioeconomic and legal distinctions among the Asian immigrant groups, internal differences among Asian immi-grants precluded efforts at cooperation. Among these obstacles were language and cultural distinctions, homeland politics, and East Asian regional conflicts. Coming from different localities and nations, "members of each group consid-ered themselves culturally and politically distinct."[9] The importation of labor first from China, then Japan, and later the Philippines, along with smaller num-bers from India and Korea, occurred over an eighty-year period as the U.S. evolved from a former colony into a global empire. Internationally, the roles of Asian nations and their leaders and rulers changed dramatically. In this context, the focus of each of the Asian immigrant groups centered on survival, home-land politics, and community building within their respective ethnic communi-ties. Each of the major immigrant groups viewed each other with suspicion and they sought to distinguish themselves from each other at critical junctures.

While Asians were lumped together for purposes of exclusion and racist treatment, they often sought to disidentify amongst themselves. David Hayano describes ethnic disidentification as the act of distancing one's group from an-other to avoid being mistaken and suffering for the presumed misdeeds of that group.[10] The Japanese immigrants of the late nineteenth century sought to dis-tance themselves from the Chinese immigrants, who had been legally ex-cluded in 1882. One Japanese immigrant newspaper editor in the early twen-tieth century condoned Chinese exclusion and presented Japanese as equal to White Americans.[11] Some Japanese immigrants, particularly those who had re-ceived substantial education in Japan before coming to the United States, viewed themselves as more acceptable than "lower class laborers who had not adapted themselves to American society." Japanese community leaders viewed industrializing Japan as an equal of European nations and China and Korea as "inferior nations" whose subjects were unworthy of equal treatment.[12]

However, despite these efforts, Japanese immigrants became the next victims of exclusion. Immigration began to slow in 1908 with the signing of the Gentleman's Agreement that, similar to the Chinese Exclusion Act of 1882, excluded Japanese laborers. Subsequently, additional anti-Japanese actions by state and federal governments restricted immigrants from owning land and culminated in the passage of the 1924 Immigration Act. This act prohibited entry of immigrants who were ineligible for citizenship and established quotas for admission based on the 1890 census, when only a handful of Japanese resided in the U.S. Furthermore, Japanese immigrants in the United States were also disqualified from becoming naturalized U.S. citizens by the courts.[13]

Throughout the exclusion era, many Chinese immigrants grew alienated from America and instead reinforced their identification with China. China's rising national consciousness and its 1911 Revolution produced a new sense of ethnic identity.[14]

Due to the U.S. colonization of the Philippines, Filipinos who migrated to work in the pineapple plantations in Hawai'i and then to the mainland had a separate status that enabled their continued migration when other Asian immigrants were barred. This created differences in immigration status and political influence for a short period. Filipinos, however, were effectively excluded in 1934 by the Tydings-McDuffie Act, which granted autonomy to the Philippines but sanctioned the U.S. government exclusion of future Filipino migration.

One example of the internal divisions that arose among Asian immigrants occurred in Stockton, California. Japanese immigrants had by 1930 established a minor presence as small business owners in places such as Stockton. That year, significant tensions arose between Filipinos and Japanese businesses catering to them over an incident concerning a potential marriage between an American-born Japanese woman and a Filipino laborer. Leaders of the Japanese community viewed the relationship as unacceptable. They applied public and private pressure to end it, which sparked a community boycott by Filipino laborers. *Issei* (first generation) leaders were responding to efforts to group all Asians together, and their own prejudices derived from Imperial Japan. Filipinos for their part sought to establish an independent presence and form their own local businesses. In response to the boycott, Japanese business leaders began to recruit more Mexican laborers into the area to replace the Filipino workers on their farms.[15] In this elaborate mosaic of racial and class differences, they didn't envision a future where Filipino and Mexican workers would one day unite to form the United Farm Workers union (UFW) and organize against the *Nisei* (second-generation Japanese American) and White growers in California's Central Valley.

In addition to the desire to maintain distinct identities, regional conflicts among Asian nations limited cooperative efforts in this country among Asian

Americans. Japan's capture of Korea in the early twentieth century and later invasion of other Asian nations heightened animosity among Asian immigrants toward Japan and reinforced nationalistic sentiments. Koreans in the United States supported the Korean independence movement, providing financial aid and military training centers to resist Japanese aggression. Many students and political activists were active in setting up support for resistance to Japanese aggression in Korea and China. In the Chinese community, there were significant efforts to raise funds for the war relief effort in China; these initiatives raised more than $25 million during the eight-year war of resistance in the 1930s.[16] Chinatown populations also organized large demonstrations against Japanese aggression in China, and protestors picketed at several West Coast ports in attempts to halt scrap iron shipments to Japan.[17]

POLITICAL ORGANIZING
EFFORTS BEFORE WORLD WAR II

Before World War II, the high water mark for labor and other forms of social movement organizing occurred in the 1930s as unemployed workers, displaced homeowners and renters, youth, and the organized labor movement built broad-based social movements. The labor movement was multi-racial and included large numbers of African American workers in the North and Asian agricultural workers in the fields out West. In urban centers, Chinese workers and other left-wing elements built alliances with the labor and political organizations. At this juncture in Asian grassroots organizing, Chinese, Japanese, and Filipino immigrant workers were often the core of incipient efforts in Asian communities and part of broad-based left-wing organizing of the labor movement.

Community institution building by the first generation of Asian immigrants preceded the mass organizing efforts of the 1930s. Before World War II, Asian Americans' political activities were limited to court challenges to discrimination, support for homeland political issues, organizing for labor rights, and circumscribed participation in electoral politics. While these reflected acts of contentious politics, they were not part of a broad social movement among Asian immigrants. Efforts instead focused on building community institutions and economic and political survival in a hostile nation. New immigrants relied on ethnic specific mutual aid societies such as the Chinese Consolidated Benevolent Association (CCBA), Japan Association of America, and Korean National Association. The ethnic Asian communities also used community-based religious centers for protection, economic survival, and for maintaining community and political unity.

By necessity some of the most significant organizing activities to achieve equality took place outside of the electoral theater. Asian immigrants could not naturalize; only those Asian Americans native to the United States held citizenship. Even the small numbers of Asians eligible to vote were mostly young and just becoming engaged in political activities.

Immigrant workers, who sought to achieve better working conditions, carried out much of the Asian organizing efforts. They joined radical and communist-led trade unions that had by the 1930s begun to accept Chinese, Filipino, and other Asian workers into their ranks. One of the most notable efforts at labor cooperation between Japanese and Filipino workers took place in Hawai'i in 1920 when ethnic-specific labor associations jointly struck for higher wages. The primarily Filipino and communist-led Agricultural Workers Organizing Committee of Southern California organized Japanese and Mexican workers in the state's agricultural fields in 1927. Chinese workers in urban areas joined labor unions and helped lead strikes for higher wages. The Chinese Workers Mutual Aid Association formed to encourage Chinese to join U.S. labor unions. In San Francisco, the International Ladies Garment Workers Union (ILGWU) organized workers employed at the National Dollar Store factory. In New York City, laundry owners and workers founded the Chinese Hand Laundry Alliance in 1933 and worked closely with the labor movement. Filipinos, the primary contingent labor force following the 1924 exclusion of all Asians, led several militant organizing efforts in the agricultural industry, including California farm workers and Alaska cannery workers.[18] These Asian American organizing efforts were closely tied to other ones led by the Congress of Industrial Unions.

In addition to mutual aid associations and labor organizing, Asian Americans constructed civil rights groups to fight for citizenship rights. Second-generation community members led these efforts. Activists formed the Chinese American Citizens Alliance in 1915.[19] A cohort of second generation Japanese Americans formed the Japanese American Citizens League (JACL) in 1930. These organizations promoted their respective communities as loyal Americans. Second-generation Japanese Americans became active in California politics, and both the Democratic and Republican political parties, seeking to expand their base of support, courted them. Groups such as the Nisei Voters League, the Japanese American branch of the Republican Party, and the Young Democratic Club formed in California and began to participate in state level party politics in 1938.[20]

The left-oriented political organization most active among the various Asian ethnic groups was the Communist Party of the United States of America (CPUSA). They organized primarily along ethnic lines in the Asian communities, in agriculture, and in urban workplaces where Asians worked. Japanese and Chinese in the CPUSA put out a declaration in 1928 addressed to workers and farmers of China, Japan, and the United States that called for the withdrawal of Japanese troops from China. In 1931 and 1932, the Agricultural Workers Industrial Union, led by its Japanese section, organized more than twenty strikes in Chico, Lodi, Fresno, and the San Gabriel Valley. There were also numerous other strikes and organizing efforts in the fields involving Japanese, Korean, and East Indian participants.[21] Outside of agricultural organizing efforts and at multi-ethnic rallies against Japan, however, the CPUSA didn't work to bring Asians together. The lack of pan-Asian cooperation became apparent with the outbreak of hostilities between the United States and Japan in 1941.

The period before the war thus laid the groundwork for future activism through comparable grievances that were similar albeit distinctive for all Asian groups—immigration restrictions, circumscribed socioeconomic mobility, denial of legal and political rights, cultural vilification, and physical violence. Their continual efforts to resist reached their fullest expression with the expansion of communist and other radical organizing that began with the late 1920s depression era. Those efforts as well as those of nascent civil rights organizations also began to expand the Asian communities' infrastructure beyond homeland-oriented organizing and organizations. Though new groups such as the Chinese Hand Laundry Association in New York City formed the first democratic mass organizations in the community,[22] Asian political mobilization remained far short of generating a sustained movement directed at changing the conditions of Asians in America. This history, however, of grievances, the creation of the first cohorts of activists and organizers, the efforts at coalition building as part of larger social movement, and broadening of the community infrastructure would survive to contribute to the later emergence of the AAM.

DISIDENTIFICATION WITH JAPANESE AMERICANS IN WORLD WAR II

The experience of Japanese Americans during World War II is illustrative of the challenge of building a strong social movement by Asians in America before the 1960s. The next section of this chapter will explore in depth the gulfs between the Asian ethnic groups. The isolation of the Japanese immigrant community from others in the United States, the anti-Japan sentiments triggered by Japan's military aggression abroad, and the Japanese community's own internal contradictions over how to view the place of Japanese Americans in U.S. society prevented a united resistance to their incarceration in 1942.

Japanese military forces had occupied Korea in the 1910s, but the U.S. government viewed the issue as a regional matter. When the Japanese military invaded and occupied a large area of northeastern China in the 1930s, the U.S. government also declined to intervene. The invasion of the Philippines and attack on military forces at Pearl Harbor in Hawai'i on December 7, 1941, finally drew the United States into war. The U.S. government response included the roundup of suspected Japanese agents, many of whom were first generation community leaders, and eventually the incarceration of all Japanese, including U.S. citizens, residing on the west coast.

Paradoxically, Hawai'i, then a United States "territory," didn't organize a wholesale detention of Japanese on the islands after the December 7 attack. The U.S. military declared immediate martial law and imposed restrictions on foreign language speakers. While there were calls for wholesale removal of all Japanese descendants to West Coast facilities, only about three thousand were interned. Many of those removed to the mainland were judged "not productive or essential to the economy." The Japanese, nearly 40 percent of the island chain's residents, were employed in strategic parts of the local economy. Most *Nisei* continued to work in the war industries and serve the U.S. military forces stationed on the islands. Nevertheless, they did not escape persecution. They suffered various forms of harassment and intimidation for labor and union activities, exclusion from higher-paying defense jobs, and relegation to agricultural and service jobs. The military also suppressed Japanese and other Asian cultures by closing down all language schools and Buddhist churches and imposing other harsh measures.[23]

On the mainland, one observer noted, "a growing racist 'yellow peril' clamor, led by the Hearst and McClatchy newspaper chains, the nativist Sons and Daughters of the Golden West, the American Legion, and some AFL unions and groups,"[24] whipping up anti-Japanese sentiments. Other Asian ethnic groups were mostly silent, and liberal and progressive elements in the United States supported incarceration. The CPUSA rationalized the incarceration because of the U.S. government's role in "the international united front against fascism." Prominent civil rights groups such as the National Association for the Advancement of Colored People (NAACP) failed to speak out "out of fear of repercussions of appearing to be unpatriotic."[25] Defense of a minority's civil rights had taken a back seat to war hysteria and opposition to fascism and military aggression. Acquiescing to public opinion, the courts and other government institutions dutifully supported the Presidential Executive Order 9066 for the mass incarceration of a racial minority. Without strong dissenting voices from religious or civil rights organizations or the left, opposition to the proposed mass incarceration failed to develop.

With the outbreak of war, Asian ethnic minorities remained as divided as when they entered this country. The dominant conservative voices in the Chinese and Japanese communities had no interest in building solidarity among fellow Asian immigrants. The two communities were generally monolingual and focused on the problems and issues of their ethnic community and respective homelands. The other ethnic Asian minorities were too small in numbers and strongly opposed Japanese militarism. Though in several cities Filipinos lived as part of larger Chinese enclaves, many Filipinos were migratory workers in fluid situations and often pitted against other ethnic group workers.

While Japanese Americans were preoccupied with preserving their safety, proving their loyalty to the United States, selling off their property, and moving to the incarceration camps, the Korean and Chinese communities continued their efforts to raise money to oppose the Japanese occupation in China and Korea. These communities were more concerned with their homelands' liberation from the Japanese Imperial Army than the plight of the Japanese in America. The national media played an important role in heightening the wartime racist hysteria. National magazines ran articles that highlighted "how to tell friends (Chinese) from Japs." Filipinos, Koreans, and Chinese sought to distinguish themselves from Japanese Americans. Some wore buttons that identified themselves as non-Japanese. Others placed signs in their businesses stating they were not Japanese owned. Others bought up land and property from Japanese Americans being interned. The weight of homeland and regional conflicts combined with class hierarchies, national chauvinism, and language barriers among the Asian ethnic groups closed off possibilities of support for Japanese Americans.

Some groups and individuals notably voiced opposition to the incarceration. The American Civil Liberties Union (ACLU) opposed it on the grounds of the violation of civil liberties and took up evacuation test cases on the West Coast, including those of Gordon Hirabayashi, Fred Korematsu, and Minoru Yasui.[26] Certain agricultural industry associations were among the strongest oppositional interest groups. The Beet Growers Association opposed the imprisonment of Japanese Americans and later sought to allow Japanese American workers to leave the camps to harvest their crops. While most of organized labor supported the incarceration of Japanese Americans, the International Longshoremen's and Warehousemen's Union (ILWU) vigorously dissented. Louis Goldblatt, then Secretary of the California CIO state council, and later Secretary-Treasurer of the ILWU, criticized the incarceration as a violation of the civil rights of Japanese Americans.[27] The American Friends Service Committee's public opposition included active efforts to provide aid to those interned and finding ways to get individuals out of the camps to attend school and work. Activists in the Methodist Church, including many *Nisei*, influenced it to oppose the incarceration. Another dissenting voice was the Socialist Party. A few individuals and organizations in the Asian communities such as the Chinese Workers Mutual Aid Association refused to get caught up in the war hysteria.

The lack of solidarity weakened the ability of Japanese Americans to ward off their impending incarceration. Furthermore, the U.S. government agents' roundup of Japanese *Issei* (first generation) leadership left the American born *Nisei* (second generation) to provide leadership. The *Nisei*-dominated Japanese American Citizens League (JACL) decided immediately after the bombing of Pearl Harbor to support the war effort against Japan, affirm their loyalty to the United States, and "to disassociate themselves from their parents' generation, particularly from its leadership, which they regarded as misguided and even subversive."[28] They also aggressively opposed any efforts to challenge the U.S. government's right to incarcerate Japanese Americans living on the west coast.

The JACL openly criticized any individual who challenged the evacuation in the courts or resisted the draft.[29] Unfortunately, the JACL's actions at the outbreak of war stifled a fuller discussion and debate about the potential civil rights violations taking place. Within the Japanese American community, the JACL's suppression of opposition and criticism remains a sensitive and unresolved legacy of World War II.

For Asians of non-Japanese descent, World War II brought a dramatic, albeit short lived, change in status. The U.S. government and the American public changed their attitudes particularly toward Filipinos and Chinese, who had become allies in the war against Japan. The U.S. government incorporated the Philippine army into the United States armed forces, and thousands of Chinese and Filipinos either enlisted or were called up in the draft. Many Chinese went to work in war industries such as shipbuilding. Public opinion toward them began to change as newsreels and newspaper headlines publicized the heroism and courage of Filipino troops. Filipinos enlistees, who were U.S. nationals, became U.S. citizens through mass naturalization ceremonies before induction.[30]

In 1943, Congress repealed the Chinese Exclusion Act as reward for the Chinese government's struggle to defeat Japan; however, the annual quota of Chinese allowed to be naturalized was restricted to 105 worldwide. Most Chinese immigration came through other non-quota categories such as war brides, wives of citizens, refugees, and as derivative citizens. People of Indian descent and Filipinos had to wait until after the war in 1946 to be allowed to naturalize, while Japanese and Koreans had to wait until 1952, with the passage of the McCarran-Walter Act.

ASIAN AMERICANS IN THE LATE 1940s AND 1950s

After World War II, the grievances of various ethnic Asians, took new turns. One change was that global politics would now be front and center in determining the future of Asians in America. This new dynamic continued to unfold with direct consequences for Chinese Americans. The world's balance of power shifted from Europe to rising new actors—the United States and the Soviet Union. These two countries became embroiled in a lengthy "Cold War" between the U.S. capitalist system and the Soviet Union socialist system for control of the world's resources and political dominance. This period was characterized internationally by this ideological, military, and economic competition but, as well, developing nations' national liberation efforts against colonial powers. One of the most significant changes in the developing world was in the 1949 establishment of the People's Republic of China. The impact of this social revolution was to reverberate across the Pacific Ocean to Chinese and other Asians in America.

The United States recognized, in the new international political equation, that Japan, a recent war adversary, was now useful as an ally against the growing communist influence in Asia. On the other hand, U.S. tensions with socialist countries, the Soviet bloc and now China, intensified, and a "red scare" gripped the country.[31]

Asian American labor activists in particular were singled out for harassment and arrest. In Hawai'i, seven members with the ILWU, including Koji Ariyoshi and Eileen Fujimoto, were arrested for their radical ideas in 1951. Many perceived that the large Hawai'ian plantation owners, in tense negotiations with the ILWU, were in part responsible for the government's actions.[32] In Seattle, in the early 1950s, the U.S. Immigration and Naturalization Service (INS) investigated members of the Cannery Workers Local 7 and accused them of Communist Party membership or other subversive activities. The cannery workers union charged the Alaska Salmon Industry with a hand in the efforts to have union leaders deported. These efforts were overturned by three important Supreme Court cases, Mangaoang v. Boyd, Gonzales v. Barber, and Alcantra v. Boyd.[33] Attempts to intimidate other Asian American labor activists also occurred throughout the West coast during the Cold War.

The INS cast its widest net in the Chinese community. In the early 1950s, it created the notorious "confession" program for that community. As part of provisions in the 1952 Immigration and Nationality Act, 30,000 people who confessed to being in the country illegally were granted naturalization conditional on disclosing everything they knew about others residing without proper documents or involved with "subversive" activities. This program sowed widespread fear and suspicion amongst the Chinese community.

Chinese immigrant political activists were singled out and harassed for their support for the People's Republic of China. When the Chinese revolution toppled the U.S.-supported Chinese nationalist government, the U.S. government intensified its surveillance of the Chinese immigrant community. Anyone who harbored sympathies for the new Chinese government was now viewed antagonistically, and many were harassed and deported as part of the "confession" campaign. Government agencies also elevated anticommunist groups as community's unitary voice. These organizations, most notably the Chinese Consolidated Benevolent Associations (CCBA), suppressed dissenting voices. Domestic security bodies, particularly the Federal Bureau of Investigation (FBI), intervened in the Chinatown enclaves in a hunt for "Red Chinese."[34]

Hysteria intensified when the United States entered the Korean War in the 1950s. The small Korean immigrant population represented no perceived threat to the United States. However, the entrance of China into the conflict on the side of the North Korean communists accelerated U.S. government efforts to harass elements in the Chinese community.

Cold War politics, increasing numbers of non-quota immigrants, and uneven efforts at building ethnic community life dominated the late 1940s and 1950s. Cold War hysteria resulted in the passage of the McCarran-Walter Immigration Act of 1952, which reaffirmed the quota system, expanded the ideological and moral bases for denying admission to the United States, and facilitated deportation. The highly restrictive legislation kept quota levels for Asian immigrants extremely low. However, through non-quota means, immigration increased in almost all ethnic Asian communities. Asian ethnic groups brought over spouses and war brides, and Asian women became a more permanent fixture in the Asian American community. Post–WW II restrictions on Japanese immigration to the United States limited non-quota immigration, and the pre-war allowance permitting Japanese males to bring brides lessened their demand for it, while other ethnic communities such as Filipino and Chinese took advantage of these openings. With limited numbers of immigrants before 1965, American-born second and third generations became the predominant segment of Japanese and Chinese communities, the two largest Asian communities at the time.

The Cold War also resulted in U.S. tolerance for dictatorial allies against communist insurgents. The heavy hand of intimidation in the Filipino community accompanied the rise of the Ferdinand Marcos regime in the Philippines. Agents of the Marcos government expanded to U.S. soil to suppress oppositional organizing overseas. Similarly, U.S. support for Korean military strongmen led to a tolerance of Korean government surveillance and intimidation of Korean Americans.[35]

In the Japanese American community, the end of WW II meant the possibility of a return to the west coast, and the attempt to reestablish community life. Structural and individual level hostilities directed at Japanese Americans were frequent. However, Japan's utility as an anti-communist ally of the U.S. government prompted the United States to make a token gesture at restitution to the Japanese American community. It passed the Japanese-American Evacuation Claims Act of 1948. However, the act, which paid out claims of $38 million in lost property claims, required proof of property losses, documentation that most Japanese Americans found impossible to obtain in the few days given to them to prepare themselves before incarceration.[36]

The growing influence of the second-generation American-born Japanese was evident in the active participation of the JACL in civil rights efforts. In 1952, the JACL Anti-Discrimination Committee successfully lobbied to restore seniority rights to all *Nisei* civil service workers who were discriminated against by World War II federal government policy. The JACL also submitted an amicus curiae brief in support of the NAACP's lawsuit in the 1954 Brown v. Board of Education case that ended formal segregation in public education and participated in the 1963 March on Washington.[37]

The 1950s also marked the drive for U.S. statehood for the Hawai'ian Islands. In 1898, Hawai'i was annexed by the United States as a territorial colony. From that date to the mid-twentieth century, a White Republican settler oligarchy ruled Hawai'i politically and economically.[38] Agricultural labor was recruited from various Asian nations and Puerto Rico to work in the Hawai'ian plantations. Asian workers participated in forming militant trade unions and establishing a permanent presence in the island's politics. In 1954, the Democratic Party, in alliance with the ILWU and *Nisei* political activists, won a landslide victory and captured both legislative houses of the territory and ushered in a new era of local Asian political power. The establishment of Hawai'i as the fiftieth state in 1959 was bittersweet. On one hand, it created a positive image for Asian Americans; community members were elected to seats in both houses of Congress, positions providing both visibility and self-pride. On the other hand it exacerbated the further loss of sovereignty and land for Native Hawai'ian peoples. The contradiction of the colonization of the Hawai'ian Islands continues today with strong pan-Asian electoral representation and growing calls for return of lands and sovereignty to indigenous Hawai'ians.[39]

ETHNIC ENCLAVES, SUBURBANIZATION, AND CULTURAL CONTROL

Another new set of grievances focused on the fate of the traditional enclaves that laid the background for the future defense of historical communities.

Post-war domestic development shifted attention to the localities where Asian immigrant communities—Chinatowns, Manilatowns, and Japantowns— resided. As each Asian ethnic group continued to be preoccupied with their respective communities' issues, they came under attack by local redevelopment policies that sought to force vulnerable communities from their homes and places of business to make way for capital's progress. Most of the west coast Asian ethnic enclaves were either destroyed or dramatically reduced in size by redevelopment and local economic development policies. For example, in Oakland, California, the construction of the Nimitz Freeway in the 1950s meant the demolition of several blocks of Chinatown's housing and small businesses.[40] In San Francisco's Japantown during the same decade, a large government redevelopment project began in the area that subsequently removed thousands of residents.

Asian American communities were struggling out of century-long environments of racial segregation, deprivation, exploitation, and political repression. Through the war, few social service agencies beyond the local churches or temples addressed the needs of the population in these enclaves, and public institutions overlooked the customary services accorded other communities in the U.S. society. Native-born Asian Americans founded a few secular service agencies such as the Chinese American Citizens Alliance, but this generation, who sought to assimilate and were limited to private, voluntary resources, could address issues only at the margins. In the late 1940s and 1950s, a fraction of the pre-War Japanese American population returned to the *Nihonmachis* (Japantowns). A different population had displaced them during their internment.[41] Playing a diminished role for a more dispersed, restructured community, Japanese Americans, long the only investors and residents in the *Nihonmachis*, now had to find other locations to live.

The leadership in Chinatowns, while revitalized by new immigration flows, still detached the community from the larger society. Bernard Wong's study of New York Chinatown describes how this leadership benefited from their patron role and consequently "maintained the ethnic boundary."[42] As for the CCBA in the Chinatowns, Ling Chi Wang, an early organizer at the Youth Services Center in San Francisco, observed,

> The so-called Chinese leadership, under increasing criticism and pressure from labor unions and young activists, became more conservative and reactionary. It persistently denied the existence of any social and economic problems and insisted that Chinatown could take care of its own problems.[43]

Manilatowns were havens for the *Manongs*, men who labored seasonally and itinerantly in agriculture and packing. Complexes of rooming houses and services supporting this aging, single male population, Manilatowns were often appended to other Asian ethnic enclaves and lacked community infrastructure to support the newer influx of families that began arriving in the 1950s and 1960s. These families settled outside the enclaves.

While external forces were busy working to gain control of urban ethnic communities, within the various Asian communities, the post-war period brought a dramatic change. The G.I. Bill enabled Asians who served in the military during World War II to go to college, to hold positions outside the traditional enclaves, and to purchase homes with low down payments and low interest financing. Many Asians took advantage of this program to seek housing in neighborhoods surrounding Chinatowns and Japantowns or in middle class suburbs that were largely inhabited by Whites. The broadening of their experience in the military, on campuses, and in other communities gave this generation a glimpse of a different status and lessened their tolerance for the discrimination that they still faced.

Asian Americans, however, faced illegal but defacto restrictions. There was "yellow-lining" of where Asian Americans could live. Returning Asian American G.I.s and Japanese American internees found real estate brokers unwilling to sell them homes in numerous towns.[44] While some realtors' practices and sellers' fears of "block busting" by racial minorities kept some areas off limits for Asians, more and more places began to open up by the 1960s. For example, in Gardena, a Los Angeles suburb, *Nisei* were recruited to purchase homes and develop businesses. Asian Americans moved into communities such as the Crenshaw in Los Angeles, the Richmond District in San Francisco, and multiple locations across the West and East Coasts and in the Midwest.

As ethnic Asians moved into suburbs and attended college, they came into contact with each other. For the first time, Asian Americans were exposed to other Asians of different ethnic backgrounds. Previously, the ethnic enclave economies kept most Asians insulated from each other. In the rural communities, WWII dramatically reduced the numbers of Japanese American farmers who returned to their farms after the war. As young Asian Americans began to attend schools, play sports, and attend dances together, many of the preceding generations' hostilities toward one another began to dissolve. One indicator of this increasing contact is that the census identified only four cities—Chicago–Gary, Los Angeles, Sacramento, and San Francisco—with multiple Asian ethnicities having five hundred or more youth between the ages of fourteen and twenty-one in 1950. By 1970, the number of metropolitan areas with such co-resident populations increased to eighteen.[45] By the 1960s, Asian Americans became more socially integrated with other people of color and with Whites. It was not unusual, for example, to find Asian Americans playing in soul bands with African Americans to large audiences of pan-Asians.

Another new set of grievances revolved around cultural suppression of Asian ethnic cultures. The larger society exerted strong pressure on Asians in America to conform and assimilate into the "melting pot." As some native born Asians began to succeed academically, they were held up as the "model minority" that, unlike other racial minorities, steered clear of crime and drugs and instead succeeded through study and hard work. Pressure to conform to the dominant culture and values was extremely strong in the 1950s. Chinese were confronted with red baiting, harassment, and deportation and sought to find ways to demonstrate their loyalty to the United States. The Korean Americans watched as their homeland became embroiled in Cold War politics, which encouraged assimilation into the dominant society. The Japanese American community, still in shock from the devastation of World War II, felt the necessity to assimilate to prove themselves as Americans.

On the mainstream stage, norms were narrow and "white." Asian Americans were advised to conform and avoid controversy. Role models and standards of beauty, behavior, and success were homogenous, exclusive, and undermined any visible reinforcement of Asian American cultures. The few characterizations of Asian Americans in popular culture were derogatory. Young Asian Americans recognized these sentiments, mocked or real, in *Roots*:

1) tall, 2) handsome, 3) manly, 4) self-confident, 5) well-poised, 6) protective, 7) domineering, 8) affectionate, and 9) imaginative. These are all the Prince Charming characteristics that all White women instill in their daughters for the ideal mate.

My future-husband seems to possess all of them, and he's also White.

It seems that Oriental girls who marry White men are looking for this stereotype and will not settle for the short, ugly, unconfident, clumsy, arrogant Oriental man that we are all plagued with.

and

I hate my wife for her flat yellow face
and her fat cucumber legs, but mostly
for her lack of elegance and lack of
intelligence compared to judith gluck.[46]

Prior to the war, popular views of Asian Americans were completely pejorative. Robert Lee tellingly categorized these views as successively "pollutants," "the coolie," "the deviant," or "the yellow peril."[47] In the 1950s, the new "model minority" stereotype of Asian Americans emerged. Few young Asian Americans took comfort in this image.

CONCLUSION: EMERGENT CONDITIONS FOR MOVEMENT

The history of Asian American communities before the 1960s most particularly affected grievances and indigenous resources. Factors affecting the framing of ideas also arose.

Previous to World War II, the Asian American communities had accumulated a storehouse of grievances. The larger U.S. society perceived Asians as perpetual foreigners. They were brutally attacked in the nineteenth century, discriminated against in almost all aspects of their daily lives, and, by the 1920s, with the exception of Filipinos, effectively excluded by restrictive immigration. The period during and after the war compounded and complicated grievances for Asian groups. During the war, Japanese Americans were punished and dispossessed while the status of other Asian American groups improved. In the post-war period, on one hand, legal and political restrictions were generally relaxed, mass physical violence lessened, and socioeconomic mobility increased. On the other hand, political persecution of large segments of the population developed, traditional enclaves were undermined, and cultural domination persisted. Thus, each Asian ethnic group brought into the AAM period a history of specific and common unresolved grievances.

These communities had also developed constrained but real resources. In the 1930s, Asian immigrants were actively organizing for labor and other rights, and many participated in the large social movements of the Great Depression era. The domestic cold-war regime drove many organizers from those previous decades underground, but they continued to be active and hold their beliefs. Moreover, the exposure of both Asian American wartime workers and soldiers to a more liberalized environment and the opening up of educational opportunities for Asian Americans would generate new actors dissatisfied with secondary status. The post-war generation began to cross ethnic boundaries, and new ways of thinking began to present themselves. The Asian American communities had also developed and expanded organizational infrastructures, though the country's political regime reinforced the domination of conservative community actors.

The Asian ethnic communities before World War II remained separate and distinct from one another. The influence of homeland governments on Asian origin communities remained strong throughout this period. During World War II, the historic differences among distinct nationalities of Asian origin immigrants were heightened. Other Asian ethnicities failed to defend the civil rights of Japanese Americans, while internal conflict within the Japanese American community grew sharp and at times violent. However, a new generation unattached to these differences and attitudes had begun to grow. They were cohorts that had begun to intersect and overlap in their experiences.

This chapter highlights the obstacles that prevented Asians in America from joining or generating social movement activism. While many of Asian American communities' actions and campaigns previous to the 1960s were significant and challenged discriminatory laws and racist treatment, they did not rise to the level of a social movement. Some of the necessary elements — grievances and resources — were present; others — political opportunity, a resonant framework of ideas and mobilizing conventions — were not. Yet, the unique community conditions and forces external to the Asian communities created small windows of opportunity for Asian Americans to begin to work together. Previously they lacked the awareness of their common experience of group grievances that is a necessary precondition for social movement formation. The social distance among Asian Americans previously limited their ability to develop a common experience and identity; however, this social separation was now evaporating as a new generation of young Asian Americans arrived on college campuses. The next chapter discusses the critical period of the 1960s and examines both international and domestic factors that created the Asian American Movement.

NOTES

1. Tomás Almaguer, *Racial Fault Lines: The Historical Origins of White Supremacy in California* (Berkeley: University of California Press, 1994), 191–203.

2. Charles J. McClain, *In Search of Equality: The Chinese Struggle against Discrimination in Nineteenth-Century America* (Berkeley: University of California Press, 1994).

3. U.S. v. Wong Kim Ark, 169 U.S. 1898.

4. Lucy E. Salyer, *Laws Harsh as Tigers: Chinese Immigrants and the Shaping of Modern Immigration Law* (Chapel Hill, NC: University of North Carolina Press, 1995), 116.

5. Salyer, *Laws*. 162–69.

6. Ronald Takaki, *Strangers From a Different Shore: A History of Asian Americans* (Boston: Little Brown, 1989); Carlos Bulosan, *America is in the Heart, A Personal History* (Seattle: University of Washington Press, 1974); Shih-Shan Henry Tsai, *The Chinese Experience in America* (Bloomington, IN: Indiana University Press, 1986; Yujii Ichioka, *The Issei: The World of the First Generation Japanese Immigrants, 1885–1924* (New York: The Free Press, 1988); Joan M. Jensen, *Passage from India: Asian Indian Immigration in North America* (New Haven, CT: Yale University Press, 1988); Chris Friday, *Organizing Asian American Labor: The Pacific Coast Canned-Salmon Industry, 1870–1942* (Philadelphia: Temple University Press, 1994).

7. Omi and Winant, *Racial Formation*.

8. Rachel F. Moran, *Interracial Intimacy: the Regulation of Race and Romance* (Chicago: University of Chicago Press, 2001), 4.

9. Espiritu, *Asian American Panethnicity,* 19.

10. David M. Hayano, "Ethnic Identification and Disidentification: Japanese American Views towards Chinese Americans," *Ethnic Groups* 3, no. 2 (1981): 157–71.

11. Roger Daniels, *Asian America: Chinese and Japanese in the United States since 1850* (Seattle: University of Washington Press, 1988), 113.

12. Ichioka, *The Issei,* 191, 250.

13. Takaki, *Strangers From a Different Shore*, 208–209.

14. Him Mark Lai, Joe Huang, and Don Wong, *The Chinese of America 1785–1980: An Illustrated Catalog of the Exhibit* (San Francisco: Chinese Cultural Foundation, 1980), 62.

15. Eiichiro Azuma, "Racial Struggle, Immigrant Nationalism, and Ethnic Identity: Japanese and Filipinos in the California Delta," *Pacific Historical Review* 67, no. 2 (May 1998), 163–99.

16. Him Mark Lai, "Roles Played by Chinese in America during China's Resistance to Japanese Aggression and during World War II," *Chinese America: History and Perspectives*. 11 (1997), 94.

17. Lai, Huang, and Wong, *The Chinese of America 1785–1980*, 62.

18. Chan, *Asian Americans,* 99; Lai, Huang and Wong, *The Chinese of America 1785–1980,* 60–61.

19. Sue Fawn Chung, "Fighting for Their American Rights: A History of the Chinese American Citizens Alliance," in *Claiming American: Constructing Chinese American Identities During the Exclusion Era*, ed. K. Scott Wong and Sucheng Chan (Philadelphia: Temple University Press, 1998), 102.

20. Jere Takahashi, *Nisei/Sansei: Shifting Japanese American Identities and Politics* (Philadelphia: Temple University, 1997), 67–74.

21. Karl Yoneda, *Ganbatte: Sixty-Year Struggle of a Kibei Worker* (Los Angeles: UCLA Asian American Studies Center, 1983), 102; Karl Yoneda "A Partial History of California Japanese Farm Workers," in *Racism, Dissent and Asian Americans from 1850 to the Present: A Documentary History,* eds. Philip S. Foner and Daniel Rosenberg (Westport, CT: Greenwood Publishing, 1993).

22. Peter Kwong and Dusanka Miscevic, *Chinese America: the Untold Story of America's Oldest New Community* (New York: The New Press, 2005), 188.

23. Him Mark Lai, *Becoming Chinese American: A History of Communities and Institutions* (Walnut Creek, CA: Alta Mira Press, 2004), 296; Gary Y. Okihiro, *Cane Fires: The Anti-Japanese Movement in Hawai'i, 1865–1945* (Philadelphia: Temple University Press, 1992), 267, 271.

24. Yoneda, *Ganbatte*, 121.

25. Eric K. Yamamato and Susan K. Serrano, "The Loaded Weapon," Parts 1 and 2, *Amerasia Journal* 27, no. 3 (2001); 28, no. 1 (2002) (double issue): 51–62.

26. The ACLU went through sharp internal debate over how to protect the civil rights of the individuals without appearing to be aiding the enemy of the United States. See R. Jeffrey Blair. 2000. "Fighting the Japanese Internment in Federal Court: The A.C.L.U. During World War II."

27. Yoneda, *Ganbatte*, 122.

28. Daniels, *Asian America*, 209.

29. Daniels, *Asian America*, 221–22.

30. Judy Yung, *Unbound Voices: A Documentary History of Chinese Women in San Francisco* (Berkeley, CA: University of California Press, 1999), 479–85; Yen Le Espiritu, *Asian American Women and Men: Labor, Laws, and Love* (Thousand Oaks, CA: Sage Publications, 1996), 50–51; Gary R. Hess, "The Forgotten Asian Americans: The East Indian Community in the United States," in *The History and Immigration of Asian Americans,* ed. Franklin Ng (New York: Garland Publishing, 1998), 591–92.

31. Ellen Schrecker, *Many are the Crimes* (Princeton, NJ: Princeton University Press, 1999).

32. Koji Ariyoshi, *From Kona to Yenan: The Political Memoirs of Koji Ariyoshi* (Honolulu: University of Hawai'i Press, 2000), 1–5.

33. Arleen De Vera "Without Parallel: The Local 7 Deportation Cases," *Amerasia Journal* 20, no. 2 (1994): 20–25.

34. Mai M. Ngai, "Legacies of Exclusion: Illegal Chinese Immigration during the Cold War Years." *Journal of American Ethnic History* 18, no. 1 (Fall 1998): 24–25; Him Mark Lai, "To Bring Forth a New China, to Build a Better America," in *Chinese America: History and Perspectives* 6 (1992): 3–82. See also the film, *The Chinatown Files* by Amy Chen (2001, 57 minutes) which documents the harassment and suppression of the left in U.S. Chinatowns.

35. Woon-Ha Kim, "The Activities of the South Korean Central Intelligence Agency in the United States," in *Counterpoint: Perspectives on Asian America,* ed. E. Gee (Los Angeles: UCLA Asian American Studies Center, 1976), 140–45; Chalmers Johnson, *Blowback* (New York: Henry Holt and Company, 2000).

36. Mitchell T. Maki, Harry Kitano, and S. Megan Berthold, *Achieving the Impossible Dream: How Japanese Americans Obtained Redress* (Urbana, IL: University of Illinois Press, 1999), 52–55.

37. Maki et al., *Achieving the Impossible*, 59.

38. Candace Fujikane, "Asian Settler Colonialism in Hawai'i," *Amerasia Journal* 26, no. 2 (2000): xvi–xxii.

39. Daniels, *Asian America,* 310–11; Haunani-Kay Trask, *From a Native Daughter: Colonialism and Sovereignty in Hawai'i* (Honolulu: University of Hawai'i Press, 1999).

40. L. Eve Armentroit Ma, *Hometown Chinatown: The History of Oakland's Chinese Community* (New York: Garland Publishing, 2000), 113.

41. This history of a number of Nihonmachis is captured in a special issue of *Pacific Citizen* in 2002 "Our Town: the Past, Present, and Future of the Asian Ethnic Enclave" vol. 135, no. 11.

42. Bernard Wong, *Patronage, Brokerage, Entrepreneurship and the Chinese Community of New York* (New York: AMS Press, 1988), 251–92.

43. L. Ling-chi Wang, "Chinatown in Transition" (paper presented at the Asian American Concern Conference, University of California–Davis, 1969).

44. Chan, *Asian Americans,* 140; Takahashi, *Nisei/Sansei,* 161.

45. Integrated Public Use Microdata Series (IPUMS): Version 3.0 [Machine-readable database]. Minneapolis: Minnesota Population Center [producer and distrib-

utor], 2004. It should be noted that the admission of Hawai'i as a state in the intervening period added Honolulu to the number of 1970 Metropolitan areas.

46. "White Male Qualities," *Gidra*, January 1970; Ron Tanaka, "I Hate My Wife for Her Flat Yellow Face," in *Roots: An Asian American Reader*, ed. Amy Tachiki, Eddie Wong, and Franklin Odo (Los Angeles: UCLA Asian American Studies Center, 1971), 44–47.

47. Robert G. Lee, *Orientals: Asian Americans in Popular Culture* (Philadelphia: Temple University Press, 1999).

Chapter Three

Swelling Rhythm: The 1960s Era and the Conditions for Change

I don't blame racism for every problem in my life, but up until this time I was not even conscious of the devastating and pervasive influence it had on all aspects of my life. With this consciousness came a whole new perspective on life. Rather than turn my anger, frustration and rebellion inward in the form of drugs, gangs, anti-social, anti-everything, I could focus my energy on changing the system responsible for the social ills of the time. I could fight for a better society rather than fight against society. Poverty, unemployment, war, all the ills of modern capitalism were no longer acceptable as individual problems.

The idealism of the movement overwhelmed me. Social injustice, genuine equality, concern for the collective above the individual; these were the first lessons I learned.[1]

The 1960s period produced dramatic international developments that would provide the context for the formation of the AAM in this decade: the competition among the three worlds of the United States and Europe, the Soviet camp, and the developing world including Asia; the growth of international capital and resultant competition for global resources; and the need of U.S. capital to import relatively inexpensive skilled and professional labor from Asia and cheap labor from throughout the world for agricultural work and marginal industries. The nation's most significant internal uprisings by non-Whites also framed this period. In the space created by the Civil Rights Movement and the Black Liberation Movement, other people of color were soon organizing similar struggles for equality, identity, and political power. Among women, the growth of the feminist movement for equal rights highlighted the gender inequities in society. The demographic changes in the Asian American population generated new community actors.

Coming out of the repressive and assimilationist 1950s, the rigid con-
formity that post-war conservatism dictated was beginning to make way for
a new liberal period catalyzed by the Civil Rights Movement, from which
activism could spring. The passage of the Civil Rights Act in 1964 and the
Voting Rights Act of 1965 represented important steps in ending decades of
restrictive discrimination in the workplace and voting booth. The movement
that secured passage of this legislation consolidated a new generation of activists, and the escalation of U.S. involvement in Vietnam led to growing
numbers of Americans opposed to U.S. involvement. In the labor movement,
the first half of the 1960s witnessed the growth of farm worker organizing in
California, including the 1965 strike of Filipinos that led eventually to the
merger of two agricultural worker organizations into the United Farm Workers of America Union (UFW). The UFW became another rallying point for
young activists.[2]

Most importantly, conditions among those in power opened up the political opportunity for change. Growing and widespread doubts about U.S. foreign policy and its pursuit of the war in Vietnam undermined support for established leadership. Political elites were sharply divided on the social issues
that roiled the country. The liberal wing of the Democratic Party, then dominant in government, moved concessions to many of the period's most significant movements. They expanded the welfare state in the 1960s by expanding
support for families with dependents; they also launched an effort to significantly reduce poverty in America, introduced affirmative action to help cor-
rect for previous discrimination, and changed immigration guidelines to
strike down decades-old restrictionist policies. This wing of the Democratic
Party, led by presidential candidate Robert Kennedy in 1968, openly supported the UFW grape boycott, the Chicano high school "blowouts" in East
Los Angeles, and opposition to continued U.S. involvement in the Vietnam
War. This support opened up space to activists calling for radical reform or
more extreme changes in American society.

This decade was also a period of greater social interaction and socialization
of Americans born of Asian descent during and after World War II. English-
speaking Asian Americans began to work, socialize, and interact with each
other on a more routine basis. They had less connection to homeland politics
and the Cold War than their parents' generation. Old world antagonisms also
declined because American-born Asian Americans did not maintain the historical hostilities that influenced previous generations.

In one of the earlier Asian American studies courses in 1970, Ron Low described the suppression of identity against which the new American generation would react—growing up enduring racism from students and teachers
alike as well as daily physical abuse in school.

I was also ashamed of my family because of our different culture, customs and language. By the sixth grade I had developed a philosophy. 'There were only two groups of people in the world, Blacks and Whites, and if you're going to make it in this world you'd better be part of one or the other.'[3]

For the activists like Ron Low, who sprang from this population, the Asian American Movement (AAM) changed everything. It gave a new way of interpreting the United States, their communities, and their parents and the world that they were living through. "Oppose U.S. Imperialism" reflected the influence and inspiration of looking anew at international events. The efforts of the United States to maintain its post–World War II dominance through its "Cold War" containment policies against communism translated into hot proxy wars in developing countries. The war in Southeast Asia particularly repulsed many young Asian Americans while China's pursuit of a socialist society and leadership role among developing countries broadly inspired the new activists of the Asian American Movement. The struggles for democracy in Japan, Korea, and the Philippines, as well as anti-colonial struggles in Africa and Latin America, affected smaller but significant subgroups of activists.

The AAM took root in many of the participants' home terrain, the campuses and the *Nihonmachis*, Chinatowns, and Little Manilas. Many of the AAM activists grew up or their newly immigrated parents lived in these enclaves, which became areas to defend. It shook the dusty and dirty workplaces where their parents, workers who were no longer sources of embarrassment but of pride for their endurance and dedication, toiled. The popular contemporary slogan "Serve the People" meant working particularly with the Japanese elderly, Filipino farm workers, Chinatown street youth, and restaurant workers of all groups in these communities.

The pan-ethnic movement of Asian Americans began on college campuses and on community streets in the late 1960s. One of the first organizations began in 1968 when Asian American students joined together at the University of California– Berkeley under the banner of the Asian American Political Alliance (AAPA). Their actions inspired other student groups to take the same name at San Francisco State College and other campuses, even on the East Coast. The organizations represented the culmination of efforts by Asian American individuals and organizations to coordinate and work together as part of larger coalitions including Black, Chicano, and Native American students in campus Third World Liberation Fronts.[4] These Third World student coalitions formed to demand ethnic studies courses, hire faculty of color, and provide more resources to historically unrepresented minority students. At the same time, street youth formed disparate groups such as Asian American Hardcore, Yellow Brotherhood, Leways, and Yellow Seed on the West Coast to address issues like police abuse, violence, and drug abuse that they witnessed in their own neighborhoods. They created drop-in centers, peer counseling programs, and service programs with a militant edge. The campus and community trends informed each other.[5] The one notable exception to youth leadership of the new movement was New York's Asian Americans for Action, begun by two older *Nisei* women. "Triple A" seeded a number of movement institutions in the New York area.[6]

This chapter will examine the components of social movements in the Asian American context. These components gave shape to the AAM that arose.

GRIEVANCES

Though the post–World War II period to the 1960s was a time of advancement for Asian Americans,[7] their initial conditions were so egregious and changes so incremental that the "baby boom" generation central to the AAM observed and experienced sufficient grievances to seed the new social movement. In Victor and Brett De Bary Nee's oral histories, *Longtime Californ'*, Lisa Mah captured Asian Americans' sense of the elusiveness of mainstream tolerance in this period.

> My family was very aware that they were embattled Chinese in a white district, that they had spent many years finding that place to live, and that at any moment you could be thrown out. And somehow a quality I sensed out of all this, about being Chinese, was vulnerability. So you had to watch your step and you had to be very clever, you had to placate, you had to maneuver.[8]

In 1960, Japanese Americans, Chinese Americans, and Filipino Americans comprised 80 percent of the Asian American and Pacific Islander population (see table 3.1). The populations had overlapping and similar histories of manual labor and surviving institutionalized discrimination. The parents were primarily working class, from the plantations, farms, railroads, mines, laundries, factories, and restaurants. There were also a significant number of small shopkeepers and merchants. A native-born, second-generation population had grown to become the majority of the population. Nevertheless, they faced discrimination and prejudice that, while no longer legally sanctioned, was socially pervasive. Over two-thirds of each of the Chinese, Filipino, and Japanese populations in 1960 were still in laboring and service occupations (see table 3.1)—clerical, food, laundry service, garment production, crafts, and agricultural labor—that were often marginal in their working conditions and low in their compensation.[9]

Table 3.1. Occupational Categories of Employed Chinese, Filipino, and Japanese over 14 years of age in 1960

	Employed Males	Males in Laboring and Service Occupations	Employed Females	Females in Laboring and Service Occupations	Total Employed (with identified occupations)	Total Employed in Laboring and Service Occupations
Chinese	66,704	42,014	25,630	19,474	92,334	61,488 (67% of Total Employed)
Filipino	53,937	38,694	11,572	8,236	65,509	46,930 (72%)
Japanese	113,472	71,498	71,271	61,295	184,743	132,793 (72%)
Total	234,113	152,206	108,473	89,005	342,586	241,211 (70%)

Source: U.S. Census Bureau, 1962

While the need for professional, technical, and management skills was a significant factor in the passage of the 1965 Immigration Act, the resultant growth of Asian immigrants included both low- and high-skilled workers. Immigrants with fewer choices helped to revive Chinese enclaves. Filipino nurses were recruited to work in the health care industry.[10]

Asian immigrant workers were quickly employed in the low wage service and manufacturing industries in ethnic enclaves or other workplaces in the area. Many of them were hired into industries that unions had historically neglected due to their low pay and stature. Chinese in the enclaves, for example, went into the garment and other light manufacturing factories and restaurants that had absorbed previous immigrants. Working conditions in many of these workplaces were appalling. These were the workers whom the AAM would primarily gravitate toward and champion.[11]

Within the enclaves, substandard employment and housing practices, gangs and youth issues, and discriminatory public enforcement and policies haunted these communities. Most Chinese enclaves had the highest housing densities in their respective cities, while Japantowns were dilapidated and decaying. In a 1969 New York Chinatown survey, over one in five of the five hundred respondents said that they had been robbed, and 42 percent of the housing in that community was estimated to be overcrowded. Over 90 percent of its residents worked in services or blue-collar employment.[12] Immigrants lived in tenement housing that had survived beyond its time and within neglected sections of town.[13] Gangs that attracted the disaffected cohort of arriving immigrant and baby boom native youth sprouted up throughout Asian enclaves, with names like the White Eagles, Flying Dragons, Wah Ching, Joe Boys, Ghost Shadows, and the Beacon Hill Boys.

Yet, even these mean, historical refuges were under siege. Urban renewal programs, at the time a healthy and growing federally supported series of initiatives, targeted nearly every one of these enclaves for urban redevelopment.

A NEW FRAMEWORK FOR THE TIMES

A new social interpretation, a new framework, also contributed to the emergence of the Asian American Movement. The AAM started after the height of the Civil Rights Movement during the Black Power movement. As Rocky Chin observed at the time, "It was the recent 'Black Power' Movement which caught on among the young of all colors, but particularly the poor and oppressed. Young Asian Americans (most often American-born) began to adopt 'Black Power' rhetoric and ideology."[14] The politics of the Black Power or Black Liberation Movement (BLM) were more explicitly antigovernment, with strong sentiments for self-determination and the radical transformation of society alongside demands for civil rights and equality. Building upon the Black Liberation Movement's contemporary critiques of U.S. society, the AAM drew from its explicitly antigovernment stance, strong sentiments for self-determination, and the radical transformation of society. The civil rights movement was largely a southern and church-based non-violent movement for equality that culminated with the passage of civil rights legislation in the mid-1960s. Young urban African Americans, who were frustrated with the slow pace of reforms by the U.S. government and the civil rights establishment's calls for patience, led the Black Liberation Movement.[15] They demanded community control of institutions and an end to the police violence in Black communities. These ideas, fused with a strong anti–U.S. imperialism message, appealed to Asian Americans, mainly young and fed up with the U.S. government's role in Vietnam and the racism and discrimination at home.

The BLM also promoted positive views of their communities, looking for the roots of minority issues in sociohistorical contexts, not in the communities' inherent failings. It emphasized collective action and discipline as first steps to solving these issues. One Asian American political organization in summarizing its history captured the BLM's powerful impact: "the Black liberation movement rose in an unprecedented storm and shook the capitalist system to its very foundation. The struggle of Black people inspired and set an example for other oppressed people, the Chicanos, Puerto Ricans, the Asian nationalities, Native Americans and others."[16] Karen Umemoto (1989) has pointed out however that, while the AAM would adopt much from the BLM framework, it also incorporated its own approaches.

The formation of AAM groups occurred where there were high concentrations of Asian Americans, in the San Francisco Bay Area, New York, Los Angeles, and on college campuses, locations where the BLM and the Black Panther Party influence was strong. This cross-fertilization of issues, coalitions, and ideas drew Asian and Black activists together. In addition, the development of Puerto Rican, Chicano, Latino, and Native American political power movements also took hold in overlapping locations and contributed other strong influences on Asian American political activists.

International issues also informed the AAM's framework. Asian countries, part of the "Third World" in the contemporary international political structure, were active and vital sites of resistance. They had thrust themselves onto the world stage. Such dramatic events as the Cultural Revolution in China, the creation of the Non-Aligned Movement from an international conference in Bandung, Indonesia,[17] and war in Southeast Asia demanded the world's attention, including that of young Asian Americans.

On each of the international arenas, narratives of intense drama, grand challenges, and great sacrifices produced larger-than-life figures. Figures who looked like Asian Americans straddled the world stage and commanded recognition. Asian American activists found the grandfatherly Ho Chi Minh, leader of the Communist partisans in Vietnam, and the dignified Madame Binh, spokesperson for the National Liberation Front, challenging the world's greatest superpower. The Cold War had also resulted in U.S. tolerance for dictatorial allies whose intelligence services abused dissidents among Asian American populations. These activities polarized and radicalized sectors of the changing Asian American communities.[18] Asian Americans also saw the students laying down their lives to fight martial rule in Korea or U.S. military bases in Japan. Mao Tse-tung (Mao Zedong) and Chou En-Lai (Zhou Enlai)'s China confronted a global imperialist legacy, leading the poorer, darker southern and eastern countries. They also launched the Cultural Revolution within China, where the young overturned institutions to create 'permanent revolution.' In the Philippines the New People's Army in the jungles and cities carried out the continuing struggle against U.S. domination since 1898. In the decade of the 1960s, these figures were part of the tide that struck at an immoral colonial legacy, a legacy where the United States played a morally ambiguous role.

As one Filipino activist, "Luis," described it,

> One has to appreciate what was happening in Asia at the time. Asians were thrown from the periphery to the center of the maelstrom. Through identification with Asia, our status looked completely different. Spiritually, feelings of racial inferiority changed to pride.[19]

In contrast, on the domestic stage, Asian Americans saw no models other than the Fu Man Chu and Charlie Chan caricatures; they were "visible" only to personify threats to the U.S. social structure or as figures of amusement.[20] Asian Americans were absent and "invisible" among decision makers in government or corporations, popular idols in sports and culture, and role models offered by mainstream institutions.

Rapid changes between the end of the war and the late 1960s in the Asian American population created the basis for a third element to this framing process. With the repeal of immigration restrictions after World War II and the resultant growth of second and third generations, American born Asians grew to outnumber immigrants. As the Asian population became a native-born community, linguistic and cultural differences began to decrease. Assimilation to the United States and its cultural values increased among the American-born generations. Younger, English-speaking Asian Americans from different ethnic groups began to work, socialize, and interact on a routine basis. Except in historic ethnic enclaves, the insular communities were beginning to dissolve. New housing patterns also drew more Asian Americans together in urban and suburban social settings. These relationships played an important role in socializing young Chinese, Japanese, and Filipino Americans together, people who faced similar issues in development in a society that could barely distinguish them.[21]

As young Asian Americans entered college campuses in the late 1960s, they demanded the right to study their own history. In doing so, they discovered divergent narratives. Rather than being the hyper-successful "model minority," most Asian immigrants were workers with limited education and job skills and had endured much since their arrival in this country, struggling for better working conditions, safety, and equal treatment.

There were many other influences. Mary Choy was a second-generation Korean American activist in Hawai'i at that time. She described, in addition to the Vietnam War and land eviction struggles, the particular heady confluence stew of ideas that in her case led to the formation of a revolutionary organization there:

> It was called Kokua Hawai'i. We studied Mao, liberalism, monopoly capitalism, etc. Our inspiration came from the Black and Puerto Rican movements. Leaders from the revolutionary Black Panthers and the Young Lords parties were invited by the Ethnic Studies Program to come to Hawai'i to share their experiences with us. What a consciousness-raising time that was.[22]

The influences then that allowed a new belief framework to percolate during the AAM's formative period were the Black Liberation Movement, national liberation struggles in the developing world, and the interaction between the young Asian American ethnic communities. The ideas of the BLM induced Asian American activists to adopt a skeptical view toward the social structure, a desire for self-determination or local control, self-pride, and collective action and organization. The AAM was particularly sensitive to international solidarity and a global view in political events. The willingness of Asian people and figures to confront great odds called upon Asian Americans themselves to take risks and offered hope in creating change, inspiration in challenging injustices. From international models, they inferred socialist ideas, the leading role of the working class, daring undaunted by the established order's enmity, and the spirit of sacrifice. The international environment provided unifying symbols, and guides to deciphering their environment. Each Asian subgroup found sources of inspirational sustenance in their ancestral lands. The increased intermingling of the Asian American subgroups at home and on the campuses also created a unifying, pan-Asian sense of common values and fate.

POLITICAL RESOURCES

Individuals motivated to forge a collective effort must find others of a like mind and then coalesce to build a movement organization, a critical element in sustaining social movement efforts. Who were the participants in the formation of the AAM? Three types of activists collectively built the AAM: students, community youth, and veteran community and labor organizers.

The first group, and by the far the largest segment of the AAM, were the new generation of Asian American students. In the 1960s, increasing numbers of American born Asians began to attend college, particularly at many large public universities. Immigrants, recently arrived from Asia, also began to attend college. International students from Asian countries added to these ranks. Some had already been politicized from their experiences in their native countries, and others became politicized during the turbulent 1960s and joined in campus protest activities.

On hundreds of college campuses, there was widespread dissatisfaction with the U.S. role in Vietnam and its failure to solve longstanding domestic problems such as poverty, unemployment, and affordable housing. On several college campuses, Asian American and international students participated in anti-war protests as individuals or as members of ethnic clubs or political organizations. Similar to other students of color, they demanded relevant course materials including the study of Asian American history. At San Francisco State and UC–Berkeley, students of color in 1968 took the lead in forming "Third World Coalitions" and demanded the study of racial minorities and Native Americans as part of their curriculum. They called for the establishment of institutions to serve the needs of students of color, including outreach and retention programs, such as the Educational Opportunity Program initiated in California in 1969. They also demanded ethnic studies programs, the hiring of faculty of color for the courses, and the diversification of other academic departments. Black and other students were critical in building a culture of resistance against existing institutions.

The U.S. military's killing of Vietnamese peasants caused Asian American student activists to question their own loyalties. Did they have more in common with the Vietnamese guerrillas fighting the U.S. government or with the regime in South Vietnam being supported financially and militarily by their own government? As one typical flyer of the time concluded:

> We must begin to draw our forces together, and address ourselves to our problems that we face in America. We must also examine the struggle our sisters and brothers are waging in Asia, and determine how we can best five [sic] our support and solidarity.[23]

They also began to recognize their common interests and connections with fellow Asian Americans of different ethnicities. Pan-Asian cooperation and new organizations emerged. Challenging traditional stereotypes of passivity, Asian American women led some of the new organizational formations such as the Asian American Political Alliance chapter at San Francisco State.[24]

The poverty and social problems in urban centers also spawned a second group of AAM activists who lived and worked in traditional ethnic enclaves, community youth, both immigrants and American born.[25] Their involvement came through community-based institutions including social service centers, War on Poverty programs, churches, and informal familial networks. These activities helped generate Asian American youth active in community affairs around youth leadership and other community problems. In Los Angeles, the formation of the Japanese American Community Services—Asian Involvement of Southern California by second generation Japanese Americans in the early 1960s, spawned numerous organizations and activists in the late 1960s and early 1970s.[26] Asian community youth, many of them involved with petty crimes, were caught up in the criminal justice system and faced harassment and brutality from local law enforcement agencies. Some became politicized, attracted by the AAM's more positive alternative vision of drugs and crime.[27] More established peers formed groups like Chinese for Affirmative Action in 1969 to get equal access to construction jobs.[28]

The third group was veteran labor, political, and community activists. Many had ties with the Communist Party or had worked with political groups in their birth countries; others were independent of organized left groups, while still others were part of the left wing of the Democratic Party. They provided a bridge from the previous generation of activists, offering organizing experience and working class militancy. They interjected a strong class character to the AAM. These individuals were involved in the community with small businesses, associations of overseas Asians, tenants, church groups, medical care, youth service, and elderly service providers.

In the Japanese American community, for example, one group of *Nisei* was civil rights activists active around the Golden Gate Chapter of the Japanese American Citizens League (JACL). While the JACL chose to work with the U.S. government during World War II, a few chapters and individuals sought to raise broader issues and challenge this perspective within the JACL. Following World War II these activists carried out quiet organizing. However, events of the 1960s brought them into action on numerous fronts. A long-time labor and community organizer describes the activities of one JACL chapter in the 1970s:

Dissatisfied with the conservatism of the existing chapters . . . they organized this new chapter as a vehicle through which to broadly share social and political philosophies. . . . The JACL Bay Area Community Chapter supported the Asian Anti-War Coalition, United Farm Workers Union, Coalition to Cut Military spending and Greater Chinese American Sewing Company strikers.[29]

These *Nisei* activists had strong ties to the community. Many of these community activists became involved not only in anti-war activities but also anti-redevelopment campaigns and later the Japanese American redress and reparations movement.

In the Chinese community, activists who were not deported during the McCarthy era became reenergized with the emergence of the AAM. Many of them were fiercely loyal to China and supported the liberation of the Chinese people from imperialism. Some worked on independent community newspapers and supported the emergence of the People's Republic of China. These community elders such as Happy Lim, a labor activist who had been active in the Chinese Mutual Aid Association, were an important link to past generations of resistance in the Chinese community. In the 1950s and 1960s, these activists had been isolated by the dominant business and anticommunist elements in the community. The energy and confrontational politics of the AAM opened up more political space, and many veteran voices were able to more openly speak out for normalization of relations with China and other issues.

The *Manongs* had a long history of labor organizing and played an important role in educating students about the history of labor and community organizing by Filipinos. Other older activists, students, and community members became active through community, labor, and anti–Vietnam War actions, similar to other Asian Americans. Both recent Filipino immigrants and those raised in the United States "would challenge the old guard in the community, demonstrating progressive and radical sensibilities which sharply contrasted with the conservative orientation that dominated Filipino American politics."[30] A major formation that politicized Filipinos on the West Coast was the annual Filipino People's Far West Convention, a conference of Filipino American students and professionals.

Some "veteran" activists dated their experience from participation in a more recent struggle, the Civil Rights Movement. Having lived and worked in that upheaval sharpened the impatience of Asian Americans against discrimination in housing, employment, education, and other areas. It elevated the aspirations of young Asian Americans not just for better conditions but also for equal rights. Shared values of democracy and fairness that highlighted the Civil Rights Movement became issues for Asian Americans as well. Individual Asian Americans who participated in the Civil Rights Movement returned, ready to bring their heightened political skills and ideals to their own communities.

The Movement drew from these three streams—students from college campuses, community youth, and progressive community and labor activists. Along one of the early centers of the Asian American Movement, you could see representatives of all these streams on the Kearny Street block between Jackson and Washington Streets in San Francisco. People like Steve Yip, Priscilla Kojimoto, and Carolyn Wong were students from UC Berkeley who helped out at Asian Community Centers and Asian Legal Services, respectively, on that block. Brothers Alex and Ray Hing and Patsy Chan were street youth who patronized the Leways storefront and the Red Guard organization, while elderly residents of the block's International Hotel Etta Chung and former farm worker Felix Ayson, worked in the International Hotel Tenants Association.[31] They were all instrumental to and provided the creativity and boldness necessary for building the AAM.

ORGANIZATIONAL RESOURCES

Individuals, however, by themselves aren't sufficient to build movements; for this, organization is also needed. The Asian American Movement had virtually no outside economic or political support or strong community institutional support. Whereas Black churches and colleges provided a base for the African American Civil Rights Movement, in many cases the conservative, established community leaders and organizations within the Asian American communities actively opposed the AAM activists. Traditional community institutions, tied to business interests, were unreceptive to the ideas and beliefs—support for the People's Republic of China and the Vietnamese and other national liberation struggles in the developing world—that Asian American activists espoused. Community youth had to build political support and funding sources without mainstream and community institutional support. There were, however, a small minority of churches such as the Methodist Church in the Japanese American community and Cameron House in San Francisco Chinatown where social and recreation programs existed.[32] Indigenous community resources were limited to these few churches and social service organizations.

Young AAM activists created an alternative initial support system out of what was at hand—the university environment—and the sympathetic niches in the community. Some universities developed community involvement programs. A communication system developed to support the new activist community through the college networks. Since many of the activists came out of those in colleges, access to higher education resources provided means of networking through the organizing of conferences and sponsorship of speakers, such as the 1969 "Yellow Identity" conference at Berkeley, among the earliest of a number of national Asian American conferences.[33]

The common characteristics of both these campus and community organizations included efforts at democratic functioning inclusive of both sexes in leadership, membership of immigrants and American born, and the encouragement of grass roots participation. They stood in stark contrast to the closed academic hierarchy on campuses and the traditional organizations in the ethnic communities based around business interests.

Political organizations sprang up on numerous campuses. The University of California–Berkeley Asian American Political Alliance (AAPA) inspired various AAPAs on different campuses. The San Francisco State AAPA was a significant actor in 1968 San Francisco State strike for ethnic studies that was catalytic for many Asian American student activists. Other politically oriented student groups at UCLA, Yale, and Columbia organized themselves as AAPAs. Different campuses saw Asian students organize under different terms. They took up a variety of issues, including community outreach issues and the incorporation of Asian American history, sociology, and culture into their campus curriculums. They achieved some success in winning Asian American studies programs, faculty, and staff and institutionalizing Asian American student groups. Asian student groups grew, and Asian American studies programs were established, particularly in public colleges on the West Coast and in Hawai'i.

Where Asian American studies programs were created, they became "counter-hegemonic" centers. They operated as democratic, anti-hierarchical entities where service to the community was a fundamental value. For example, University of Hawai'i's Ethnic Studies Program saw "fighting institutional racism" and "developing activism and student participation in both community struggles and the running of the [Ethnic Studies] program" as two core purposes. Curriculum and decision making involved students and community leaders. "Our History, Our Way!" became the program's rallying cry.[34]

The expanding Asian American population at colleges and universities allowed the AAM to continue to utilize the resource base of the educational system. Students accessed campus resources and organized fundraisers to help start community organizations and support campus and community causes in the fledgling Movement. This nexus between campus and community is evident in student Pam Tau Lee's description of her introduction to volunteering in Chinatown:

> And I go in there. It was to answer phones for a group called the Asian Legal Services. That was at one table. So I was at the Asian Legal Service Table. It looked just like this . . . metal table. And that's because the metal table came from UC Berkeley! [laughter] That's because the Department of Ethnic Studies

paid for the table, paid for the chairs, paid for the phones, because that was the big fight, you know, to have people go to the community and the university should offer that kind of education so that people can help their people.[35]

Administration hostility constantly threatened the stability of these programs and blunted their capacities. Tenure-track positions were grudgingly and incrementally yielded. Because of the transitory nature of the student activism, which destabilized campus organizations' effectiveness, campus groups were soon overshadowed by the growth of community-based political formations.

All over the country, the convergence of grievances and contesting ideals led many newly politically active youth from campuses and the streets back to the gritty passageways and fields of their enclaves to mobilize and create new avenues to better the conditions.[36] They would join veteran labor and community activists to challenge established norms.

At first, young people created shoestring operations that operated out of basements or borrowed space. Japanese American Community Service–Asian Involvement (JACS–AI) was one example. Leways, a youth center, and the North Beach Youth Council in San Francisco similarly scratched out havens for politically conscious young activists.[37] Over time, new and more numerous organizational forms were created in the community that provided sites for resistance and opposition to the status quo.

The community passed around new, dramatic, grassroots, printed media—eight- to sixteen-page newspapers, some bilingual, that functioned as voices and evangelists of these groups. *Rodan*, *Gidra* (both named after Japanese movie creatures), *Chinese Awareness*, *Kalayaan* ("Freedom"), and *Getting Together*, and later magazines like *Bridge*[38] gave those wrestling with new-found ideas alternative visions for their old communities. Readers, informed by a deeper understanding, gained a sense of participating in a broader social activity. Since Movement literature was often shared and saved by individuals and student organizations, the readership would easily exceed the print runs. Young Asian Americans roamed from one urban area to another, taking buses, hitchhiking, or driving old jalopies, to "check things out" or participating in more formal meetings. These intersections spread viral ideas that captured a new generation's desire for change.

The somewhat unique activities of Yellow Seed, which began as "part gang, part social club, and part paramilitary organization" in Stockton, California, gives a sense of the Movement's trajectory:

What did we do with our new knowledge of the Asian Movement? At first, we just ran a clubhouse for ourselves. We put on dances and car washes as fundraisers. Then, we started to do more activist things. We collected clothes for the Native

Americans on Alcatraz. We put on a Thanksgiving dinner for Asian cannery workers and their families. We started and ran a recreation center for Asian children. In
order to develop more knowledge we advocated for Asian American studies at the
University of the Pacific, we put on our own Asian conference, and we encouraged members to enter and finish college.[39]

One of a number of new political Los Angeles groups,[40] the *Gidra* collective, primarily Japanese American students from University of California–
Los Angeles, opened offices on the west side of Los Angeles to operate a
community-oriented newspaper in 1969. Operating completely as a volunteer effort, the five founders began the paper by contributing $100 each.[41]
Gidra would develop a press run of about 4,000 copies, with about 900 to
1,300 local subscribers.

Other groups appeared in New York, Seattle, Boston, Detroit, Honolulu,
Philadelphia, Chicago, and other cities on the west and northeast coasts that
Asian Americans populated. The Asian Community Center, politicized col-
lege youth from University of California–Berkeley, and Kalayaan in San
Francisco appeared. Third Arm, a spin-off of the radical activists of "the
House" at University of Hawai'i's ethnic studies program, went into Honolulu's Chinatown to defend single room occupancy elderly residents. In contrast to opening storefronts in urban areas, Hawai'ian youth, who came out of
a 1970 youth conference, went back to the land to defend pig farmers in the
Kalama Valley who were being evicted for up-class development. They
would form an organization, Kokua Hawai'i, and continue to fight all over the
island chain against the taking and redevelopment of Hawai'ian land.[42]

Later in 1971, activist and radical nationalist groups such as the J-town
Collective in San Francisco's *Nihonmachi* neighborhood, Free Chinatown
Committee in Boston, and Yellow Seeds in Philadelphia Chinatown formed.
In 1972 in Chicago, Chinatown activists formed the New Youth Center; the
same year in Los Angeles, a number of individuals, predominantly Japanese
Americans from organizations and collectives including the Community
Workers Collective, JACS–AI, and *Gidra* formed the East Wind Collective, a
revolutionary organization of Asian Americans. In diverse localities a spontaneous network of activist groups sprang up, nurtured by the pure idealism
and spirit of challenge that was the climate of the time.[43]

The AAM reflected varying political trends from liberal to radical. Revolution was only one of two major trends in the new Asian American Movement. While all of these activists viewed themselves as part of a shared force
for alternatives, they did not all have the same goals and philosophies. Some
looked to work "within the system" to change it. They found service provision or advocacy to be the most feasible means of change. Other than tradi-

tional associations and churches, few entities had provided services to Asian American communities.

Some activists built hopeful structures like food and garment co-ops.[44] Organizers structured the entities to be worker-run and worker-owned businesses. Others, particularly in Los Angeles, formed self-help groups, such as Asian Sisters to counsel female gang youth or services for drug abusers, parents, and low-income community members.[45] Law students, medical students, and educators tried to practice their newly learned professions in novel ways that mirrored their ideals. Many of these, the first in their families to be college educated, returned to the community to fill the vacuum of services and forwent more lucrative paths. Money was scorned. Bell-bottomed, long-haired youth prized the commitment exhibited by voluntarily "serving the people."

Many of those forming service organizations were movement activists who wanted to adopt a more cautious approach to their ideology. The Food Co-op founders in New York sought to demonstrate socialism in practice.[46] New York's Chinatown Health Fair, which in 1971 offered one-time free health screening and testing, wanted to restructure health care. It evolved into an initiative for more permanent services; the Chinatown Health Clinic began in borrowed space on a second floor walkup on Catherine Street.

Initiatives began as voluntary efforts, but many service-oriented groups quickly realized that public funds were available to address the most flagrant needs in their communities. The federal government had begun to provide new resources that the AAM could employ by establishing various programs. The new resources responded to the widespread defiance and upheavals in minority communities, particularly African Americans.[47]

Under the Lyndon Johnson administration, ambitious and significant "Great Society" programs were created to address the discontent and a number of urban and minority issues. Anti-poverty spending quintupled between 1965 and 1980. Funds for programs such as Model Cities flowed into urban areas. In the Asian American ethnic enclaves, traditional leadership organizations were ill equipped to take advantage of these funds. In their stead, new organizations and agencies with better language and professional skills sprang up and grew, supported by the new inflow of resources. Seeing funds as resources long owed to the community, these organizations in Asian American enclaves organized themselves to access many of these funds.[48] One indication of the breadth of the growth is provided by Richard Hung's study.[49] In the ten metropolitan areas with the largest numbers of Asian Americans, 48 non-profit organizations had been incorporated prior to 1960, while 129 incorporated in the following decade, and 339 from 1971 to 1980. This growth substantially changed the organizational structure in Asian American communities.

CONCLUSION: CONDITIONS FOR CHANGE

The twenty-odd years from the end of World War II to 1965 established the cohort who would lead the AAM and other aspects of community life. Building upon resource bases on the campuses and in the community, these activists created new agencies and groups to provide services like English classes and legal programs and make claims on rights and institutional resources. They demanded immediate answers to social injustices and inequities affecting the Asian American population. They could provide access to mainstream public and private programs or negotiate institutional procedures. They imagined community health clinics and youth counseling and other services to address the myriad issues of different segments of the community, whereas the previous generation of leadership was limited by the community's internal resources.

Dramatic population growth, beginning with the implementation of immigration reform legislation in 1965, would create a popular base for the new organizations and agencies, while weakening the hold of the traditional structures. The new working class immigrants provided constituencies for the new organizations, who were often in a better position to serve their needs. A more diverse immigration flow and a new influx of professionals and managers who entered through the third preference category[50] in the 1965 immigration statutes were also more independent of the traditional organizations. They not only saw things differently but also were less dependent on the services they offered.

The new organizations represented dramatic change. They had resources— paid staffs, volunteers, funds, and technical capacity—that could be applied to community issues. They had different approaches to dealing with community needs and issues and new ideas about community governance and who should participate. The new organizations also brought different ideas about the place of Asian American communities within the larger society. With established institutions uncertain and divided, they had greater possibilities in realizing their new ideas. Breaking out from the traditional leadership's insularity, the new activists took advantage of these factors to make greater demands and bring Asian Americans into the mainstream of American polity by engaging in coalitions and in issues shared by other social sectors.

NOTES

1. Kenwood Jung, "The Forces of Revolution Were on the Rise," *Amerasia Journal* 15, no. 1 (1989): 135–37.

2. Joe Virata, "Memories of America: A Conversation with Philip Vera Cruz," in *Gidra: the XXth Anniversary Edition*, ed. Gidra Staff (Los Angeles: Gidra, 1990), 10.

3. Ron Low, "A Brief Biographical Sketch of a Newly Found Asian Male," in *Roots: An Asian American Reader,* eds. Amy Tachiki, Eddie Wong, and Franklin Odo (Los Angeles: UCLA Asian American Studies Center, 1971), 345.

4. Asian American Polical Alliance. "Asian American Political Alliance Statement," in *To Serve the Devil*, eds. Paul Jacobs and Saul Landau (New York: Vintage, 1971), 269–70.

5. Miyashiro, Sheri, "Yellow Brotherhood," in *Gidra: the XXth Anniversary Edition,* ed. Gidra Staff, (Los Angeles, CA: Gidra, 1990), 122–23; Nagai, "Yellow Seed," 7; Nick Nagatani, "'Action Talks and the Bullshit Walks': From the Founders of the Yellow Brotherhood to the Present"; Ray Tasaki, "Wherever There's Oppression," both in *Asian Americans: The Movement and the Moment*, eds. Steve Louie and Glenn Omatsu (Los Angeles: UCLA Asian American Studies Center Press, 2001), 81–86, 148–55.

6. Diane Fujino, *Heartbeat of Struggle The Revoluationary Life of Yuri Kochiyama.* (Minneapolis: University of Minnesota Press, 2005), 234–74. See also Wei, *The Asian American Movement,* 28–29.

7. Daniels, *Asian America.*

8. Lisa Mar, "Lisa Mar, 36," interview by Victor Nee and Brett de Bary Nee, in *Longtime Californ': A Documentary Study of an American Chinatown,* V. Nee and B. Nee (New York: Pantheon Books, 1972), 166.

9. Bill Ong Hing, *Making and Remaking Asian America Through Immigration Policy, 1850–1990* (Stanford: Stanford University Press, 1993) ; Chan, *Asian Americans*; Bureau of the Census, *Statistical Abstract of the United States*. Bureau of the Census (Washington DC, 1962). Hing draws from a number of sources to estimate that there were nearly 900,000 Chinese, Japanese, and Filipinos as well as 11,000 Koreans and a little over 12,000 Asian Indians. The United States's western frontier, including Hawai'i, brought in successive waves of Asian agricultural and other types of "coolie" workers to develop and build the infrastructure for these areas. As the immigration flow of the preceding ethnic Asian population was restricted, workers from another Asian country replaced them. In addition to agriculture, these laborers had in common participation in the fishing and mining industries and domestic service. They also often had in common peasant roots. The 1960 U.S. Census only enumerated Chinese, Filipino and Japanese Americans.

10. John Liu and Lucie Cheng, "Pacific Rim Development;" Paul Ong and Tania Azores, "The Migration and Incorporation of Filipino Nurses," both in *The New Asian Immigration in Los Angeles and Global Restructuring,* eds. Paul Ong, Edna Bonacich, and Lucie Cheng (Philadelphia: Temple University Press, 1994).

11. Getting Together, *Chinese-American Workers: Past and Present: An Anthology of Getting Together* (San Francisco: Getting Together, 1973); Michael Liu, "Chinatown's Neighborhood Mobilization and Urban Development in Boston" (Ph. D. diss., University of Massachusetts–Boston, 1999); Doug Chin, *Seattle's International District* (Seattle: International Examiner Press, 2001); Nee and Nee, *Longtime Californ,'* 253–61.

12. Chinatown Study Group, "Chinatown Report 1969" (New York, Columbia University's Urban Center, 1970), Photocopy.

13. Nee and Nee, *Longtime Californ'*; Jan Lin, *Reconstructing Chinatown: Ethnic Enclave, Global Change* (Minneapolis: University of Minnesota, 1998); Rocky Chin, "New York Chinatown Today: Community in Crisis," *Amerasia Journal* 1, no. 1 (March 1971).

14. Andrew Hsiao, "The Hidden History of Asian American Activism in New York City," *Social Policy* 28, no. 4 (Summer 1998): 23–31; Rocky Chin, "New York Chinatown Today": 7.

15. Kwame Ture (formerly Stokely Carmichael) and Charles V. Hamilton, *Black Power: The Politics of Liberation* (New York: Vintage Books, 1992), 50–51.

16. League of Revolutionary Struggle, *Statements on the Founding of the League of Revolutionary Struggle (Marxist–Leninist)* (San Francisco: Getting Together Publications, 1978), 28; Hsiao, "Hidden History."

17. The Bandung conference of Asian and African states beginning in 1955, organized by Indonesia and other leaders of the Non-Aligned Movement, brought together twenty-nine states in an attempt to form a non-aligned bloc opposed to colonialism and imperialism. The participating states adopted five principles—non-aggression, respect for sovereignty, non-interference in internal affairs, equality, and peaceful coexistence.

18. Most notably in Korean and Filipino communities.

19. Miriam Ching Louie, "'Yellow, Brown and Red': Towards an Appraisal of Marxist Influences on the Asian American Movement," Pacific And Asian American Center For Theology And Strategies Collection, Graduate Theology Union, Berkeley, 1991: 8.

20. Fu Man Chu and Charlie Chan were popular figures in U.S. culture representing Asian Americans. Fu Man Chu was a despot bent on world domination while Charlie Chan was a mincing protagonist. Caucasian actors in "yellowface" always played both characters.

21. Espiritu, *Asian American Panethnicity*.

22. Mary Choy in *Autobiography of Protest in Hawai'i*, Robert H. Mast and Anne B. Mast (Honolulu: University of Hawai'i Press, 1996), 182.

23. Asian Alliance, "Today's Hiroshimas," authors' collection, circa 1970, mimeographed.

24. P. Wong, "The Emergence of the Asian American Movement;" Umemoto, "On Strike!"

25. Alex Hing, "Alex Hing: Former Minister of Information Red Guard Party and Founding Member of IWK," interview by Fred Ho and Steve Yip, in *Legacy to Liberation: Politics and Culture of Revolutionary Asian Pacific America*, ed. Fred Ho (San Francisco: Big Red Media and AK Press, 2000), 279–96.

26. Rocky Chin, "The House that JACS Built," *Bridge* 2, no. 6 (August 1973): 5–10.

27. Tasaki, "Wherever There Is Oppression."

28. Warren Mar, "From Pool Halls to Building Workers' Organizations: Lessons for Today's Activists," in *Asian Americans: The Movement and the Moment*, eds. Steve Louie and Glenn Omatsu (Los Angeles: UCLA Asian American Studies Center Press, 2001), 32–47.

29. Yoneda, *Ganbatte*, 197.

30. Helen Toribio, "Dare to Struggle: the KDP and Filipino American Politics," in *Legacy to Liberation,* ed. Fred Ho (San Francisco: AK Press, 2000), 31.

31. May Chuan Fu, "Keeping Close To The Ground: Politics And Coalition in Asian American Community Organizing, 1969–1977," (Ph. D. diss., University of California–San Diego, 2005); Pam Tau Lee, conversation with Michael Liu, San Francisco, CA, 1 March 2006.

32. Other churches that played this role in other cities were the Chinese Christian Church in Boston and the St. Peter Claver Center in Seattle.

33. On the East Coast around the same time the 1970 Asian American Reality Conference at Pace College brought the newly formed community groups, student organizations, and curious activists together from many parts of the East Coast as well as representatives from the West Coast.

34. Ibrahim G. Aoude, "Introduction to the Ethnic Studies Story: Political and Economic Environment" and Miriam Sharma, "Ethnic Studies and Ethnic Identity: Challenges and Issues, 1970–1998," both in *Social Processes in Hawai'i* 39 (1999): xv-xxxvi, 19–42.

35. Pam Tau Lee, "Community and union organizing, and environmental justice in the San Francisco Bay Area, 1967–2000," interview by Carl Wilmsen, 2003, Regional Oral History Office of the Bancroft Library, University of California–Berkeley.

36. A. Hing, "Alex Hing."

37. Fu, "Keeping Close To The Ground;" Pam Tau Lee, conversation; "From the Pool Halls."

38. *Rodan,* and *Kalayaan* appeared in San Francisco, *Chinese Awareness,* and *Gidra* developed out of the Japanese American community in Los Angeles, while *Getting Together* and *Bridge* were based in New York.

39. Nagai, "Yellow Seed," 7.

40. Roy Nakano, "Marxist-Leninist Organizing in the Asian American Community: Los Angeles, 1969–1979," Los Angeles: UCLA Asian American Studies Center, 1984.

41. Mike Murase, "Toward Barefoot Journalism," in *Counterpoint: Perspectives on Asian America*, ed. E. Gee (Los Angeles: UCLA Asian American Studies Center, 1976), 307–19.

42. Grace Lee Boggs, *Living for Change* (Minneapolis: University of Minnesota Press, 1998), 196–97; Nelson Nagai, "I Come from a Yellow Seed (for Bobby)," in *Asian Americans: The Movement and the Moment,* ed. Steve Louie and Glenn Omatsu (Los Angeles: UCLA Asian American Studies Center, 2001), 248–61; John Witeck, "The Rise of Ethnic Studies at the University of Hawai'i: Anti-war, Student and Early Community Struggles," *Social Processes in Hawai'i* 39 (1999); 10–18.

43. M. Liu, "Neighborhood Mobilization"; R. Nakano, "Marxist-Leninist Organizing"; Tasaki, "Where There Is Oppression"; Laura Pulido, *Black, Brown, Yellow and Left in LA: Radical Activism in Los Angeles* (Berkeley, CA: University of California Press, 2006), 105–11: New Youth Center, *Chicago Chinatown Newsletter* 1:1 (May 1972), New Youth Center: Chicago, IL.

44. The Food Co-op in New York and the Garment Co-op in San Francisco are examples of such efforts. Co-ops were attempted in Los Angeles. See Nee and Nee,

Longtime Californ,' 360–71, and Dean Lan, "The Chinatown Sweatshops: Oppression and an Alternative," *Amerasia Journal* 1, no. 3 (1971): 40–57.

45. Alan Nishio, "Personal Reflections on the Asian National Movements: Alan Nishio," *East Wind* 1, no. 1 (1982): 36–38.

46. Virgo Lee, interview by Michael Liu, New York, 23 December 2001.

47. The BLM led to the unleashing of long restrained anger among minority communities. Riots and marches often followed attacks on Blacks. The Watts section of Los Angeles was one of several cities that saw uprisings in the years 1965–1967. Other minority groups like the Puerto Rican Young Lords Party and Chicano Brown Berets followed the example of Black militancy.

48. Y. Espiritu, *Asian American Panethnicity*; G. Burtless, "Public Spending on the Poor," in *Confronting Poverty: Prescriptions for Change*, ed. S. H. Danzinger (Cambridge, MA: Harvard University Press, 1994), 529; Stephanie Fan, interview by Michael Liu, tape recording, Brookline, MA, 17 February 2004. Though researchers have varied on the exact accounting of the War on Poverty spending and whether they include programs directly associated with it or all social program spending, the flow of funds into urban areas rose several multiples in a relatively brief period.

49. Richard Hung, "Asian American Participation in Civil Society in U.S. Metropolitan Areas," Paper presented at the Association for Research on Nonprofit Organization and Voluntary Action Annual Meeting, Montreal, Canada, November 2002.

50. The 1965 legislation established a hierarchy of preferences. The third preference, "professional, scientists, and artists of exceptional abilities," emphasized skills and education, while most other preferences ranked applicants' familial relations with U.S. citizens.

Chapter Four

The Birth of the Movement: Stepping Toward New Values and New Community

Asian American Movement (AAM) activists developed a passion for systematic change. This passion was channeled into an extraordinary new attitude, which was critical and confrontational toward U.S. policies.

The new conditions converged on someone like Sadie Lum, who grew up in the Ping Yuen projects in San Francisco Chinatown. The daughter of a resourceful single mother, she developed within the enclave's environment and adopted its prevailing norms, judging her life's worth as a woman by who she would marry. A teenage mother, she endured unfruitful relationships and struggled to raise her daughter. She was also resigned to her poor material circumstances.

However, the contemporary social convulsions—the Vietnam War and minority rebellions—touched and stirred interests outside her difficult domestic situation. The role of women fighting in Southeast Asia and the fight against racial injustice inspired her. Friends participated in the San Francisco State strike and formed the Red Guard Party, working out of a new youth center in the community. She began participating in their work of draft counseling and youth organizing. The influence of progressive ideas and a new supportive social network gave her the strength to leave her abusive relationship. In her own words, the movement gave her a new outlook on herself and on life. She joined and became a leader in the Red Guard and then I Wor Kuen.[1]

The values that the AAM embodied were to confront the areas of justice, race, and class. Through these lenses, the AAM sought to change the world, attain full racial equality, and improve the lives of working people.

This chapter will first examine in detail these values and then survey the work that the AAM took up. To give greater depth to describing this work, it will end by referencing two organizations—I Wor Kuen and Inter•Im in Seattle—that occupied overlapping but differing positions in the AAM.

A BETTER WORLD

Zeal to change the world motivated the new generation of activists. International issues were primary influences. The Vietnam War was a unifying and central issue that permeated the Asian American Movement's consciousness.

Pieces like "Sam Choy" in *Getting Together* newspaper, "The Nature of G.I. Racism," and "G.I.s and Asian Women" in *Gidra* that described the military's institutionalized racism resonated alongside the racism that activists perceived in the society around them. In "Winter Soldiers," Mike Nakayama, a Vietnam veteran, describes his perceptions of other contemporary veterans' testimonies about military abuses,

> In Vietnam, racism presented itself in the GIs' attitudes of Asian people as less than human and as having no regard for human life. This reinforces the GIs' fear and hatred of the Vietnamese and Asian people in general. One example cited by an Asian brother was his hearing a Marine sniper complain of receiving credit for only one kill when he shot a pregnant woman.
>
> This racism involves all Asian people, according to testimony of an Asian veteran who told of being advised to "watch your back." One brother was taken to the hospital as an emergency case after being wounded with schrapnel (sic). He was treated last because hospital personnel thought he was a "gook"! The U.S. military presents itself as the most overt racist tool used against all Asian people.[2]

Such stories only consolidated existing antipathy for the War. Asian Americans mobilized broadly and constantly to stop the war. The AAM voiced the perspective that race colored U.S. war policy, an issue that the primarily White anti-war mainstream avoided. From interpreting the war, young Asian Americans developed broader and more critical analyses of the policies and failings of U.S. society. Mike Murase, a *Gidra* staff member, in advocating for an Asian American contingent at anti-war demonstrations, articulated such a broader critique:

> Asian Americans must demonstrate our opposition to U.S. aggression in Southeast Asia not only as concerned human beings but as Asians living in the U.S. because: (1) American policy is a policy of genocide. (2) Genocide is racism because it justifies the extermination of an entire people, who are fighting to be free, with the lie that Asian people place less value on life. (3) The systematic dehumanization of "gooks" in the military affects Asians in America as well because it is to America that trained killers of Asians return.
>
> In Southeast Asia, the lives of millions of Asian men, women, and children have been destroyed so that the rich in America can rob and plunder the lands belonging to other peoples. The racism which results is not just an unfortunate by-product of any war as some contend. It is the result of a well calculated and institutionalized policy.[3]

Another major segment of the Movement emphasized building support for China as the leader of the Third World, the countries of Africa, Asia, and Latin America. The success of China, as in many socialist countries, in health, education, housing, and eliminating inequalities held out new possibilities. These were the issues that were most salient for the poorest social sectors, on whom activists focused. Many AAM activists would engage in the campaign to restore diplomatic relations between the United States and China.

The struggle for democracy in Korea and the Philippines moved many others, particularly activists with roots in those countries. Students, professionals, and workers from Korean *chaebols* would struggle against the troops of military-backed strongmen on the streets of Korean urban centers. Elsewhere the guerillas of the New People's Army fought alongside the peasants on the outlying islands of the Philippines to oppose the martial law regime of Ferdinand Marcos. The U.S. Army supported and patronized these authoritarian leaders. One participant's analysis of Filipinos' efforts in the United States at the time observed, "Political movements from minority communities often seek redress of grievances for its members. This movement was not about grievances. Rather, it was in opposition to an overseas government which was perceived as a client state of the United States and its goal was to change US Policy towards this government."[4]

Issues of imperialism, race, colonialism, collectivity, socialism, and democracy were fused in the AAM's desire to create a better world. They generated models of what the AAM wanted and rejected in their society. In its preamble to a proposed treaty with Vietnam, Asian Americans for Peace, the vehicle for the Los Angeles Asian American anti-war organizing in the early 1970s, wrote,

> Be it known that the American and Vietnamese people are not enemies. The war is carried out in the names of the people of the United States and South Vietnam but without our consent. It destroys the land and people of Vietnam. It drains America of its resources, its youth and its honor.
>
> We hereby agree to end the war on the following terms so that both peoples can live under the joy of independence and can devote themselves to building a society based upon human equality and respect for the earth. In rejecting the war, we also reject all forms of racism and discrimination against people on the basis of class, sex, national origin, and ethnic grouping which form the basis of the war policies, past and present, of the United States government.[5]

AN END TO RACISM; "THIRD WORLD" UNITY

Domestically, foremost among the articulated changes was the demand to rectify a system of racism in the United States. Beyond the realm of ideas, systemic racism was seen as part of a system that was at the root of the problems facing Asian Americans. Fighting racism meant both directly addressing its symptoms through providing services and changing or replacing the institutional structures that perpetuated them. I Wor Kuen's direct call, "We demand an End to Racism," was based on an analysis that the Berkeley Asian American Political Alliance (AAPA) shared and expanded on. "We believe that the American society is historically racist," AAPA stated, "and one that has systematically employed social discrimination and economic imperialism, both domestically and internationally, exploiting all non-White people in the process of building up their affluent society."[6]

The Asian Community Center described the situation, in a notion popular for the times, as "internal colonies which this racist society uses to exploit our manpower and labor for low wages" and confronted this situation with cooperative food, film, and summer youth programs and a drop-in center.[7]

These views and consequent programs of self-help and militant demands were a seminal challenge to the established community leadership, a charge that contemporary power and economic relations were unacceptable. The traditional leadership accepted subordinate power positions within U.S. society and hoped and worked for the gradual improvement of conditions. The new activists, on the other hand, demanded full equality. And to the dominant society, the call by a generation of Asian American activists for full rights flew against the dominant construct of a "model minority."

Rooting out racism was a concept that could rally many of the disaffected, the young, and the risk-takers in their communities. Those who witnessed a history of injuries and prejudice saw a force to rectify historic wrongs.

It was also a concept that linked Asian Americans with other "Third World" people—Puerto Ricans, Blacks, Chicanos, and Native Americans. Given the inspirations of the AAM, such Third World unity was a central thread of the new movement. Formations such as the Black Panthers, Young Lords, Brown Berets, and Third World coalitions enabled the development of the AAM, and the AAM pursued tactics that incorporated cooperation with other communities of color.[8]

"YELLOW POWER" AND SELF-GOVERNANCE

The AAM sought the achievement of political power most concretely in greater self-governance for Asian Americans in the United States. The slogans of "self-determination," "community control," and "yellow power" voiced these demands directly and indirectly. For the AAM, self-governance was necessary because the community could then bend institutions to meet its needs rather than being exploited by them.

I Wor Kuen's "Twelve Point Program" began with demands for self-determination for Asian Americans as well as Asians and included a demand for "Community Control of Our Institutions and Lands." Less militantly but in the same vein, *Chinese Awareness* in Los Angles editorialized, "Our community has been divided and ignored by the dominant society for too long. We need to challenge the system and make it pay attention to our needs. Otherwise the system must be altered. The manner in which the change is to take place must be determined by a united community."[9] The idea of self-governance even resulted in the fleeting formulation of an Asian nation in Hawai'i, where Asian Americans could exercise self-rule.

Such a view was consistent with the AAM's development of numerous self-help programs around youth, health, and education, and self-determination appeared feasible in the enclave communities where many activists focused. The demand for local control extended to land and public services and institutions that activists had seen as failing the communities. One of the most immediate arenas for "community control" were the schools. In New York, the demand for community led to a decade-long struggle between numerous communities of color and the powerful New York Federation of Teachers. Other urban areas saw variations of this theme, including the Josiah Quincy community school in Boston, which released its facilities to the Chinatown community after academic hours.

"YELLOW IS BEAUTIFUL"; EMBRACING THE PEOPLE

The articulation of identity for Asian Americans was a complex cornerstone of the AAM. One aspect of this articulation was self-pride, "Yellow is Beautiful"[10] was directly modeled on the Black Liberation Movement's "Black is Beautiful" slogan. Numerous articles deconstructed the self-loathing inherent in past practices of body manipulation and manners of dress to imitate White Americans.

This new self-pride was integrated with the creation of a new Asian American identity that superseded the ethnic identities that young activists had grown up with. Many of the reasons for their ethnic disidentification had diminished for young Asian Americans. Previous scholarship has focused on the pan-ethnic dimension of the new identity. This social construction of identity was certainly, as Espiritu suggests, a political construction but not made out of whole cloth. For the AAM generation, it was grounded in material conditions in their various shared communities' experiences and the society's racialization of them. Hawai'i's pan-ethnic, heavily Asian American population and activism also played an influential role on contemporary thinking. The early activism at the University of Hawai'i, its dramatic land and labor struggles, and the U.S. colonial history attracted Asian American activists' attention.

The articulation of a new identity also led to reevaluation of Asian Americans' own culture, history, and people, particularly the worth of working people. Asian American studies and other university classes, movement newspapers, and veteran labor activists introduced the role of workers and class struggle.

As the young generation of Asian Americans sought to learn about the struggles of Asian and other workers, the United Farm Workers Union campaign for unionization and call for a nationwide boycott of table grapes became prominent during the years 1965 to 1970. This struggle drew many Asian Americans to support these efforts, including boycotting grapes and getting them out of Chinatown and Japantown stores.

Asian Americans learned of and reflected on the plight of Asian workers. This led to a reimagining of the Asian American population's disadvantaged circumstances that many at an earlier age found humiliating. Seeing these conditions as a result of larger, impersonal forces and within a historical progression removed the stigma from their communities and directed it toward social elites and institutions. Activists saw the endurance, difficulties, and grievances of workers in a new, more valued light and their strength as models to emulate.

Karl Yoneda, the labor organizer, captured this new attitude:

> There are many heroes whose records are unsung and unknown. We can enrich ourselves from the past in order to create the kind of society all of us are hoping and striving for. Asian immigrants contributed greatly in enriching the US mine, railroad, farm, sawmill, fishing, cannery, sugar and pineapple industries. We, their descendants, have every right to have a say in its destiny.[11]

The AAM folk music trio of Chris Iijima, Joanne Miyamoto, and Charlie Chin, in a different media, boasted of this new identification in their song "We are the Children." "We are the children of migrant workers, of the concentration camp, of the railroad builder" they said, "who leave their stamp on Amerika."[12]

In embracing themselves and their communities, the AAM also took on the responsibility to qualitatively better conditions. And in the optimism of youth, they imagined changing them.

THE WORK OF THE NEW MOVEMENT

The activism that the Asian American Movement fostered spanned a range of political views. While trends could be traced between the more politically oriented, revolutionary groups and reform-minded service ones, there were numerous formations that spanned the space between these different poles.[13] The new activism generated a spirit of creativity, improvisation, and optimism that profoundly affected their communities. This was given voice in the cultural flowering described later in this chapter. The AAM also occupied itself with a wide spectrum of issues and projects. From that spectrum, this text will look specifically at the Vietnam War and international support, labor, student, community, women, and culture.

THE VIETNAM WAR AND SUPPORT
FOR INTERNATIONAL STRUGGLES

When the AAM emerged in the late 1960s, the Vietnam War and the struggle for civil rights were the dominant issues confronting the nation. Opposition to the war was a unifying and central problem in the Asian American Movement. The communist-led Vietnamese liberation movement had defeated French colonialists in 1954 after nearly a decade but then faced a subsequent undeclared war by the United States. The U.S. government characterized the struggle as a civil struggle in which it was supporting the anti-communist side, but many saw it as a continuation of a war for liberation, where the United States had taken on the role of the France. While the AAM was only one of many organized trends in turmoil around the war, mobilizing around it was one of the primary arenas where Asian Americans recast their relationship with U.S. society.

Young people from all parts of the AAM opposed the war, not simply out of a self-interested avoidance of risk but from seeing themselves in the faces of those wearing the black Viet Cong uniforms. The seeming mismatch between a "superpower" like the United States and a small Southeast Asian country created a natural empathy for the underdog.

The revelation about U.S. bombing of Cambodia in 1970[14] electrified many youth. The U.S. "incursion" expanded the war, disregarding the sovereignty of Asian nations and the vulnerabilities of another Asian population. The application of Agent Orange defoliant and napalm upon a peaceful population in a neutral country seemed like criminality.[15]

Anti-war protest was a regular and continuing activity of most AAM groups. They engaged in the panoply of activities—military draft counseling, working with soldiers, issuing literature, organizing teach-ins, writing songs and skits, and organizing public protest. Some visited Vietnam. Others organized delegations to visit with counterparts in third countries. The war provided many of the symbols around which young activists rallied, symbols visible in posters on apartment walls and on pins on jackets and bags and articulated in chants during marches.

The war helped to build the Asian American Movement, drawing in successive cohorts of young people. From first interpreting the war, young Asian Americans developed broader and more critical analyses of the policies and failings of U.S. society. Each new point reopened the doubts about the United States's legitimacy and drew in more young people in protest, Asian Americans among them. Asian Americans also looked critically at other contested parts of the globe. Vietnam became the AAM's portal to the desire for global justice. As Buck Wong remembers it:

> The Vietnam War changed my life as it did the lives of millions of people. In a relatively short time, I went from "not wanting to be killed in a war" to "questioning war as a method of resolving conflict" to "disagreement with America's foreign policy."[16]

In time they felt the need to organize separate vehicles reflecting their perspective. On the West Coast, Asian American marchers appropriated the Snake Dance, originated by Japanese students, to distinguish their contingents in anti-war marches. Looping and undulating in a long line from one side of the street to the other as they inched forward, the Snake Dance also asserted their distinct perspective on the war.[17] The Snake Dance visibly signified that the Asian American Movement would pursue an independent course in activism.

The AAM introduced the perspective that race colored U.S. policy in the war, an issue that the primarily White anti-war mainstream avoided. Asian Americans held signs such as "Stop Asian Genocide" or "Stop the bombing of Asian People." The Brandeis Asian American student group held a typical view. Their statement on the war began:

> We feel very strongly that U.S. involvement in Vietnam, both military and political, is an imperialist and racist involvement, in keeping with America's inhumane policies and that it must be recognized and opposed on this basis. Our own experience with discrimination, racist manipulation, and particularly with the denial of the existence of racism against Asians in America magnifies our concern with the present struggle.[18]

The San Francisco area developed one of the most organized, distinct Asian responses to the war. The Bay Area Asian Coalition Against the War (BAACAW) formed in 1972 to build an Asian presence in the large anti-war movement in the San Francisco Bay area. Asian anti-war activists made repeated failed efforts to transform the politics of the larger anti-war movement.[19] They perceived a narrow focus on American youth involved in the war epitomized by the mainstream anti-war slogan of "bring the boys home." AAM activists wanted a broader, anti-imperialist perspective that called for solidarity with the Vietnamese people in their struggle for self-determination from U.S. domination.

BAACAW was organized into several regions, with each region serving as a mini-movement center. For example, in the East Bay area, the center was the Asian Student Union on the UC Berkeley campus in San Francisco, there were several centers including San Francisco State College, Japantown, and Chinatown/Manilatown.

The coalition's orientation was pan-Asian. The focus of activity was on organizing and mobilizing the entire Asian community to oppose the war and support the efforts of Southeast Asians opposed to U.S. aggression. Its membership was broad-based and typical of most AAM activities of the period. The coalition included wide participation from ethnic-specific groups, student organizations, religious figures, church organizations, civil rights groups, and leftist organizations. The coalition linked the broad issues involved in the war to community issues and problems. The war promoted hostility and violence toward Asian Americans and consumed resources that many felt should be used to solve community needs. Hundreds of Asian Americans mobilized as part of larger anti-war rallies; they also participated in teach-ins on college campuses and in ethnic communities.

Outreach had modest success in reaching Asian community members in low-income communities, many of whom were recent immigrants faced with immediate issues of daily life.[20] The coalition was more successful in reaching young Asian Americans, many of whom became active in the AAM. BAACAW carried out organizing and agitational and educational activities until the war ended in 1975.

Without resources or support, Asian American groups carried out continuous anti-war protest over several years. Rather than being conciliatory, these anti-war activists raucously stood up for their views and organized independently, confronting both established institutions and the mainstream protest leadership. The work against the war was the starting point from which the AAM expanded their vision to root out racism and imperialism globally in search of a better world.

As the war progressed and peace talks began, the issue of the war for the AAM moved from the center to a place alongside other issues. Other areas of work rose in importance. The war, for some, had drawn them into lifelong international concerns about other countries and more systemic critiques about capitalism, and they continued to pursue these other concerns with similar passions. For others, the resolution of the War concluded the urgency of the Movement, and they focused on more daily issues.

Transitions are evident in examining two disparate, contemporary publications, *Yellow Seeds* newspaper in Philadelphia, the publication of a small community group, and Basement Workshop's *Bridge* magazine in New York. The early years of *Yellow Seeds* carried occasional articles about the war explaining the relation between domestic and social issues. After 1975, the articles exclusively focused on domestic issues except for an article on the death of Mao Tse-tung. Similarly, *Bridge* magazine editorialized from time to time about the war from 1971 to 1975, speaking on the Vietnamese cease-fire in 1973, U.S. prisoners of war, and the My-Lai massacre of Vietnamese civilians. After 1975 and a special retrospective issue on Vietnam, *Bridge* turned more exclusively to domestic issues for the next two years, focusing on issues such as Asian American theater, electoral politics, children's literature, and poetry.

While the Vietnam War was a dominant inspiration, other international contests also drove Asian American activism. One example is the enduring involvement of Filipino Americans in the struggles of the Philippines. A steady stream of Filipino nationals began arriving in the 1960s; these immigrants eventually formed locals to support the national democratic movement in the Philippines. In New York, they formed the Support Committee for a Democratic Philippines. In San Francisco, the Kalayaan Collective formed and produced a nationally distributed newspaper and also "initiated the call to organize a national formation"[21] that would focus on the Philippines as well as on other issues.

Efforts were underway in the fall of 1972 to establish a national formation when President Ferdinand Marcos declared martial law in the Philippines. This led to the establishment of the National Committee for the Restoration of Civil Liberties in the Philippines, a broad coalition of opponents to martial law. In addition, other organizations in the Filipino community also began to organize against Marcos, including elements of the Philippines ruling elite who came to the United States seeking refuge from the Marcos regime. Among its most visible representatives was Raul Manglapus, a former Philippines senator, who came to the United States a few months after Marcos declared martial law and sought to have the United States invade the Philippines to oust Marcos.[22]

Members of the leftist Katipunan ng mga Demokratikong Pilipino or Union of Democratic Filipinos (KDP) also helped form the Friends of the Filipino People (FFP), composed predominantly of non-Filipinos concerned with U.S.-Philippine relations. This group conducted lobbying in Washington, D.C., to reduce U.S. aid to the Marcos regime.[23] For the rest of the 1970s and into the 1980s, KDP continued to conduct anti-imperialist work around the Philippines, including forming the Anti-Martial Law Alliance in 1974–1975, which coordinated work between KDP and the FFP.

IMPROVING THE COMMUNITY CONDITION: SERVE AND FIGHT FOR THE PEOPLE

Activists of the time of nearly all stripes tried to improve the environment within their communities. They attacked the panoply of problems with much of the same energy and creativity that they applied to protest. They preoccupied themselves with the issues of education, police harassment, housing, working conditions, health conditions, women's and youth issues, and legal rights. They addressed these issues by directly providing these services and making claims upon institutions.

As volunteers, many activists tried to provide for the needs of their communities that "the system" ignored. Free legal counseling, youth activities, child care programs, English as a second language (ESL) and tutoring classes, and elderly and children's breakfast programs sprang up, created simply out of the inspiration and of youthful ideals. Activists solicited material elements — books, food, medical supplies — for the new services from local institutions and small businesses or paid for them themselves. Volunteers provided the people power. JACS–AI activists, for example, supported themselves with occasional youth service positions and began drug abuse, legal aid, and support programs for elderly and youth.[24] Enclave residents, those previously forced to fend for themselves[25] and others, part of the new immigration flow and unaware how to meet basic needs, flocked to these new services.

When the services saw the need to become more stable, the resource demands for such transitions exceeded volunteer capacity. Steady sources of support were needed. Activists, some warily, began to take advantage of public funds. They needed the support but were leery of conditions that would limit the delivery of services and dependencies that would integrate them into "the establishment." A few decided that the system owed their communities these resources and that they could work for "change within the system." The infusion of funds for services greatly expanded what the new service organizations could do, especially as they concluded that funds did not restrict their essential mission to help their communities.

Asian Health Services started as a volunteer effort in a single room in Oakland Chinatown, providing information and referrals. By 1979, it secured federal funds to establish a formal community health clinic.[26] Founded in 1972, Search to Involve Pilipino Americans (SIPA) began as a vehicle to introduce young Filipinos to Filipino culture. SIPA sought to reconnect Filipino youth to their identity and community issues, sponsoring trips to the International Hotel, a focus of struggle for California Filipinos. It expanded its work to health services, drug counseling, youth employment, and tutoring.[27]

Serving and fighting for the people took divergent paths into the mid-1970s. Modest, service-oriented organizations grew into established service providers. Those more committed to systemic change, who initially provided many services, began to emphasize the importance of fighting for change. While they continued to provide services in limited forms, either informally or through modest programs, they developed a more consolidated role for themselves as organizers. Others continued to work in service programs for employment while doing organizing for change outside of work hours.

The development of these services brought changes to the ethnic enclaves in two ways. They vastly broadened and improved programs that could address the specific issues of Asian Americans. With a primarily working class immigrant population, these issues were myriad and had gone unaddressed. Second, the services, by working within existing social service networks, became a major channel connecting the enclaves to the larger society. They were a significant means of breaking these enclaves out of their isolation.

CAMPUS CRUCIBLE

One of the driving constituencies of the AAM was the student population. Students had the opportunity to examine and consider social systems, energy to act on their beliefs, and freedom to challenge the system. While the campus-community interrelationship was a seminal concept of the AAM and many students returned to their communities, campuses remained sites of struggle for succeeding student cohorts.

In the academy's curriculum, Asian Americans were people without a historical or cultural presence or a political role in the United States. Within these domains, white authority figures often delivered a White person's narrative, and representation within academic programs, institutions, and the faculty and staff was lacking. The norm of academic "objectivity" separated students from the communities that they cared about.

The formation of the AAPA was a milestone in the history of Asian Americans as it brought different individuals together under a pan-Asian racial and organizational identity. Those who started the AAPA at UC–Berkeley first coined the term Asian American.[28] The trend only accelerated with the news of the 1969 SF State Third World Liberation Front's strike for ethnic studies. Asian American Political Alliance, Intercollegiate Chinese for Social Action, and Philippine-American Collegiate Endeavor all helped to establish the nation's first School of Ethnic Studies; many of the strike participants carried this militancy forward on campus or in the community. Their example inspired many other third world students of color. Instead of study, Asian American student activists learned how to organize, spending long evenings in meetings rather than classes, hunched over flyers instead of books, and built alliances, coalitions, networks, and strike centers rather than résumés.

Student activists demanded Asian American studies programs, Asian American faculty, open admissions, community-campus programs and fought against later cutbacks in the programs established across California, the East Coast, and Hawai'i. Michael Murase, a founder of *Gidra*, observed the breadth of student activism as taking place "On the West Coast . . . on virtually every campus of the University of California system as well as California State University at Los Angeles, Loyola, Claremont, and Pepperdine."[29] In 1970 University of Hawai'i students established an ethnic studies program, beginning a successful seven-year battle for permanent status, an emphasis on local history and activism, and student participation in governance. In 1971 Asian American students at City College in New York led three hundred Black, Latino, and Asian American students in a three-day takeover. Their efforts secured free admissions for Asian American students, an Asian American Studies program, and new Asian American faculty and staff and similar concessions for other students of color.[30] In the same period, Seattle Central Community College students took over the administration building and demanded to know "Where's the community in our community college?" Such student struggles won the first Asian American studies courses and then programs, representation in the academy, liberalized admissions policies, student roles in governance, coalitional structures between organizations of color, urban community service, and studies from a more global perspective.

The campus was a crucible. The campus conditions that Asian student activists sought to change began with organizing themselves, articulating an analysis of their position and goals, and confronting university power structures to transform policies and practices. Ideologically, Asian students were looking at both the revolutionary liberation movements internationally and at the oppression of Asian and third world peoples in the United States. University of California–Berkeley's AAPA newspaper stated:

> We Asian Americans realize that America was always and still is a white racist society. Asian Americans have been continuously exploited and oppressed by the racist majority and have survived only through hard work and resourcefulness, but their souls have not survived. . . .
>
> We Asian Americans support all oppressed peoples and their struggles for liberation and believe that Third World People must have complete control over the political, economic, and educational institutions within their communities.[31]

What would these ideas look like in practice on a college campus? Two slogans capture the sentiment: Serve the people and Self-determination! Realizing

these involved political education study groups, sponsoring educational outreach programs to reach new potential members, collaborating with community groups, and trying to make accessible the colleges' resources to Asian
communities and working class Asian students.

One example of this evolution was the formation of pan-Asian student organizations at UC–Berkeley. The Asian Student Union (ASU) described the
conditions that led to its formation in 1972, illustrating the array of issues on
campus that confronted Asian students:

> a period when political activity among Asian students at UCB was inconsistent and
> without definite direction, often working from crisis to crisis. This was reflected in
> the Asian Ad hoc Committee that spontaneously formed around a triple strike situ-
> ation on campus; (1) the Boalt Hall Law Students strike around Third World spe-
> cial admissions, (2) the campus trade union strike, and (3) the bombing and mining
> of Hanoi and Haiphong. Students saw the need to have an organization that could
> do consistent work around political issues affecting Asian students.[32]

The ASU struggled over the next two years to establish an active organization that reflected "the participation, interests, and politics of a broad sector of students through its activities, events and struggles." Berkeley students
were actively involved in numerous community struggles and in linking them
with other Asian students. For example, they supported the Kiku and Mandarin restaurant workers in San Francisco for better working conditions,
against management use of immigration restrictions to intimidate immigrant
workers, and for unionization. The ASU then summarized that they had focused too little effort on Asian students and overemphasized events in general; they changed their main focus toward "the Berkeley campus and the
ASU." By 1974-1975, the ASU had grown into a large organization with six
committees: Asian studies, Women's Caucus, newsletter, political action,
study discussions, and publicity/outreach. The ASU learned important lessons
about building a student base through trial and error and evaluating its experiences. This constant assessment, from the influence of the Asian American
Movement, was a hallmark by the end of this first period of the Movement.[33]

In the process of trying to understand and transform these relationships,
students developed skills and ideas that have become, in Karen Umemoto's
term, foundational.[34] Throughout the 1970s, Asian American student activism
grew, established itself, and spread to more campuses.

FIGHTING FOR WORKING PEOPLE

In the world of labor, veteran labor activists crucially aided the new generation of organizers. A number of the first generation of immigrant Filipino,

Chinese, and Japanese labor organizers and activists had continued to organize throughout this period. The figures such as Philip Vera Cruz in the United Farm Workers and Karl Yoneda in the Longshoreman's union educated young Asian Americans about their labor experiences. They spoke about the role of Asian immigrant workers in the 1930s and in the post-WWII period. They highlighted the important struggle of Filipino and Mexican farm workers for better working conditions. Asian Americans on campuses and in communities supported the call to boycott table grapes to support the farm workers' campaign against pesticide exposure and other dangerous conditions in the fields.

Where these issues and other factors converged were in immigrant worker organizing, racism in the mainstream labor movement, and recognition for Asian American workers. In the early 1970s, only a handful of Asian Americans were union organizers or elected union leaders. This void compelled non-unionized immigrant workers to self-organize and deliver their votes to unions, and it was left to the AAM to build support and publicize this upsurge of Asian immigrant worker struggles.

Organizing workers in ethnic enclaves, where familial ties and institutional control by small-business owners were prevalent, was extremely difficult. Feudal culture was influential, and some workers lacked legal immigration status. In many of the large commercially profitable Japanese restaurants, owners pitted different races against each other, while in Chinese restaurants, complex forms of subjugation were used to keep workers divided. In the manufacturing industries, workers were exposed to both health and labor rights violations.

During the early phase of the AAM, the new generation of immigrant workers staged numerous organizing drives to win unionization and respect on the job. Some of these campaigns occurred in the garment industry such as Gold Factory in San Francisco and health care such as Gouveneur Hospital in New York's Lower East Side. Asian Americans also opposed hiring discrimination in the construction industry. Other campaigns took place among hotel and restaurant workers—the Nam Yuen and Asian Gardens restaurants in San Francisco's Chinatown, and the outlying Mandarin Restaurant. These seminal campaigns were a few of the many that largely immigrant workers carried out in this period, typically without union support or recognition.

One major struggle occurred in San Francisco during the summer of 1974. One hundred and thirty-five employees of the Great Chinese American (Jung Sai) Sewing Company, mostly Chinese immigrant women, went on strike for better working conditions, job security, and higher pay. The Jung Sai garment factory was one of a bevy of contract shops that sewed materials for Espirit de Corp, owned by "hip" capitalist Doug Tompkins. Jung Sai was an atypical sewing factory because of its relatively large workforce and its direct ownership by the manufacturer. However, its working conditions were typical of most contract sweatshops; workers barely made $2 per hour and were forced to punch out and return to work "off the clock" to avoid overtime pay. They were also denied regular bathroom breaks.

Three times the immigrant workers sought to organize themselves into a union. Repeatedly, a line of middle-aged women in patterned blouses, carrying handbags and umbrellas against the sun, intermingled with young community supporters, marching outside the factory. On the third unionization attempt, 90 of the 135 workers secretly signed pledge cards. When the union, the International Ladies' Garment Workers' Union (ILGWU), contacted the management to negotiate a contract, one of the leading workers was fired. The workers went out on strike in protest.[35]

The grueling seven-month strike would involve sit-downs and arrests, culminating in an incident where the management attempted to force through bins loaded with cloth, hospitalizing several workers. In the end, the workers agreed to a compromise settlement, but Jung Sai never reopened.[36] Nevertheless, the strike was a breakthrough in demonstrating the potential militancy of Chinese women workers and their willingness to stand up and fight for labor rights.

Issues of race, class, and gender were hotly debated throughout the campaign as various forces involved sought to influence the politics of the struggle. The union sought to downplay the political significance of the first major strike in Chinatown in decades. Two groups associated with the new left movement based in Chinatown, I Wor Kuen (IWK) and Wei Min She (WMS), disagreed about the significance of the "national question," the issue of race, on Asian Americans. I Wor Kuen highlighted the fact that the struggle was both a labor issue and a question of the "national oppression" of Chinese Americans. Wei Min She saw the strike primarily as part of a larger struggle of all working people. There were also disagreements about the role of the union. IWK sought to change the union by capturing union positions and in this context sought to cooperate with the current union leadership, while WMS believed change came from rank and file action rather than by obtaining union leadership positions. The debate over the significance of race and ethnic-specific issues in the struggle against capitalism would continue in the left movement for many years. While the differences among the two left groups were sharp, as one activist recounted later, "to their credit, these organizations made far reaching efforts to work together despite their differences in order to avoid hurting the strike support."[37]

Asian American workers also tried to break into mainline industries. In 1974, Chinese community activists, led by Asian Americans for Equal Employment (AAFEE),[38] in New York's Chinatown demanded construction jobs for Chinese workers. They targeted the construction company hired to build Confucius Plaza, a large, federally funded housing project in the heart of the community. Hiring demands were won after arrests at the work site, daily demonstrations, and public pressure on the construction company. Similar efforts to hire Chinese workers on projects were launched in San Francisco's Chinatown by Chinese for Affirmative Action. In Boston, Chinese workers united with Black and Latino workers through the Third World Jobs Clearinghouse, sometimes in physical confrontation with White construction workers, to break into the construction industry.

AAM activists also had to confront racist campaigns. KDP was heavily involved in defending Filipino immigrant nurses and other health workers against deportation and denial of work certifications. During the early 1970s, U.S. unions began to adopt anti-Japan "Buy-American" campaigns as growing volumes of imported goods began to enter the U.S. market. In August 1972, the ILGWU published a poster in New York City featuring an American flag with "Made in Japan" superimposed over the front of it. A coalition of Asian American community activists launched a campaign to oppose the racialization of the import crisis.[39]

While many of the organizing campaigns were spontaneous, lacked union or financial support, and most often failed, they nevertheless mobilized support from the Asian American community and working class supporters. These struggles exposed not only the exploitation of workers but also the class distinctions inherent within ethnic communities between workers and their employers. These class differences would be another recurring theme in Asian ethnic communities. The adversarial or compromised roles of unions also informed future community-labor relations.

These campaigns elevated the issues of working women. Immigrant women often led the struggles of Asian American workers. They overcame many obstacles to immigrate to this country and shouldered the triple roles of mother, wife, and worker. Their strong stands for justice and decent working conditions in the face of recalcitrant employers, unsympathetic government agencies, and passive union leaders inspired many. Their struggles heightened awareness about the role and importance of working women.

Reports such as the one below reported by *Getting Together* sensitized many activists to the acute conditions that Asian working women faced.

I worked in a garment factory sweatshop in San Francisco Chinatown. From my own experience and from talking with my fellow workers in the garment factory, I found out a lot about the sweatshop situation. There are a lot of them up and down the block, probably at least one in every single block. Most of them are illegal in that they pay the workers lower than the minimum wage which is $1.65 an hour. That is why they don't put up a sign outside the door saying that it's such and such a company. How you can tell that inside is a sweatshop is usually it's a storefront, on the ground floor, either they have curtains all around the windows so you can't look inside or they paint the windows and the door is closed. But when you walk past it you can tell it's a sweatshop. . . .

The workers are not paid by the hour, but on the piece rate, between $6.00 and $8.00 a dozen, which is 50 cents to 60 cents apiece. This is the standard price in San Francisco Chinatown. The workers sew on an average of a dozen a day, and that is from eight o'clock in the morning to six-thirty or seven at night. Most of them take only half an hour to eat lunch. They eat lunch right there at the sweatshop, they either bring their lunch or cook something right there. When I said workers sew an average of a dozen a day, I meant the experienced workers. When I first worked there, I made five dresses in three days. For workers who have worked in this trade for five to seven years, some of them are super-fast, they make about two dozens a day, but that's only twelve dollars for like ten hours of work. How they get around paying the workers the minimum is by talking them into not using their social security number. The sweatshop owners have different ways of not reporting to the government.[40]

By the end of this first period of the AAM, there was growing awareness of the potential and strategic position played by workers in society. The various efforts to unionize and end discrimination against Asian American workers spurred many AAM activists into labor activism. The more political groups began serious efforts to conduct worker organizing.

A REVOLUTION OF CULTURE

The emergence of the Asian American Movement also created an opportunity for groundbreaking intellectual and cultural work. Depictions of Asian Americans in U.S. culture were dominated by demeaning stereotypes with few and restricted avenues for expression of their culture.

The AAM called for the telling of the Asian American story in a new way with a new context. Moreover, it became a vehicle for broad participation in creating a new cultural voice in U.S. society. With this voice, the experience of Asians in America would be cast as an experience of an oppressed people facing a history of social, legal, political, and cultural attack by the dominant society. And in facing this experience, Asian American life in the United States could be celebrated as determined resistance and a struggle for freedom, turning on its ear the self-image that many Asian Americans had been raised with.

On the intellectual front, this meant relating the Asian American experience to the progressive and revolutionary writings of the day, from Frantz Fanon to Che Guevara to Mao Tse-tung to Malcolm X to the Black Panthers.[41] Alongside this great intellectual ferment was the creation of images, sounds, and language that represented the Movement. Silk-screened event posters, murals depicting Asian American historical moments, poetry anthologies, skits and full length plays, music ensembles, and films all formed tangible evidence of the impact of the emerging Asian American Movement.

Significant works were created. These included *A Grain of Sand: Music for the Struggle by Asians in America*, a 1973 LP music record by Chris Iijima, Joanne Miyamoto and "Charlie" Chin. The artists toured the country giving concerts and carried out their own community organizing work in New York. *Third World Communications*, edited by writer Janice Mirikitani, produced a number of anthologies and publications—*Aion* Magazine in 1971–1972, *Third World Women* in 1973, *Time to Greez!* in 1975.

Aiiieeeee!: An Anthology of Asian-American Writers, published in 1974, was the first widely available collection of works by Asian American authors selected by an Asian American editorial team. *Aiiieeeee!* asserted a tradition of writing by Asians in America giving voice to a unique experience.

This work's introductory essay, "50 Years of Our Whole Voice," influenced cultural work in the AAM by providing an Asian American perspective on the contributions and struggle of Asian American writers. In part of that introduction, Filipino poet Sam Tagatac illustrated the new boldness as he describes an alternative insight in his poem "Starfighter." He says he "know(s) better" about the United States, seeing beyond its triumphal narrative. The conclusion following the poem proclaimed, "Only a Filipino-American can write adequately about the Filipino-American experience."[42]

Theater work during the anti-Marcos period expressed the powerful sentiments of the Filipino activism in the United States and affirmed its relationship to the Philippines. It also provided a foundation for an internationally famous theater tradition in the ensuing decades that exists on both sides of the Pacific. This tradition engendered cultural resistance in its use of language, movement, and ideas as well as serving as a vehicle for community organizing.

Performances of music, theater, dance were an opportunity for gathering and a collective experience. The creative process provided mobilizing structures for organizing as well as developing frameworks of ideas. Consequently, new and notable cultural groups were founded in this period. As part of the Third World solidarity built in the SF State Strike, artists like Janice Mirikitani built multi-racial vehicles. Kearny Street Workshop, primarily known as a writers and visual artists group, and Japantown Art and Media in San Francisco, Visual Communications in Los Angeles, and Basement Workshop in New York grew out of those times. Basement Workshop was loosely coordinated, and artists pursued different interests, but they saw their art in the context of their communities, participating in community struggles directly and through their artistic work.

The San Francisco Bay Area saw the formation of such performing arts organizations as the Asian American Theater Workshop, Asian American Dance Collective, and San Jose Taiko. Indicative of the interrelationship between culture and activism, the two primary founders of San Jose Taiko, Roy and P. J. Hirabayashi, were activists in San Jose's Asians for Community Action that, among other accomplishments, created the Asian American Studies program at San Jose State.[43]

For the most part, these organizations were products of the AAM, most often located in the historic enclave communities and embracing the "Serve The People" ethic. They served a dual function as vehicles for the individual pursuit of art and making the arts not only accessible to the community but also directly supportive of the aims of the Movement.

One early example is the guerilla theater performances that popularized the summer 1972 campaign to defend Harry Wong, a street newspaper vendor in San Francisco Chinatown. The police had long harassed Harry Wong for selling material about and from mainland China alongside other news material. He was arrested for "obstructing the sidewalk" and selling goods without a license. Mounting a campaign to defend Harry Wong, cultural activists worked alongside organizers and community attorneys. Rallies were organized, highlighted by street theater, which was performed in full dress on a makeshift stage. These skits dramatically played out the background, circumstances, and arrest of Harry Wong by six officers.[44] The campaign succeeded in seeing that the charges against Wong were eventually dropped.

Perhaps a most important outcome of the day-to-day work of these mobilizing structures was its contribution to a Movement culture. International Women's Day and International Workers Day were introduced and became annual events in the community. Beyond raising support at benefits or disseminating messages and information, the work created venues for the development of lifelong relationships, for self-examination and self-transformation, and dialogue around a myriad of burning issues in the context of experiencing a "life in the community." Thus Movement culture played a key role in popularizing the new framework of the Movement and creating a political community.

SLEEPING WOMEN AWAKE

Within the struggle for full equality for Asian Americans as a people, female activists engaged in the AAM soon perceived that the demand for equality also resonated for gender issues within the AAM. They wanted to play a full role. To do so, they extended equality to the status of women to overcome continued privileges for males in established U.S. as well as traditional Asian culture.

The AAM's ideals bred, sometimes indirectly, the development of Asian American Women's rights. The "Women's Question" was one of the early dividing points in the Movement. As Asian women became deeply involved in Movement activities, they experienced mounting dissatisfaction with their own situations as participants. The Movement called for equality and justice. Yet as activists, women consistently found themselves playing subordinate roles: "taking minutes, making coffee, typing, answering phones, handling mail."[45] Evelyn Yoshimura, a Los Angeles activist, recounts a meeting during which a man said, "This is my wife, and she has nothing to say." In fact, Evelyn states, "she wanted to be active but was unable to say something."[46] The Movement's lens, when turned inward, revealed internalization by both men and women of Asian gender stereotypes as well as Asian patriarchal traditions of female subordination. This realization required connecting the struggle for equality for Asian American women to that of Asian Americans overall and women overall in society.

In the early years, the boundaries of "significant" Asian American women's issues were introspectively focused on identity. A reader for a 1970 UCLA course "Asians in America" was typical; writers address controversial topics such as catering to White standards of beauty—"peroxided hair and scotch-taped eyes will not make Yellow pride"—or dating White men.[47]

As for the AAM as a whole, the rapidly changing international context of the early 1970s provided a significant source of inspiration for women activists. The roles of Asian women revolutionaries pushed the boundaries of Asian women's leadership as well as reemphasized the significance of the U.S. war in Southeast Asia for Asian American women.

1971 was a pivotal year in politicizing the Movement on Asian women's issues, through the intersection of the influence of Asian women revolutionaries and the definition of the Asian American women's question in the AAM. Most Asian American female activists, diverging from mainstream feminism, soon converged on fighting for gender equality as part of the overall AAM.

Fifteen women who worked on *Gidra* met separately during 1969 and 1970. Their work culminated in the January 1971 issue that strongly stated their unity, in red print just below the table of contents. These points read:

- oppose this capitalistic society which confines the role of women to a cheap labor force, or to mindless bodies completely influenced by Madison Avenue propaganda;
- resist the degrading images that a racist society has imposed on both ourselves and our brothers;
- struggle with our brothers against male chauvinism and join in constructing new definitions for self-determination in the revolutionary society.[48]

The statements reflected both boundaries rejecting exploitative roles for women and consciousness about how they would work toward change, specifically with—not separate from—men in the Movement. Through historical articles, personal perspectives, images, and analyses, *Gidra* raised the issues of women as central to the Movement and the overall question of revolution. Asian American Women also brought out the sexist dimension in various issues in the AAM, such as the Vietnam War, a topic little discussed in the mainstream anti-war movement. Evelyn Yoshimura's "G.I.'s and Asian Women," as well as a number of reproduced anti-women images from pamphlets distributed to U.S. servicemen drove this topic home. Consequently the issue of women's equality was incorporated as part of the nominal ideals of the AAM.

In April of that year, 200 North American women, 120 of whom were Asian American, attended the Anti-Imperialist Women's Conference in Vancouver, Canada, simultaneously held with one in Toronto. The conferences would highlight differences with mainstream feminism. Representatives from revolutionary groups in Laos and North and South Vietnam shared their perspectives and experiences in their struggles for liberation. In *Gidra* a survivor of the infamous "tiger cages" of South Vietnam, Dinh Thi Huong, was quoted, "The more barbarous the army is, the stronger the struggle of the people."[49]

These Asian revolutionaries made a significant impact on Asian American women attendees. Wilma Chen wrote that, "The Indochinese women legitimized our struggle by coming. As we signed a pact of mutual solidarity against U.S. imperialism, we recognized once and for all how our struggles are linked." At the same time, in analyzing some of the dynamics at the Toronto conference, she criticized the views and conduct of White women at the conference. Chen felt that White women patronized the Indochinese sisters and tried to privilege women's issues as separate and more important than the overall revolutionary struggle described by the Indochinese delegates.[50]

By 1973, Leslie Loo reported at a national Asian American Studies conference that collaborators among Northern California colleges agreed that courses on Asian women should emphasize history, community involvement, identity, and the roles of women in Third World countries. They envisioned the outcomes of these courses as fostering a sense of responsibility and initiative to make social change.[51] Loo also asserted that "In the U.S., we Asian American women have learned much from our blood sisters in Asia and have begun to rise up against our common enemy: oppression and exploitation."[52]

The AAM had also begun to focus on issues beyond professional and activist women, specifically on the conditions and burdens of working women. In IWK's publication, *Chinese American Workers: Past and Present*, a series of articles described personal accounts of the diverse oppression, burdens, and harassment that working women faced in the workplace, home, community, and home.[53] More significantly, the AAM began programs to organize working women in their workplaces and to provide services that they needed, such as childcare and language classes.

Nevertheless, dedicated women's groups were important to addressing the spectrum of women's issues. Miya Iwataki graphically described confronting violence against women in the Movement. When a sister came to a meeting after having been battered by her boyfriend, the women decided to confront him as a group. They wanted to make sure that "no one would harass any women in the community."[54] Carol Mochizuki wrote that her involvement began after she discovered that other sisters had felt a need to come together—first casually but then forming specific work groups on topics such as childcare, women's history, and women in international struggles.[55] It would be the first of numerous such groups. Sisterhood meant making it possible for full participation and mutual respect.

Thus appropriating some of the tools and sources of inspiration for the AAM, Asian women activists struggled to create new roles and expectations through creative means. Using the AAM's prism and platform, Asian American Women reinterpreted their own lives and roles and extended the demand for full equality within the AAM. Moreover, they fought for rights for Asian American Women so as to complement the overall AAM.

In the next section, we will examine how two groups acted within the new environment. I Wor Kuen and Inter•Im occupied different positions in the Movement ecosystem, but each of them had to negotiate the various issues and currents affecting it. Exploring the choices the two groups made and the roles that they played helps clarify the dynamics and culture of the period.

I WOR KUEN: A REVOLUTIONARY ORGANIZATION

The most dramatic and, given the spirit of the times, most influential groups were revolutionary Asian American organizations, those who challenged the system most directly—the Red Guard and Kalayaan in San Francisco, East Wind Collective in Los Angeles, Wei Min She, Kokua Hawai'i, and I Wor Kuen (IWK) in New York.

A dozen college and community youth, many formerly with AAA, formed IWK.[56] With roots in the student and anti-war protests, IWK's early members included college dropouts whose parents were rooted in Chinatowns such as Virgo Lee, Chinatown street youth such as Walter Lee, Japanese Americans, including Chris Iijima, the son of a Nisei activist. IWK also included a community college teacher and two lecturers at Columbia. Quitting school and collectivizing their resources and income, they opened a storefront on a low-rent New York Chinatown corner on Market Street.[57] In explaining their decision, members said, "[Serving the people's needs] could be meaningful if and only if we devote ourselves wholeheartedly to responding to the daily problems of the masses, weighing our actions in terms of their interest in every case. To that end, we must learn from the people, fight together with them everywhere and to the end. This, therefore, necessitates our living among them and together among ourselves."[58]

They became an electrifying and creative catalyst in New York's Chinatown. Beginning in 1969, in berets and sunglasses, IWK established a new tone. They were a striking change from the older, Chinese-speaking small businessmen that had functioned as spokespersons for the community and were rooted in the clan-based and district-based organizations. They also contrasted with organizations such as the Chinatown Planning Council, the community's largest service organization. Founded by older, but like IWK primarily native-born members, the Planning Council focused on services and avoided political issues.[59]

IWK's red storefront, one large open area, hosted a stream of young people who sampled the activist life style. Jean Yonemura, a California Barnard College student from Berkeley, was one of the Japanese Americans who helped establish the IWK storefront in New York Chinatown. "I had no concerns about going to Chinatown," she recalled. "We wanted our work to affect real people. It was an exciting time." She was one of the four people who worked full time to support themselves and the eight other members who worked at the storefront full-time. She did temp work that had early hours so that she could get to the storefront by the early afternoon to help out. "People knew that we were a group that would fight for Chinatown people and wouldn't back down."[60]

Like the Red Guard on the West Coast, I Wor Kuen found some inspiration from the Black Panthers. Similar to the Black Panthers, they issued a multipoint platform that included calls for self-determination and community control for Asian Americans, decent housing, childcare, and education, an end to racism and militarism, and a socialist society. IWK focused less on the militaristic aspects of the Panthers and more on Mao Tse-tung's maxims on relating to the broad working population. Their paper, *Getting Together*, proclaimed in its first issue, "All Power to the Brothers and Sisters who Love the People and Fight the Real Enemy" and "We Serve the People."[61]

As a revolutionary organization with a broad agenda, IWK over time intervened directly in all the various sectors of the AAM. Within that broad agenda, the war played an equally central role. The war drove one of IWK's initial areas of work, organizing draft counseling. This also influenced their decision to initially focus on community and street youth. They participated as part of large multi-racial anti-war coalitions such as the November 4th Coalition and other anti-war work and often traveled to Washington, D.C., for national anti-war marches. *Getting Together* regularly carried articles about the war, and IWK, as part of their film series, showed works about the War and from Vietnam.

Less remotely, I Wor Kuen developed programs to address long-standing needs in ethnic enclaves. They provided free tuberculosis tests, going door to door on the streets of New York Chinatown, which eventually grew into other free health services—pap tests, venereal disease tests, prescriptions, and check ups. Similarly, they provided free legal help for youth and established child-care programs, the Hsin Hua schools. Some of these programs lasted longer than others, but IWK continually addressed the provision of services to the Asian American communities in its work.

IWK applied confrontational tactics to defend perceived neighborhood interests. One of their first campaigns was to organize protests against tourist buses that brought tourists to Chinatown. With broad support, they successfully blocked municipal meat inspectors in New York, whose procedures had closed down small restaurants for hanging barbecued meats. IWK confronted them in the early morning hours and characterized the inspections as racist and predatory. They demanded bilingual services at local hospitals and took up youth issues and fighting police harassment. They organized 2,000 Chinese and Italian tenants against Bell Telephone Company's evictions in New York. In this campaign, taking direct action, they reopened buildings boarded up by Bell.[62] Affordable housing still stands on this site today. Later as a national organization, they were an active part of the coalition defending the International Hotel and other enclave areas such as Little Tokyos and Chinatowns throughout the country. IWK's voluntary provision of needed services to the community at large and confrontation as well as negotiations to achieve community ends were widely imitated avenues.

They directly challenged the traditional community leadership whose organizations were under the CCBA and Six Companies. In campaigns to "Free the Gym," a community recreational facility controlled by the New York CCBA, and in their support of the People's Republic of China, IWK represented a call for democracy in the community and against feudal control; it was a major and open challenge to bases of the traditional organization's power in New York Chinatown. Their call for unity with other communities of color, Black and Latino, presaged future coalition building but represented a sharp break with the inward looking traditional leadership.

While students leaving school were part of the cadre that founded IWK, they soon saw the need to reconnect with campus struggles, a continuing active area.

A number attended City College of New York (CCNY) and became involved in the struggle to shape the Asian American Studies program there, including an occupation of an administration building in 1971. They also later founded regional student networks and numerous other student groups. Many students were attracted to IWK. Butch Wing, a long-time student activist, recalled that anti-war work introduced him to IWK. He and others who joined IWK engaged in ethnic studies issues in Laney Community College in Oakland and UC–Berkeley. In student organizing, IWK took stands defending ethnic studies and reaffirming its original values—their connections with the community and student participation.

As IWK gravitated toward Marxism, it wrestled with the issue of organizing workers. They had long supported workers' struggles such as the Jung Sai. They also fought for affirmative hiring of local residents such as at Gouveneur Hospital in New York. Beginning in 1973, IWK began direct organizing in the restaurant, garment, public transportation industries, and telephone.[63] Many were industries where Asian American workers particularly concentrated.

IWK placed less emphasis on the women's and art and cultural sectors. An organization known for female leadership, their work on women's issues focused on those of working women, such as day care. IWK worked cooperatively with arts and cultural groups such as Kearny Street. Workshop and Basement Workshop, but limited its direct cultural work to popular ad hoc forms such as guerilla theater and community singing.

Through their newspaper, they were able to influence others outside of the New York area. By 1971, I Wor Kuen expanded to the West Coast and established itself as a national organization. It eventually grew to be the largest revolutionary Asian American organization.[64]

INTER•IM: WORKING WITH THE SYSTEM FOR CHANGE

Seattle's International District (ID) was cobbled together from the city's historic Chinatown, Manilatown, and Nihonmachi settlements as well as areas of concentration of African Americans in the 1950s. Though the site of a lively community life, it was an area long neglected by the city; the ID housed Asian American elderly and the poor.

In 1968, the Seattle Model Cities Program provided start-up funding to a group of local business owners and activists to create the International District Improvement Association (Inter•Im). Inter•Im's goals were initially commercial, but Model Cities funding intended support for comprehensive planning, including social service delivery and citizen participation. Inter•Im's storefront was first in the N. P. Hotel, briefly in the International Realty

Office, the Toda and Chin Building, and finally, the Bush Hotel, a single-room occupancy for elderly residents and transients, on Jackson and Maynard Streets. With a board of residents, business owners, and professionals, being at ground level kept Inter•Im close to the "street action" and easily accessible to community people.

With the hiring of Bob Santos, a civil rights activist, in 1971, Inter•Im moved to the center of Seattle's Asian American Movement, involving a spectrum of pan-Asian, cross-generation individuals. Santos recalls the roots of this activist leadership, "Our attachment to the I.D. began in youth league basketball, progressing to dances and jazz clubs when we were old enough. The political activists from the Civil Rights Movement were fearful of the losing the District [ID]."[65] Student internships, especially through the University of Washington School of Social Work, were highly successful in practical training and building a base of young professionals who would staff or give leadership to emerging community groups. Under Santos's leadership, Inter•Im emphasized networking rather than typical opposition organizing in the AAM and always incorporated political lobbying and working with local governmental bodies.[66]

Inter•Im staff participated in community confrontations with authorities and usually represented the ID in any follow-up negotiations. One typical chapter was Inter•Im's role as part of the coalition opposing the construction of the Kingdome sports stadium in the late 1960s and early 1970s. The stadium construction would destroy many buildings and houses in the neighborhood. As a group with a pan-Asian, pan-racial character and outlook that distinguished them from older community organizations, Inter•Im took part in the new militant defense of the community that was demonstrated at the Kingdome's groundbreaking ceremony in 1972. Asian Americans disrupted the proceedings, throwing mud balls at the distinguished establishment speakers while chanting "Down with the Dome." The activists continued their struggles and demands for respect for the residents and businesses of the ID as "Concerned Asians for the International District." Evaluating that the Kingdome was inevitable, however, they decided to particularly focus on elderly housing. Their efforts, including a march on the local Housing and Urban Development office, eventually led Seattle to include a provision to maintain the area's Asian character and to rehabilitate the area for housing and small businesses in 1973.

Inter•Im also supported the Milwaukee Hotel occupation. In the 1977 Milwaukee Hotel occupation, activists responded to the threatened closure of one of the many dilapidated hotels in the area. Such hotels served to house many of the elderly single men who lived in the district; thirty hotels would be eventually destroyed. Inspired by the I-Hotel struggle to the south, the Seattle radicals sought to keep what was precious to the resident community but was dispensable in capitalist logic. Without support from the owners, they mounted a 24-hour fire watch, repaired the building's code violations and raised money to improve conditions. After months of occupation, while eventually having to abandon the building, they changed the direction of planning around community housing in the area.

While Inter•Im did not lead many of these militant actions, their support was significant in strengthening coalition efforts and by promoting youth involvement through internships and activism. Inter•Im's leadership was most evident in gaining recognition by city government as the "primary community-wide agency representing the area"[67] and in founding the Seattle Chinatown–International District Preservation and Development Authority, a public development corporation. While both challenging and collaborating with government institutions, Inter•Im identified low-cost housing as a priority relatively early in their struggles and steadily pursued that goal.

The focus of Inter•Im's work was on community development, but it often facilitated the direct provision of services, such as providing desk space for a free legal clinic staffed by law students and young attorneys or serving as the fiscal agent for the International District Health Clinic. While Inter•Im did not directly organize students, it created opportunities to involve students and encourage their initiative. One spin-off project that remained under Inter•Im's umbrella was the Danny Woo Community Garden. Elderly residents of the ID expressed a desire for a community garden and a place to be more physically active. Bob Santos persuaded property owner Danny Woo to donate use of a vacant, overgrown lot located near some of the new elderly housing units. Volunteer crews of students, elderly gardeners, and professionals built 100 terraced garden plots, using over 1200 donated railroad ties from Burlington Northern, a company that had historically relied on Chinese and Japanese workers to build the original tracks.

Inter•Im and IWK were both community-based. However, Inter•Im focused more on city infrastructure such as social services and low-income housing that reformed Seattle's ID. IWK politicized and organized activists to work toward long-term transformations of capitalism. In the Asian American Movement, Inter•Im provided a stable organization that mobilized resources while IWK articulated the framing ideology and analysis of the AAM and recruited and trained activists.

THE MEANING OF THE EARLY AAM

Many of the best and the brightest in the Asian American communities took up the challenge and provided critical leadership to the nascent AAM. While taking the community to territories far divergent from their experience, they gave heart to these new efforts and provided the abilities to build a skeletal structure for a new movement.

The range of activities that the new AAM undertook was broad and varied. Critical issues included opposition to the Vietnam War, establishment of ethnic studies on college campuses and building a student movement, women's organizations, preservation of historic ethnic enclaves, and the generation of a new art and culture movement.

What united these efforts were new concepts—self-reliance, self-determination, equal treatment, rectification of historic wrongs, and the belief that they were changing fundamental aspects of their communities. Just as World War II thrust Asian American individuals into the mainstream U.S. industries, the determination of this new generation of activists to engage in these issues thrust the Asian American communities into the primary civil turmoil within various localities. This upsurge connected their communities with a new universe of people and recast their role in U.S. society.

The example of the International District, International Hotel, the Jung Sai Strike, and the other work of the AAM demonstrate the changed world that the early Movement shepherded in. Highly motivated and committed, the activists unveiled new attitudes, developed new methods of organization, and mobilized surprising, unconventional resources that changed the terms of debate and the actors on contentious issues.

In urban development, normally the most critical and contested item on urban agendas, activists organized tenants and residents, taught themselves both professional and manual skills. They learned how to best organize watches, frustrate law enforcement, form human barricades, and about legal procedures, land development regulations, urban planning, and building repair. As they fought these battles, they learned and taught community participants alternative methods of confronting and dealing with established authority and developed a new framework of interpreting community history and vision.

They moreover altered the course of development and drew in new actors, residents, tenants, and activists, around future development that led to permanent community institutions. In the case of Seattle's International District, it was the group Inter•Im that transformed into a community development corporation. In the case of San Francisco's International Hotel, it was the Kearny Street Housing Corporation, an advisory group.[68] In doing so, they democratized the process of urban planning and engaged the population.

The new community infrastructure and competing leadership represented a major shift in Asian American ethnic enclave organizational structure. Once dominated by more compliant associations, a more heterogeneous mix including action-oriented, service, social, and cultural groups, led by native-born, uncompromising and far-reaching leaders, qualitatively broadened Asian American social structures. Where only counsels for moderation were once heard, calls for change and equity now rang out. It added a completely new layer of community infrastructure and institutions for Asian Americans.

The involvement of Asian American activists in the defense of ethnic enclaves was repeated across the country. Urban renewal efforts effectively threatened the remaining significant resident constituency in many Asian American communities, and Movement activists organized to counteract them. In Los Angeles activists fought the eviction of primarily Latino tenants and community organizations in Little Tokyo's Sun Hotel. Honolulu's People against Chinatown Evictions sat in the city development office to forestall evictions of the Chinese and Filipino residents and businesses in Chinatown. In San Francisco's Japantown, Committee Against *Nihonmachi* Eviction mounted 24-hour watches to oppose the evictions of residents and destruction of buildings when the city wanted to make way for a massive Japanese development project on Sutter and Buchanan Streets. In Hawai'i 600 farmers of taro, sweet potatoes, and vegetables fought the Marks family for several years on 1,500 acres in the Waiahole-Waikane valley. In Philadelphia, activists fought the Vine Street Expressway that threatened the local Chinatown's church and gymnasium. Boston's Chinatown has carried out perhaps the most sustained grassroots struggle to preserve its community. From organizing the community's first demonstration against hospital expansion in the 1970s, it has continued to protest, even organizing its own referenda on gentrifying development in the present day.[69]

Similarly in other movement activities, Asian American activists organized with the same resourcefulness and passion, introducing new ideas, ideals, energy and creativity into many areas of the broad community and creating new relationships with the larger society. They addressed chronic problems and inequities, undeterred by the lack of institutional support, experience, or expertise. As a consequence, they created new community structures, Asian American studies programs, community services, grassroots organizations, and coalitions that persisted to address the problems and issues. The AAM refashioned their communities.

The development of the Asian American Movement arose out of a confluence of factors. The most important was the development of a new generation who questioned the established order within the community and Asian Americans' place within the larger social structure. Imbued with the challenging spirit of the times, they were willing to take risks and make sacrifices to carry out their ideals. They were willing to turn their critique upon themselves and challenged ingrained sexist and class attitudes. They were able to build upon a storehouse of historic and current grievances that determined Asian Americans' unequal status and to draw on the experience of a cadre of older Asian American organizers. They drew from parallel movements in other minority communities and a contentious and contested international stage for inspiration, symbols, and frameworks. The popular skepticism toward the Vietnam War and divisions among the governing class fed and encouraged their rebelliousness. Being the first Asian American generation to attend college as a matter of course, they were in a position to appropriate resources from the higher education system. They used those resources to establish and build a new social movement on campus, in the workplace, and within the enclave. These processes supported the diverse creation of groups, which became tributaries to the flow of young people welling up against the walls of the system

NOTES

1. Sadie Lum, "Asian American Women and Revolution: A Personal View," *East Wind* 2, no. 1 (Spring/Summer 1983): 46–50.

2. Mike Nakayama, "Winter Soldiers," authors' collection, circa 1971, mimeographed; Evelyn Yoshimura, "G.I.s and Asian Women," *Gidra,* January 1971, 4.

3. Mike Murase, "Why an Asian Contingent?" *Gidra,* May 1972, 13.

4. Enrique de la Cruz, "The Opposition Movement in the Filipino American Community" (California State University–Northridge, n.d.).

5. Asian Americans for Peace, "Joint Treaty of Peace Between the U.S. and Vietnamese People," *Gidra*, April 1971, 9.

6. I Wor Kuen, "Twelve Point Platform and Program"; Asian American Political Alliance, "AAPA Perspectives," both in *Roots: An Asian American Reader,* eds. Amy Tachiki, Eddie Wong, and Franklin Odo (Los Angeles: UCLA Asian American Studies Center, 1971), 251, 296.

7. "Asian Community Center," *Rodan* 1:5 (November 1970) in *Roots: An Asian American Reader,* eds. Amy Tachiki, Eddie Wong, and Franklin Odo (Los Angeles: UCLA Asian American Studies Center, 1971), 273–75.

8. Pulido, *Black, Brown, Yellow, and Left*; Daryl J. Maeda, "Black Panthers, Red Guards, and Chinamen: Constructing Asian American Identity through Performing Blackness, 1969–1972," in *American Quarterly* 57, no. 4 (2005): 1079–1103.

9. *Chinese Awareness* (Los Angeles) 1:3 Oct. 1971, 2.

10. Filipino Americans, of course, took exception to the initial expression.

11. Karl Yoneda, "One Hundred Years of Japanese Labor History in the USA" in *Roots: An Asian American Reader*, eds. Amy Tachiki, Eddie Wong, and Franklin Odo (Los Angeles: UCLA Asian American Studies Center, 1971),150–58.

12. Chris Ijima and Nobuko Miyamoto, "We are the Children" (NewYork: Paredon Records, 1973).

13. For example, in the early days of New York's Chinatown Health Clinic, IWK merged their free health clinic into the latter's services; Tomio Geron, "The Asian

American Movement in New York City, 1968–1975," authors' collection, 1996, photocopy.

14. Secret bombing campaigns in Cambodian territory had begun two years earlier.

15. A criminality that Christopher Hitchens has chronicled in "The Case against Henry Kissinger" in *Harper's Magazine,* February 2001: 49–74, March, 2001: 33–58.

16. Buck Wong, "Public Record, 1989," *Amerasia Journal* 15, no. 1 (1989): 119.

17. While Asian Americans took it as their own, it should be noted that other parts of the anti-war movement had also learned the Snake Dance.

18. Brandeis Asian American Student Association, "Asian American Views on the War," authors' collection, circa 1971, mimeographed.

19. *Kalayaan*, 1972.

20. During this period, for example, San Francisco's Chinese community had sued the SF School District over the lack of bilingual educational services, which was upheld in the landmark *Lau v. Nichols* suit.

21. de la Cruz, "The Opposition Movement," 3, 32.

22. de la Cruz, "The Opposition Movement," 6.

23. Toribio, "Dare to Struggle," 35.

24. Merilynne Hamano Quon, conversation with Michael Liu, 13 May, 2003; Rocky Chin, "The House that JACS Built," *Bridge* 2 no. 6 (August 1973), 5–10.

25. To a limited extent, traditional associations provided for some needs in selected areas such as in the event of death, disputes, and immigration problems. Basic human needs such as health, education, housing, and food were largely left to the individual.

26. Asian Health Services,"The History of Asian Health Services," Asian Health Services, www.ahschc.org/history.htm (25 January 26, 2008).

27. Estella Habal, "How I Became a Revolutionary," in *Legacy to Liberation,* ed. Fred Ho (San Francisco: AK Press, 2000), 197–210; Ester Soriano-Hewitt, "The Bayanihan Spirit: The Search to Involve Filipino Americans," in *Gidra: The XXth Anniversary Edition,* ed. Gidra Staff (Los Angeles: Gidra 1990), 128. The International Hotel's significance will be described below.

28. Espiritu, *Asian American Panethnicity*, 34.

29. Mike Murase, "Ethnic Studies and Higher Education for Asian Americans," in *Counterpoint: Perspectives on Asian America*, ed. E. Gee (Los Angeles: UCLA Asian American Studies Center, 1976), 205–23.

30. These gains would prove temporary and would be critically reversed during New York City's financial crisis of 1975.

31. Asian American Political Alliance Newspaper, "Understanding AAPA," in *Roots: An Asian American Reader,* eds. Amy Tachiki, Eddie Wong, and Franklin Odo (Los Angeles: UCLA Asian American Studies Center, 1971), 44–47.

32. Asian Student Union, *Asian Students Unite* 4:1 (Fall 1975), Asian Student Union, University of California–Berkeley: 2.

33. Asian Student Union, *Asian Students,* 2–10.

34. Umemoto, "On Strike!"

35. I Wor Kuen "Political Summation of the Jung Sai Strike," *I.W.K. Journal* 2 (May 1975): 49–72.

36. Joyce Maupin, *Union Wage* 1974. Ten years after the end of the unionization effort, the workers were able to obtain a settlement.

37. Harvey Dong, "The Origins and Trajectory of Asian American Political Activism in the San Francisco Bay Area 1968–1978," (Ph. D. diss., University of California–Berkeley, 2002): 156.

38. Peter Kwong, *The New Chinatown* (New York: Hill and Wang, 1987); Wei, *Asian American Movement*.

39. Dana Frank, *Buy America: The Untold Story of Economic Nationalism* (Boston: Beacon Press, 1999).

40. Getting Together, *Chinese American Workers,* 59.

41. Frantz Fanon, author of *Wretched of the Earth*; Che Guevera, a Argentinean-born revolutionary, who was a leader in the Cuban revolution and participated in fomenting insurgencies in other parts of Latin America; Malcolm X, the Black nationalist, who grew to fame as a leader in the Black Muslim group, the Nation of Islam.

42. Oscar Peñaranda, Serafin Syquia, Sam Tagatac, "An Introduction to Filipino-American Literature," in *Aiiieeeee!: An Anthology of Asian American Writers* ed. Frank Chin et al (Washington DC: Howard University Press, 1974); lxii–lxiii.

43. Stan Shikuma, "The Making of a Modern Folk Art: Taiko in the Pacific Northwest/Canadian Southwest Region," (paper presented at the Annual Meeting of the Association for Asian American Studies, Toronto, Canada, March 2001).

44. Asian Legal Services Committee to Defend Harry Wong, "American Justice and Harry Wong," authors' collection (circa 1972), offset printed.

45. Susie Ling, "The Mountain Movers: Asian American Women's Movement in Los Angeles," *Amerasia Journal* 15, no. 1 (1989): 53.

46. Evelyn Yoshimura, interview by Julie Bartolotto, 1 May 1995. "Women's History: Asian American Women's Movement Activists," *The Virtual Oral/Aural History Archive, California State University, Long Beach*, January 24, 2007, www.csulb.edu/voaha

47. Gil Dinora, "Yellow Prostitution," *Gidra*, April 1969.

48. *Gidra*, January 1971, 2.

49. The overseas organizations included the Laos Patriotic Women's Union, the Vietnam Women's Union of North Vietnam and the Women's Union for the Liberation of South Vietnam. "Tiger Cages" were open cages used to imprison Viet Cong and North Vietnamese prisoners.

50. Wilma Chen, "Toronto Women's Conference," *Gidra*. May 1971.

51. Excerpts from the Proceedings of the National Asian American Studies Conference II, University of California Davis, July 6–8, 1973: "Asian Women's Panel— Pat Sumi, Leslie Loo, Cynthia Maglaya," in *Concerns of Asian American Women,* Washington Commission on Asian American Affairs, Task Force on Asian American Women: Olympia, June, 1976, 17.

52. Excerpts, 16.

53. Getting Together Newspaper, *Chinese-American Workers.*

54. Miya Iwataki, interview by Sherna Gluck and Angela McCracken, 8 March 2004, "Women's History: Asian American Women's Movement Activists," *The Virtual Oral/Aural History Archive, California State University, Long Beach.* January 24, 2007, www.csulb.edu/voaha

55. Carol Mochizuki, "Women's Group," *Gidra*, June, 1971.

56. For an alternative profile of a revolutionary group, see Harvey C. Dong's dissertation on Wei Min She. I Wor Kuen literally translated as Fists of Righteous Harmony, popularly known in the West as the "Boxers."

57. Virgo Lee, interviews by Michael Liu, New York, NY, 23 December 2001, 28 May, 2006.

58. *Asian Americans for Action Newsletter* 2:1 (February 1970), Asian Americans for Action, New York: 3.

59. In other Chinatowns, particularly California, these reform oriented groups had political expressions such as the Chinese American Citizens Alliance. In outlook they were similar to the JACL.

60. Jean Yonemura Wing, interview by Michael Liu, tape recording, Berkeley, CA, 24 October, 2003.

61. *Getting Together,* Feb. 1970.

62. *Getting Together*, Sept. 1970–Dec. 1970.

63. League, *Statements on Founding*, 49–53.

64. Franklin Ng, ed., vol. 3 of *The Asian American Encyclopedia*. (North Bellmore, NY: Marshall Cavendish Corporation, 1995), 628.

65. Bob Santos, interview by Tracy Lai, tape recording. Seattle, WA: 30 August, 2006.

66. Much of the following account of development of Seattle's International District comes from Chin, *Seattle's International District.* See also Bob Santos, *Hum Bows, Not Hot Dogs* (Seattle: International Examiner Press, 2002).

67. Chin, *Seattle's International District*, 81.

68. After the evictions at the International Hotel, those activists who remained around the issue coalesced over the years in the Kearny Street Housing Corporation.

69. For a detailed account of this issue, see Leong in *Amerasia Journal* or Lai et al, "The Lessons of the Parcel C Struggle: Reflections on Community Lawyering."

Chapter Five

The Mature Movement (1976–1982): Weaving through New Surroundings

As the Movement matured, the community's resources—its organizational infrastructure and human capacity—expanded, and its guiding frameworks became more sophisticated. These sources of strength helped overcome an increasingly unfavorable social and political environment and internal divisions within the movement.

The Nixon and Ford administrations began to restructure Great Society Programs under the policy of a "new federalism." New federalism consolidated specific programs that had supported urban activism, such as Head Start, job training, and Model Cities, into block grants where local power structures gained increasing control over federal funds. Beginning a lengthy trend toward neo-liberalism, the succeeding Carter administration began shrinking welfare programs and the role of government. Carter also extended collaboration among local elites by directing that federal urban programs include private sector investment and diverting funds toward the suburbs. The new administrations initiated a conservative political reaction and aggressively attacked the gains of labor and minority groups achieved in the past decade.[1] Local political opportunities for change contracted with each such development.

The international situation introduced new problematic issues for the Movement. Global politics became more complex and ambiguous. The clarity of the anti-imperialist struggles internationally, which contributed the symbols and models for the early movement, became less definite in the late 1970s and 1980s. The victory of communist forces in Vietnam and Southeast Asia removed a central unifying issue for AAM activists. The end of the war also raised questions about tactics for their other work. As one former IWK member related,

It was a big debate about how fast or how far to push ideology, or how to carry the ideological message in the community. It was always an ongoing debate, and it was primarily driven by the fervor in the anti-Vietnam War movement . . . there was never a question whether ideology should take a low profile during the peak of the anti-War movement. It was only when it began to appear that the war was going to end that it became an increasing level of doubt, if you will, as to whether this was the right way to organize in the community, whether the ideological message was the right way to go, which was putting the ideology first. . . . As far as whether there should an IWK in the community, it was not that level of enthusiasm to maintain that level of commitment. It didn't have the Asian connection, so to speak. You know, the Vietnam War was connected to organizing in the community because the oppression was indicative of the American government's oppression of Asians both as a minority in the United States and internationally against the people of Vietnam. That whole driving force disappeared, diminished. Now there was no war. Why do we need this kind of radical, revolutionary type of organization? [2]

The issues of democracy in Korea and the Philippines, while uniting Korean Americans and Filipino Americans respectively, distinguished those subgroups from other Asian Americans. While other Asian Americans could express support, these issues primarily united the respective subgroup. Rather than being inclusive, it challenged the panethnic Asian American concept, prompting E. San Juan, prominent analyst of the Filipino American condition, to observe that

now is an opportune time to assert our autonomy from the sweeping rubric of "Asian American," even as we continue to unite with other Asians in coalitions for common political demands. There is a specific reason why the Filipino nationality in the United States . . . needs to confront its own destiny as a dislocated and "transported" people; that reason is of course the fact that the Philippines was a colony of the United States.[3]

Finally, the communist victories in Southeast Asia created ancillary complicating effects for activists. An influx of Southeast Asian refugees, wards of the U.S. government, added to the changing community landscape. The creation of communities of bedrock anti-communist Vietnamese and other Southeast Asians complicated the "people" in whose name activists organized. The relatively more uniform, working class, native-born constituency with whom they had begun their passage was rapidly changing.

Lifestyles and organizations matured. More conventional household arrangements replaced the collective households that youth and spartan lifestyles accommodated. The development of family life competed for time and energy with the demands of activism. While the Movement drew in additional

Alaska Cannery Workers Union. 1940. Photo: Unity Newspaper

Chinese Workers Mutual Aid Association in San Francisco Chinatown, 1941. Photo: Unity Newspaper

San Francisco's Leways street youth group laid the groundwork for the Red Guard circa late 1960s. Photo: David Wong

LEWAY INC.

A NON-PROFIT ORGANIZATION
TO HELP FIND EMPLOYMENT AND
RECREATION FOR THE YOUTH OF
OUR COMMUNITY

Demonstration against Ferdinand Marcos, Philippines president, who declared martial law in the 1970s. San Francisco Bay Area. Photo: Unity Newspaper.

China unification demonstration, opposition to the ruling party in Taiwan, in New York City Chinatown. 1973–1974. Photo: Michael Liu.

Movement Newspapers were widely circulated in the 1960s and 1970s. Richard Siu, Asian American Resource Workshop staff member reading Getting Together *in Boston Chinatown 1977. Photo: Michael Liu*

Anti Bakke Decision (University of California Regents v. Bakke), San Francisco State contingent, part of a national effort to defend affirmative action 1977. Photo: Unity Newspaper

Free Chol Soo Lee rally in San Francisco. 4. Chol Soo Lee is a Korean American whose wrongful murder conviction and nearly ten years of imprisonment unified the Movement to successfully win his release from prison. August 1982. Photo: Unity Newspaper

Asian Americans for Jesse Jackson in San Francisco Chinatown. May 1984. Photo: Unity Newspaper

National Coalition for Redress and Reparations' Grassroots Delegation to Washington DC, July 1987. Photo: John Ota

"Spring Action": thousands mobilize for educational rights organized by Asian students in coalition with African Americans and Latinos. Sacramento, California. April 1989. Photo: Perry Chow

Chinese Progressive Association, one of a number of community-labor centers organizes P&L Garment workers. The closure of the largest garment shop in the city led to a successful fight for job retraining rights in Boston. May 1986. Photo: Therese Feng

Ward's Cove Packing demonstration protesting discrimination against Asian workers in Alaskan Canneries, Seattle 1994. Photo: Dean Wong

Korean drummers at anti-Iraq war demonstration in Boston's Copley Square, 2003. Photo: Michael Liu

young idealists, most of the most influential organizations' leadership was aging. The initial optimism that characterized a large part of the Movement and envisioned rapid and far-reaching changes in society proved naïve. Continued progress in the Movement necessitated a more sober and somber reassessment.

A Filipina single mother in the group KDP described some of the tension between political and personal responsibilities:

> I lived in a collective household especially designed by the KDP to help me with my responsibilities to my children. By now, however, my boys were about nine and ten; they started to get into trouble with the police, mainly mischievous and petty stuff—but for a mother, terrifying nonetheless. I personally could not find the time to help them with their homework. . . . Although my comrades often helped, they could not deal with the teachers and the schools. I felt that no one really understood my emotional crisis and the stress of attempting to raise two adolescent boys in the "barrio" Mission district.[4]

All these factors conspired to fray the Movement. Sectors of the Movement began to chart independent directions.

Yet, despite working within more challenging frameworks, activists had sufficient momentum to conduct more sophisticated and long-term campaigns. They were driven by a burst of organizational development, more experienced leaders, and new ideas that the first phase of the Movement produced. These were now integrated with the development of more comprehensive worldviews. There was a web of new and more acculturated organizations able to negotiate mainstream U.S. society. Outside the communities, established groups had begun to recognize the needs of Asian Americans. AAM groups could for example call upon the National Lawyers Guild, a legal advocacy group, to defend them when civil rights were threatened or to advocate around equity issues. The resource base had increased with the maturation of the Movement.

GRIEVANCES: SERVING A CHANGING PEOPLE

Another major factor in Asian American migration was global economic restructuring. By the 1960s, the post World War II economic boom had peaked, and a crisis of capitalism emerged. Growing high quality "cheap" imports threatened the economic stability of the largest economy in the post-World War II era. In response, U.S. capitalism began to restructure the economy, moving manufacturing offshore where labor costs were lower. The shift to management and services and the limitations of U.S. public education created

the need for large numbers of professionals, managers, and business entrepreneurs.

This void was a significant factor in the passage of the Immigration and
Nationality Act Amendment of 1965 Immigration Act, which drew large
numbers of Asian immigrants to the United States. The act replaced the national origins quota system with a system for allotting visas based on family
reunification and employment skills.[5]

The effects of the 1965 Immigration Act were becoming more evident in
the Asian American communities. More families arrived and were reunited. A
significant managerial and professional class arrived, creating a new and different class bifurcation. In 1969, one typical year after the Immigration Reform Act took effect, of the four largest Asian immigrant groups, 42.3 percent
of Filipinos, 20.8 percent of Chinese, 23.2 percent of Korean, and 45 percent
of the Asian Indians entered under the occupational preference for managers
and professionals.[6] Those identifying themselves as managers or professionals grew steadily; they jumped from 28 percent to 34 percent of the Asian
American population in the 1970 and 1980 censuses, respectively, exceeding
that proportion for the general population. But along with this more privileged class, a significant less-educated, less-advantaged class arrived in great
numbers. Some were undocumented. Service industry workers, particularly,
continued to comprise a significantly higher percentage for the Filipino and
Chinese populations than of the population as a whole. Despite a doubling of
the population, those identifying as laborers, service persons, and operatives
(lesser skilled blue-collar workers) were still the largest segment of the Asian
American population. By 1980, the Asian American population had reverted
to being majority foreign-born.[7]

Exacerbating grievances for the movement, the flow of the more disadvantaged created new demands for services, advocacy, and organizing in enclave communities. Institutions continued to largely overlook the needs of
Asian Americans and these new populations. However, the new service and
activist organizations strove to fill the gap to meet these demands. They began to address the previously unacknowledged issues in the communities —
poverty, employment and housing conditions, the status of women, and
gangs. And the enclaves' overarching issue of sustaining themselves as communities remained; they continued to be threatened by redevelopment and
gentrification. Redevelopment threats now came not only from highways but
also from the first projects involving growing Asian capital in the larger Chinatowns and Little Tokyos.[8]

The immigration flows also created a more diverse Asian American population, multiplying for example the relatively small Korean and Asian Indian
populations. Another significant segment was the Vietnamese and other

Southeast Asians who came under the refugee parole provisions and later the Refugee Act of 1980.[9] In a few short years there were more than 300,000 Southeast Asians, primarily Vietnamese, swelling the Asian American population an additional 10 percent.[10] Moreover, they catalyzed other grievances in addition to older ones—the rise of hate crimes stemming from resentment over the United States's defeat in the Vietnam War and the introduction of a large number of Asian Americans into new areas. Hate crimes were not simply confined to the Southeast Asians, as the 1987 "Dotbuster" attacks on Asian Indian residents in the northern New Jersey area sadly demonstrated.[11]

MARXISM AND PROFESSIONALISM

New organizations began to grow in the space created by the first wave of movement activity. The new populations that grew through the 1965 Immigration Act also drove new organizational formation.

Organizations began to adopt more comprehensive points of view to cope with more complex environments. This gave greater direction to activists, who learned to work with diverse social forces and institutions, develop long term strategies, carry out more sophisticated plans, shepherd assets, and satisfy larger and broader constituencies. The more complex, subtler points of view allowed many of the organizations to play leading roles within the communities while inspiring greater tensions among them.[12]

Differences in outlook between the political organizations and the service-oriented organizations widened. Service agencies began to adopt more professional approaches. Those that failed to, more typically the self-help and utopian groups that relied solely on voluntarism and provided free services, eventually disbanded from fragile finances and weariness. Professionalism allowed the service organizations to adapt to the demands of funders and ensured a flow of income that could stabilize and expand service provision.[13] Especially after the end of the Vietnam War, the "social service activist" became "the social service professional."

Rather than modeling themselves after the "barefoot doctors" of China, health professionals gravitated toward traditional white-robed roles for doctors. Health clinics, some initially free, developed to become health centers, supported through insurance plan and public health program reimbursements. They broadened their range of services to meet the needs of a growing and changing community and, like other nonprofits, conformed to the demands of funding sources. The Chinatown Health Clinic in New York became a multi-million-dollar service agency.[14] What began as law collectives became public interest law firms. Housing and tenant programs often shifted into development corporations. For

example, the Asian Amercans for Equal Employeeement (AAFEE), which began
by fighting for construction jobs and organizing tenants, successfully sought
funding for a housing rehabilitation project, during the last half of the 1980s, including a $1 million grant from the New York State Department of Social Ser-
vices, and went into development.[15] SIPA, while continuing a focus on youth,
expanded to other fields. According to the group's website, it became a key service provider and community development arm among the low-income and un-
derserved multi-ethnic youth and families in the Temple Beverly corridor, Los
Angeles County's "Filipinotown." Other service agencies began to specialize toward women or youth or to become one-stop multi-service centers. Many of
those engaged in expanding services considered this work a continuation of the
Movement.[16]

Regina Lee described the evolution of New York's Chinatown Health
Clinic, which she helped found:

> In the early years, we both felt a part of the AAM and somewhat different. Be-
> ing in the same building as the Basement Workshop and the Food Co-op., we
> collaborated on different projects. We worked with Lower East Side Neighbor-
> hood Health council on creating the Betances mobile health clinic. At the same
> time, we felt somewhat different. We stayed away from the contentious issues.
> Some organizations didn't want to work with traditional groups. The Health
> Clinic was willing to work all groups, as long as it improved health care services
> to the community."
>
> After six or seven years, it became apparent that a volunteer organization was
> not enough. The Clinic was overflowing. There was a two- to three-week backlog
> for appointments. We had a lot of volunteers coming in. We started getting grants.
> Then we got a big federal grant for Project AHEAD (Asian Health Education and
> Development), which was to train young people in health careers. The Clinic grew
> gradually in the 1970s and the 1980s. In the 1970s there was an effort to institu-
> tionalize community health clinics. The Clinic became a certified section 330 fed-
> erally qualified health center in the late 1970s. This was important because it
> meant that we could get insurance reimbursements.
>
> There were initial concerns about going after funding. Some were concerned
> whether we could continue to do advocacy. I thought that we could do both, to
> "bite the hand that feeds you." We advocated for more patient-centered health.

The Health Clinic did change over time. Its founders, the more activist
members, left to do other things. Other volunteers, more service oriented,
came through and replaced them. Two of the initial doctors stayed with the
Clinic.[17]

Distancing their AAM roots and methods was neither smooth nor consistent for service organizations. Health clinics, for example, were built around
certain progressive principles, serving those without access to health and ag-

onizing over funding choices that might compromise such principles. At times they also resorted to the insurgent methods of the past. When California's Proposition 13 cut taxes and consequently drastically cut funding for service agencies in the late 1970s, the executive directors of Asian Health Services and Filipino Immigration Services and four other service providers were arrested and charged for organizing a sit-in in county offices.

Service organizations were not alone in seeing the need for institutionalization. As described below, art and culture organizations and women's groups, among others, began to devote more attention to their own particular issues and interests.

Many of those challenging the system structure more closely adopted forms of Marxist thought. Marxism provided a greater discipline as well as a comprehensiveness that activists needed for the times. Marxist analysis broadened and made more effective many of these organizations. The radical organizations also became larger and/or part of other multi-racial organizations.[18] Instead of I Wor Kuen, there was the League of Revolutionary Struggle. In place of *Katipunan ng mga Demokratikong Pilipino* (KDP), there was Line of March. The Asian Study Group became first Workers Viewpoint and then the Communist Workers Party. The growing sophistication and size of organizations located in numerous cities nationwide required greater attention to internal communication and ideological consolidation around a common political "line" or perspective as well as strategic and tactical planning. On the negative side of the ledger, adopting more developed ideologies led to more infighting that often became debilitating in some areas[19] and alienated this part of the Movement from many of the service-oriented organizations, who were less concerned with ideological issues.

These tensions moreover represented real differences in how to conduct community work and where Asian American political activists would concentrate their organizing work. Among politically radical groups, some, such as the Workers Viewpoint and Wei Min She, advocated for the overriding significance of the labor movement. In reflecting their view that "The only way for Asian Americans to combat racism and national oppression is to link our struggle with the struggle of the American working class,"[20] they began over time to shift their resources from the Asian American communities to workplace organizing. They also advocated a more antagonistic approach toward other classes in the Asian American communities. Other groups like I Wor Kuen emphasized the significance of Asian American struggles as well as those of other minority groups and of working with different classes within the Asian American community on common issues. Because of this orientation, I Wor Kuen and its successor organizations continued to play a significant role in the Asian American community as it matured.

There were other differences as well. Differences about the importance of ideology versus grassroots organizing would determine how much time and effort groups would pay to organizing the population around immediate issues rather than developing political ideas. The race question in the United States affected how important organizing communities of color would be. Another major argument centered on whether to change the system "from within," meaning that revolutionary activists would change the direction of public and private institutions by working from positions of power inside rather than focus on organizing resistance from outside. The Workers Viewpoint organization developed an "American Express strategy," of embedding individuals in capitalist institutions long term to take them over rather than organize to oppose and constrain them. All these disagreements, while sometimes unnecessarily shrill and at times outlandish, were about how and where activists should organize, the type of organizing to carry out, and the relative importance of developing theory rather than organizing.[21]

It's appropriate to comment on the role of these divisions in the eventual trajectory of the AAM. Though there were relative levels of engagement in debating and competing for influence, the political differences and attitudes certainly siphoned a lot of energy from what was a relatively young mobilization. It weakened the overall political influence of the AAM, while simultaneously clarifying differing approaches and perspectives. This in turn caused groups to focus inward on political education and consolidate around the organization's perspective rather than on working together. It also exacerbated the divisions between service-oriented and more radical politically oriented perspectives. These differences were to last for most of the life of the various radical groups.

In the transition created by the withdrawal of some of these groups into workplace organizing and other concerns, broader grassroots organizations, which supported social change but did not call for alternative social systems, developed in ethnic enclaves. Though the radical groups heavily influenced these groups, the new organizations drew in older, immigrant, and more diverse membership. Chinese Progressive Associations (CPAs) in four cities, AAFEE (later Asian Americans for Equality) in New York, Asian Americans United in Philadelphia, and Little Tokyo People's Rights Organization in Los Angeles continued grassroots organizing functions in the Asian communities.

SHIFTING ISSUES:
CHANGING DYNAMICS OF INTERNATIONAL SUPPORT

A shift in focus arose around international issues, primarily affecting the political groups. The communist victories in Southeast Asia were followed by a series of tragedies that tested many activists' beliefs in alternatives to capitalism.

Hostilities broke out between socialist Kampuchea, formerly Cambodia, and Vietnam. The details of the murderous reign of the Khmer Rouge, the Communists who won control of Cambodia, seeped out in the years following. Furthermore, Vietnam's expulsion of Vietnamese of Chinese extraction created a tragic caravan of "boat people," many of whom faced death and suffering in the passage out. In 1976, Mao Tse-tung, an icon of the first phase of the AAM, passed away in China, leaving behind a major ideological legacy and also a symbolic vacuum. The year 1979 saw China and Vietnam going to war,[22] and the latter invading Kampuchea, ousting the Khmer Rouge government. The Khmer Rouge continued to fight a guerilla war against the Vietnamese.[23]

The struggles between China and the Soviet Union that began in the 1960s for leadership of the communist world deepened in the ensuing decades. They drew in many of the "Third World" countries that activists supported in their struggles against colonialism.

Beginning in 1972, China began a process of improving relations with the United States, which was realized in the "normalization of relations" between the two countries in 1979. Supporters of China within the movement, who had agitated for this milestone, viewed this as a victory for the people's movement internationally, as the United States acknowledged a socialist nation. Yet, China began adopting greater market mechanisms and more pragmatic international policies. The continuing shift of China's social structure and political positions troubled many activists. How to view China's new relationship with the United States became an issue within the Movement. This debate, while not pivotal in determining political AAM groups' domestic organizing projects, did influence which international models and resistance movements they would support.

Thus, the focal points of the international landscape for Asian American activists, Vietnam, and China, which had inspired many, had begun to tarnish themselves as alternative ideals. Interpretation of world events became more imperative. It was not simply the changing roles of the most prominent models internationally that wounded the Movement; the antagonism between them led to increased shrillness in debates among the radical groups, who often aligned themselves with one or another party in these international polemics.

There were areas of unity internationally. Support for African independence struggles or against settler domination in South Africa and Rhodesia (now known as Zimbabwe) grew.[24] Korean and Philippines support work continued unabated. Among Filipino Americans, active nationwide organizing on the latter area took place through an Anti-Martial Law Coalition directed against the continuing Marcos dictatorship.

Another issue also emerged that mobilized Asian Americans in the late 1970s. On March 28, 1979, the Three Mile Island Nuclear Power Plant near Middleton, Pennsylvania, melted its nuclear core. The incident helped ignite a broad antinuclear movement internationally. As the growth of nuclear weapons expanded and the threat of nuclear war grew between the United States and the Soviet Union, that movement grew rapidly through the early1980s.

A strong and vibrant anti-nuclear movement for nuclear disarmament and world peace among Asian Americans connected the AAM with peace and anti-nuclear activists in Asia and built new social networks of activism. Similar to the anti-Vietnam war movement, Asian American activists found themselves outside the mainstream anti-nuclear movement and built strong inter-ethnic Asian American coalitions that coordinated their work and efforts with the larger, predominantly White, middle class movement. On the East and West Coasts, Asian Americans for Nuclear Disarmament groups sprang up and raised the issue of race and nuclear disarmament. They helped educate the larger anti-nuclear peace movement about the United States's use of nuclear weapons on Japanese people during World War II and nuclear testing on the Pacific islands.

However, long before these new forms of Asian American organizations appeared, Japanese Americans who were visiting Japanese cities during and survived the application of the atomic bomb were quietly working together since 1965. They formed an organization called the Committee of Atomic Bomb Survivors in the U.S. They sought to secure health care for the *hibakusha*, atomic bomb survivors. These heroic individuals inspired many Asian American anti-nuclear activists.[25] At the massive disarmament demonstrations in New York in 1982 and commemorations in San Francisco, Los Angeles, and New York, the *hibakusha* and their supporters came out to support nuclear disarmament and call for an end to the nuclear arms race. This organizing, combining traditional methods of appealing for legislation for medical care relief for atomic bomb survivors with protests against the growing nuclear war threat, reached an entirely different and formerly inactive segment of the Japanese American community.

The changing international situation with shifting alliances and new international threats reflected an aspect of a new environment for the AAM. Asian American activists' frames had to thus negotiate a labyrinth of increased complexity, less compelling international models, and a shift toward solving more immediate problems domestically. Many former international support activists brought their experience and political acumen into this arena of political activity.

SHIFTING ISSUES II:
TRANSITION IN DEFENDING THE ENCLAVES

Another area within the Movement that reached a turning point was the campaign to preserve enclaves. Between 1976 and 1979, long-term development struggles saw major changes or were resolved.

Activists and the tenants were forcibly evicted from the International Hotel in San Francisco in 1977, the campaign that had become the touchstone for activists defending Asian enclaves across the country. Through its eight-year battle, thousands of young activists had rallied around the "I-Hotel" campaign, defending it for elderly *Manongs* and the community organizations that occupied it. Asian American activists had made the I-Hotel the primary development issue in the city over the years that they fought off eviction. Marches, demonstrations, lawsuits, legislation, and sweat to renovate the building were all part of the struggle. At one point, five thousand people formed a human chain in a show of force. It took the coordinated efforts of hundreds of members of the city's police and fire departments in the dead of night to overcome its epic defense. A network of supporters had come out on a moment's notice to face down eviction.[26]

In 1978 the state of Hawai'i resolved the threatened evictions of native farmers and farming tenants of the Waiahole-Waikane Valleys on Oahu. This struggle pitted the Marks family, the landowner and one of the most prominent families in the state, against small farmers. By purchasing the land for the farmers, Hawai'i ended one of the most intense struggles around development in its history, a struggle that had lasted five years.[27] The city of Honolulu also settled eviction battles in Chinatown in the summer of 1979, agreeing to relocation and housing concessions for the tenants.[28]

In Little Tokyo in Los Angeles, for many years, the struggle for the Sun Hotel had become the focus of energy for Asian activists in the city. However, despite hundreds of protestors, community organizations and tenants were also evicted from the Hotel in July 1977. Los Angeles's city redevelopment agency took control of the last parcel of land standing in the way of large-scale development by the Japanese multinational corporation Kajima. The agency had to agreed to major concessions in terms of suspending evictions, constructing housing, and relocating tenants and businesses. As mentioned earlier, Seattle ID activists occupying the Milwaukee Hotel evacuated it in 1979, after winning concessions.[29]

These junctures in these struggles required many in the AAM to regroup. The International Hotel and Sun Hotel evictions for example displaced a number of leading organizations in the Movement, who, in addition to putting effort into finding new housing for the displaced individual tenants, had to find new and usually more expensive quarters of their own. Many of these development challenges had achieved varying degrees of success. They had placed on citywide agendas the history, role, and constituencies of ethnic enclaves. In many instances, while activists were unable to save individual buildings and pieces of land, they won concessions for tenants, changes in the redevelopment process, and commitments toward the future.

Some continued the struggles, working to build upon these changes, but in the main the defense of such ethnic enclaves marshaled less energy than they had in the earlier period of the AAM. Other issues—redress, hate crimes, working class organizing—competed for attention. While survival of the enclaves remained a chronic issue and struggles continued, activists would return only at a later time to this issue with a renewed and different force. Within and outside the enclaves, much of the activist energy began to focus on the workplace.

THE GROWTH OF WORKING CLASS ORGANIZING

Growing numbers of AAM activists decided to organize workers for better pay and working conditions. They were influenced by the spontaneous labor struggles of immigrant workers and the growing influence of Marxism, which recognized the worker's role in producing social wealth and productive capacity. They went into workplace organizing to provide "conscious leadership" to the working class and sought to recruit workers with leadership skills and the political understanding of the need for systemic transformation into movement activists.

There were different points of view on whom and where to organize. Some left groups influential on the AAM, most notably the Revolutionary Union, believed in organizing only at the "point of production," i.e., assembly-line factories, sites that were most often located far from concentrations of Asian Americans. They considered workers working in highly organized and coordinated systems of labor to be the most able to see the need for a different society. Several groups sent their cadres to work in auto, steel, and other heavy manufacturing industries as the perceived sites of working class "advanced elements." Other groups, including IWK, promoted an alternative view that labor and community organizing were integrally linked together. They focused on organizing workers of color, who were concentrated in the "lower stratum" of the working class. This stratum was viewed as the most oppressed with the greatest potential to see the need for fundamental changes in society.

The decision to make workplace organizing a critical component of the movement's work was driven by two factors. As a practical matter, activists needed to earn a living; and second, a political imperative called to integrate with the workers, learn from their experiences, and provide political leadership to their struggles. This was part of the AAM's growing Marxist view of the working peoples' role in building and transforming society. Other activists wanted to base the movement among working class elements who were perceived as stable and grounded in the reality of survival and struggle.

The story of one young labor organizer captures the spirit and essence of what AAM activists found when they went to work:

I went to U.C. Santa Cruz for two years and studied social sciences. There were things I liked about college and other things I couldn't stand. College gives you the time and material to investigate what society is all about and a place to discuss it with people of various backgrounds . . . but no matter what your studies, it was still just study—something abstract and detached. . . . I decided to drop out for awhile and worked a series of jobs in the hotel/restaurant industry. I had always looked at waitressing as perfect for working my way through college: It required no training, it offered part-time positions and it was the kind of job I could go home and forget about. . . . I assumed that I'd be waitressing for two or three more years. But the more I got to know people at work, the more I came to identify with them and this changed the way I looked at myself and how I looked at working people.

It hit, on my first day of work that no one at the Holiday Inn looked at work the way I did. They had worked in restaurants and hotels all their lives, Most of them had worked there for over ten years. They are there, on time, five a.m. every morning, working overtime where needed; they're sick maybe once a year.

It was summertime, during the height of the tourist season, when I started work and the restaurant staff was being overworked to the breaking point. Every week, the bosses experimented with our scheduling, laying off as many people as they could and forcing the rest of us to work two jobs at once or overtime. Our supervisor would follow us around telling us we were lazy and threatening to fire us. The paranoia and exhaustion wore everyone out. One day, during our break, we noticed one of the waitresses had what looked like paint on her fingernails. She told us that her fingernails were getting torn up and the only way she could hold them together was to attach pieces of bandaids onto her nails with crazy glue. I was shocked and asked what we should do about it. A friend of mine replied, "Well, you should get out of here as fast as you can. You're going to school; you've got a chance to do something better with your life. If you stay here, you'll only ruin your heath."

How could I just quit and go on to "something better with my life"? I was the only one there who had the option of quitting. Everyone else had to stay. They had families to support and parents to take care of. And for them quitting the Holiday Inn wouldn't solve anything; conditions in the service industry were the same everywhere. I wanted to do something to help change the conditions at work.[30]

As AAM activists went to do workplace organizing, they found Asian American labor organizers already working in trade unions and in some cases holding leadership positions. The combination of young AAM activists, veteran labor organizers, and staff members enabled a broader interpretation of Asian American labor rights and organizing and fueled an upsurge in Asian American labor activity.

In the late 1970s, double-digit inflation, combined with growing cuts in benefits and wages, and soaring unemployment ignited numerous spontaneous struggles of Asian American workers. In 1978 Chinese workers in San Francisco unionized the *Chinese Times*, at the time the largest Chinese language paper in the United States. Another episode involved the California state government's attempt to raise the eligibility requirements for full unemployment benefits to twenty weeks of work per year. Most women in the canneries worked seasonally, thus failing to qualify for benefits. Hundreds of Sacramento Chinese and Chicano cannery workers mobilized and rallied at the State capitol to stop the stricter guidelines. The same year, in 1978, the Hotel Employees and Restaurant Employees Union (HERE) unionized the first Chinese restaurants in New York City. Two were four-star–rated restaurants, and these successes led to unionization efforts at other Chinese restaurants. Unfortunately, the union failed to continue these efforts with a general organizing campaign within the Chinese restaurant industry.[31]

In Los Angeles, Japanese workers were involved in labor actions that highlighted the working conditions of immigrant and low-wage workers in the restaurant and hotel business, the difficulty of unionization within those industries, and the AAM's potential to expand those struggles. These organizing campaigns were emblematic of numerous struggles that would continue to be waged in Los Angeles' Little Tokyo.

In 1979, Japanese immigrant and other workers, after years of management abuse and threats of deportation, sought union representation from HERE Local 11 in the Horikawa Restaurant. Another unionization target was the New Otani hotel, built in the late 1970s. HERE attempted to organize the hotel twice over several years. They drew support from the Little Tokyo community and students and other young activists. In both cases unionization efforts failed. However, AAM labor activists were able to couple their struggles with related ones in the community and draw support from other active sectors.[32]

The effectiveness of labor-community strategies was demonstrated in 1980. Warehouse workers at three Japanese companies went on strike, the first mass Japanese workers' strikes since World War II. Whereas historically, Japanese workers worked under substandard contracts, the workers, members of the Teamsters Local 630, demanded in this instance a contract identical to other Teamster warehouse contracts in the area. The Japan Food Corporation (JFC), a subsidiary of the multi-billion-dollar Japan-based Kikkoman Corporation, was the largest of the three companies. They refused to settle even after the other two companies had. The strike lasted for weeks, and the campaign eventually drew in the Japanese American communities in Los Angeles and San Francisco. Community supporters, led by AAM activists, rallied and leafleted in Little Tokyo and in front of the JFC warehouses. This support forced JFC, after ten weeks struggle, to agree to the workers' demands.

Another demonstration of how AAM labor activists could invigorate workers' struggles and the increasing role of immigrant workers occurred in San Francisco. Latino and Asian immigrant workers, along with Black and White workers, were to transform the city's largest union, Local 2, into a militant rank and file union. Local 2 had dramatically changed from primarily a White and Black worker force. Two thirds of its 17,000 members were minorities, and Asians, largely Chinese and Filipino, were a quarter of the union. The old guard of the union had obstructed membership participation. They opposed efforts to translate their meetings, limited rank and file participation, and refused to set up elections for negotiation committees and shop stewards.[33] In 1975, internal changes in the union's leadership led rank and file Latino and Asian immigrants, movement activists, and other left forces to challenge the local's corrupt leadership.

In 1978, hotel maids at the St. Francis Hotel decided their working conditions were intolerable and waged an eighteen-month campaign to win regular break times and a reduction in the number of rooms that they each cleaned. A core of Filipina room cleaners, believing that they were being discriminated against, led this campaign. They won their arbitrated case in April 1980, which granted them regular rest breaks and reduction in the number of rooms to clean.[34]

Meanwhile the mass agreement of the major hotels in San Francisco expired in 1980; 6,500 workers, a majority immigrant women, were organized to strike. When negotiations between hotel management and the Local 2 broke down, the union struck the major hotels for weeks. During the strike, immigrant workers, including many Asian women room cleaners, led the picket lines around the hotels. The International Union leaders and hotel management had to settle the strike out of town, away from the rank and file negotiation team.

The role of Asian women rank and file members was a particularly important part of the struggle.[35] Asian women workers were steadfast on the picket lines and in maintaining the strike. At the time, former Asian American student activists, including Pat Lee, Lora Jo Foo, and Pam Tau Lee, were working in the industry. Each of these Chinese Americans, coming from different economic and geographic backgrounds, had been active as students and provided critical rank and file leadership in their hotels, picket lines, negotiations, and the union's politics. Role models for other workers, they were a direct link between the AAM and the struggles of working people. As women leaders, they demonstrated in this significant campaign the importance of melding their political leadership with grassroots struggles of the workers. Each of them has continued to provide leadership in the labor movement and API community. This strike reverberated throughout the West Coast hotel industry; workers in other cities began to rise up and demand the pay and working conditions achieved in the San Francisco hotel strike. Looking back, Laura Foo remarked, "For years, the thousands of immigrant workers in Local 2 were a silent majority who bore the abuses of the hotels and the union. As activists from the Asian American communities, we gave voice to these immigrant workers whose first language was not English; we articulated their issues and demands."[36] In the Local 2 strike and other Japanese and Chinese immigrant worker campaigns described, AAM labor and community activists played leadership roles among the workers, helping them to win immediate campaigns and draw lessons, for themselves and the AAM.

THE COMMUNITY LABOR CENTER: NEW FORMS OF WORKER ORGANIZING

AAM activists would also create new forms of worker organizations distinct from traditional trade unions that had long neglected the potential of organizing minority workers. Workers of color were usually without union representation and relegated to jobs with the lowest pay and most difficult working conditions. Even in unionized workplaces, contract enforcement was weak, and unions often ignored their needs.

Applying more sophisticated approaches, Asian labor and community activists joined forces to form pan-ethnic Asian American worker associations to fill the void in "Asiatowns." They began working with non-unionized immigrant restaurant, grocery, and construction workers employed in enclave economies.

In San Francisco, the Asian American Federation of Union Members formed in the late 1970s. George Wong, a veteran labor activist, helped successfully unionize *Chinese Times* newspaper workers, forming the first pan-ethnic Asian American labor organization.[37]

New York Chinatown, with the exception of its garment industry, was largely unorganized. The New York HERE Local 69, according to one observer, tended to focus its energy on "expensive restaurants, and hotels, hospital, and company dining rooms: because they have a large number of workers concentrated in one place, they are relatively easy to organize."[38] Unions had no presence in the Chinatown restaurant industry, and only a limited profile in Chinese restaurants outside of Chinatown. Dissatisfied with union neglect of Chinese workers and their failure to enforce contracts in unionized shops, AAM activists and frustrated workers formed the Chinese Staff and Workers' Association (CSWA) in 1979.

The CSWA launched a major campaign in 1980 at the Silver Palace, Chinatown's largest restaurant. After a difficult fight, CSWA successfully unionized the restaurant's workers. However, instead of joining HERE, the workers voted to form an independent union affiliated with CSWA. With limited resources available to a small, worker-based union, this independent union movement failed to spread to the hundreds of other Chinese restaurants in New York, and few other independent unions formed.[39]

The formation of the CSWA posed a dilemma for the AAM and the labor movement. The CSWA was not only distinct from but also openly critical of the trade unions' role in organizing Chinese workers. Charges of union indifference and apathy for Chinese workers in New York were to a degree true. Yet, the strategy needed to address this problem was uncertain. The growth of CSWA into a large multi-service organization is evidence that an independent workers center met unfilled needs of a large immigrant worker base. However, in many cases, such as HERE Local 2, working within trade unions created significant improvement in Asian workers' lives, and this view represented a different perspective on the role of past enclave workers associations such as the Chinese Workers Mutual Aid Association (CWMAA), active in the 1930s to the 1950s.[40]

During this same period, other workers associations such as the Asian Immigrant Women's Advocates in Oakland and CPA Boston's Workers Center would form in Asian ethnic communities with differing strategies on relations with established unions. Unpaid wages, layoffs, lockouts, and runaway ownership of closed factories were typical occurrences, and the community labor centers could respond with pickets, demonstrations, and other community mobilization efforts, with occasional union support.

THE REVIVAL OF STUDENT ORGANIZING

Another area that reflected the AAM's increased strengths was student organizing. Less conscious of changes in historical contexts but strengthened by the broader perspective of Marxism, students focused more on contemporary issues. Student organizing around issues such as Asian American studies, community support, and gender equality reached levels so significant that regional networks, the Asian Pacific American Student Union (APSU) on the West Coast and the East Coast Asian Student Union (ECASU), formed in 1977 and 1978, respectively. While public schools such as San Francisco State, Universities of California–Berkeley and Santa Cruz, and Laney Community College comprised the core of APSU,[41] private, elite universities such as Harvard and Yale and a smaller number of public universities including Hunter College and University of Massachusetts–Boston led the ECASU formation. These networks comprised dozens of campus organizations. For example, a 1978 APSU conference attracted two hundred students and over thirty organizations from "California, Oregon, Washington, and Hawai'i." The common purpose was far-reaching. For APSU, they were (in somewhat abbreviated form):

- Promote unity among all Asian/Pacific students;
- Fight against racism and national oppression;
- Support Third World, women's, campus, labor, community and all other progressive struggles;
- Promote understanding of Asian/Pacific people's cultures and histories;
- Build friendship among all Asian/Pacific peoples[42;]

Later, a Midwest Asian student network formed, and there were tentative discussions of creating a national network.[43]

The major catalyst for student organizing was the campaign against the 1978 Supreme Court decision that signaled the beginning of an offensive against affirmative action programs. The Court ruled, in what became known as the Bakke decision, that the University of California–Davis Medical School's special admissions program for qualified Black applicants violated the rights of an unsuccessful White applicant, Allan Bakke.[44] Students, primarily from minority student organizations from various campuses nationally, mounted a campaign to defend affirmative action programs.

Where once the response may have been localized, bolstered by connections through the larger political movement organizations, anti-Bakke-decision coalitions[45] formed across the country, organizing demonstrations and teach-ins. Over forty Asian student groups were part of these coalitions, playing a major role in building a visible, national, multi-year campaign to defend affirmative action programs.

Asian students also organized for educational rights for low-income and students of color, building links to the community, and Asian ethnic studies programs, particularly on the East Coast, where they were and remain rare. On the West Coast, student newsletters revealed that maintaining existing ethnic studies programs was a ubiquitous and continuous battle for the Asian American students of the period.

Student support played a major role in many community struggles, supporting defense of ethnic enclaves in San Francisco and Los Angeles, laid-off garment workers in Boston, and reparations for Japanese-Americans interned during World War II. Unlike the early era, this support was not built through large numbers of students dropping out of college to go into the community but with students often working through campus resources.[46]

Another major strength of student organizing in this period was the cross-racial coalition building between students of color. In addition to cooperating in the anti-Bakke work, Asian student organizations of the time also worked with Black, Latino, and other groups around ethnic studies and educational rights. Todd Lee, who was at both Berkeley and San Jose State, remembers Third World unity as an essential component.

> There were a lot more consistent efforts to work with African American and Latino students. There were often solidarity speeches from African American student leaders and Chicano student leaders. The Chicano network in particular was very strong on the West Coast. . . . At that time, there was no question that among most activists there was a basic solidarity with Blacks and Latinos.[47]

A broader, more long-term vision guided this era's student organizing, stretching beyond local campuses and the immediate classes of activists.

ART AND CULTURE: MAKING ASIAN AMERICA

The development of Asian American art and culture captured many of the crosscurrents felt by different areas of the AAM of the mid-1970s to early 1980s period. These new conditions encouraged a developing independence of the art and culture community from the traditional Asian American Movement. While this community remained supportive of the aims of the Movement, artists and arts organizations began to focus more on their own work and opportunities to pursue funding and organizational development.[48]

Nevertheless, the Asian American Movement had created a tangible and lasting day-to-day cultural and artistic impact on the Asian American community. Poetry readings, visual art exhibitions, film festivals, concerts, dance performances, theater works, taiko performances, jazz concerts, street festivals, and dances featuring Asian American rhythm and blues and funk bands, nurtured through the AAM, had become commonplace events in major Asian American urban centers in San Francisco, Los Angeles, Seattle, Boston, and New York.[49]

Moreover, cultural work as a mass organizing method continued through community organizations and various trade unions. An important aspect of community-based work was the affirmation of the language and arts of respective homelands to reflect the experiences and values of immigrants resisting assimilation by the dominant Eurocentric culture. Movement activities widely promoted bilingualism and biculturalism as a core principle and platform for struggle. Traditional arts forms such as the Lion Dance, martial arts, taiko, and kulintang music became vehicles for expression of anti-colonial sentiment and integral elements in community organizing.[50]

Art and culture popularized values such as the common person's role in making history, the power of militant resistance and the heroism in serving the people. This became an important way to document past values and struggles. This work also provided progressive templates and themes for contextualizing struggles. The cumulative result of this activity meant that Asian American art and culture in a diversity of forms had itself emerged as a framing process for the Movement.

The maturation of the movement in the post-Vietnam era also provided challenges to artists and art and culture organizations to institutionalize. For example, the evictions of tenants from numerous community buildings not only left the elderly tenants and movement organizations homeless, it left arts organizations like the Jackson Street Gallery and the Kearny Street Workshop without a place in the community. In this context arts groups began to face the issue of institutionalization, creating non-profit organizations and seeking grants from private foundations and government sources. This began a new phase where organizations struggled to maintain their storefronts, and artists and activists tried to negotiate making a living. Between getting older and a more difficult environment to support artists, many involved in the arts had to leave the field; the few who could develop a career had to focus on income-generating "gigs."

The same issues of professionalization and movement-directed programming that affected other parts of the AAM also tore at the cultural activists. These transitions even affected the forms of art and culture. One artist described the rise of Asian American Theater in terms of the diminishing role of political activism.

> During the sixties, Americans learned there were many forms of expression. It was a time when it was important to communicate and express oneself. It was a political time. It was a time that excelled in media. Every act became a political act. Eventually people tired of both the politics and the cacophony of electronic media.
>
> When the war ended, there was a turning inward. Everyone was "into" themselves. And the theater, which was live, immediate, and less impersonal than mass communications, seemed to fit the sense of the times.[51]

The increasing divisions in the AAM and the blurring of clear values of the direction of the earlier movement caused artists to reexamine their roles. These tensions sometimes caused serious divisions and confusing decisions. In New York's Basement Workshop, members who were affiliated with Workers Viewpoint and less politically oriented artists divided the Basement Workshop's resources to settle divergent and intense differences on the direction of the organization.[52] Fortunately, in California the cultural community did not become an area of contention. In San Francisco, after the fall of the I-Hotel, there was not the same kind of physical proximity between artists and arts organizations and the organized political forces. Nevertheless, all the arts organizations suffered from declining commitment and instability.[53]

At the same time, the still vital AAM continued to initiate campaigns that inspired individual artists—the growth of West Coast and East Coast Asian student organizing, the campaign to free Chol Soo Lee, a Korean-American prisoner, the redress movement in Japanese American communities, and the drive to have the United States recognize the People's Republic of China. These generated new opportunities to create movement-based cultural work. This historical period led to new songs like Robert Kikuchi Yngojo's "Ballad of Chol Soo Lee" and "Tanforan" (for the WWII assembly center) on the LP recording, *Yokohama, California*, an unprecedented number of personal histories about the Japanese American relocation for the U.S. Commission on Wartime Relocation and Internment, and the beginning of widespread college campus cultural events featuring professional and student artists. *Hito Hata*, the first full-length film made by and about Asian Americans, in 1980 captured the contributions and hardships of Japanese Americans and connected it to contemporary Little Tokyo community issues. One of the filmmakers, Duane Kubo, was a Little Tokyo activist in the 1970s who fought to oppose redevelopment in the community. This issue was integrated into the film.[54]

WOMEN ORGANIZED AND ORGANIZING

Asian American women had staked out a space that placed them as a critical part of the Asian American Movement. They assumed leadership roles in services as executive directors and leaders of political organizations and were integrated in the Asian American movement. Because of the influence of China's slogan, "Women Hold Up Half the Sky," women's issues had a standing that few political Asian Americans could openly ignore.

As part of the overall orientation of the Movement toward workers, the Asian American women's issues differed from the mainstream women's movement in acknowledging the concerns of working women—working conditions and concern for children.[55] For example, in the mid-seventies, when Boston faced a court-mandated busing order, activists organized the Boston Chinese Parents Association around demands for safety and education. Suzanne Lee, who led that organizing for the Boston Chinese Parents Association, almost exclusively women, recalled:

The women didn't call this leadership training or use this kind of language, but that is what they are doing. They just do what has to be done, partly because it is for the children and out of practicality. One husband who didn't like his wife attending the meetings and being so active locked her out of the house. Later on, she divorced him.[56]

The conditions and needs of Asian American garment and restaurant workers were highlighted and acted upon. Activists often established day care cooperatives and emphasized organizing women workers in garment, light assembly, and other industries where they concentrated.

Nevertheless, the chronic problem of male privilege and the particular issues of women underlay the need to institutionalize dedicated women's groups. Ling characterized this as two contradictory trends—first, "a rebellion against male chauvinism in the Asian Movement and with Asian culture and at the same time a strong allegiance and identity with the same Asian American Movement."[57] The latter trend was explicitly opposed to anti-male tendencies of the mainstream feminism movement.

Divisions in the Movement then led to a multiplicity of efforts. While some put more energy into political Movement organizations, others directed their energy toward creating specifically women's groups. Dedicated federal funding often encouraged these women's organizations.[58] Pioneered by Los Angeles' Asian Sisters, Asian Women's United in San Francisco, the Organization of Asian American Women in New York, the Organization of Pan Asian Women in D.C., Asian Sisters in Action in Boston, and a number of other groups in different cities sprang up. Asian women set up women's service centers such as the Asian Women's Center in New York, addressing battering and sexual assault. They created spaces for mutual support, to discuss relationships and racial-sexual stereotyping, to organize against relationship violence and sexual harassment, and to create publications around women's issues.[59]

SEATTLE'S CAMPAIGN FOR ASSASSINATED FILIPINO AMERICAN UNION LEADERS

One campaign that demonstrated the expanded vitality of the AAM took place in Seattle. While Chinese labor activists in other cities were seeking new forms of organizing workers, in Seattle, two young Filipino rank-and-file leaders, Silme Domingo and Gene Viernes were working to reform existing unions. Local 37 of the International Longshoremen's and Warehousemen's Union (ILWU), also known as the Alaska Cannery Workers Union, represented workers in the sprawling fish canning industry that worked the waters off Alaska. Since the 1920s, large numbers of Filipinos worked the Alaskan canneries, and many lived in the Seattle area.

Silme Domingo and Gene Viernes became active in the Asian American left and labor movements of Seattle. Their talent, determination, and energy soon led them to become popular leaders. Domingo and Viernes, along with other veteran workers, had helped form the Alaska Cannery Workers Association (ACWA) in the early 1970s to bring badly needed reforms to the cannery industry.[60] In addition to a lawsuit, which challenged discrimination in the industry, ACWA fought to preserve single-room housing in the International District hotels. These hotels served as home for cannery workers.[61] They were also active in the U.S.-based movement for democracy in the Philippines and as members of KDP.

Viernes joined Local 37 in 1966 when he was only fourteen, "after lying about his age and paying a $50 bribe to a cannery foreman." He spent his summers as an "Alaskero," working in the Alaskan salmon canneries with his brothers and father. College educated, Silme Domingo, before his election to union office, chose to use his knowledge to organize in International District and around other community issues and to provide legal advice to cannery workers. For four years, they fought to rid Local 37 of corrupt leadership and end collusion with the cannery owners. Domingo and Viernes were swept into leadership of the largely Filipino union just months before their slaying; they were both gunned down inside the local union office in 1981 by local gang members connected to the Marcos dictatorship in the Philippines.

The Committee for Justice for Domingo and Viernes that formed immediately after their murders suspected from the beginning that much bigger forces were at work. They worked to build international support, coordinate legal work, and conduct a hard-nosed investigation within the community. They obtained the conviction not only of the assailants, but also of a gang leader and a local union president. They organized within the union to recall and remove ineffectual union leaders. Moreover, in the breadth of vision that characterized a more mature movement, as they continued their work over the decade, they pursued suspected connections to the Philippines government.

In 1989, in a result unprecedented in U.S. history, they prevailed in a legal strategy that resulted in a court ruling that a foreign head of state, Ferdinand Marcos, had ordered the killings and had to pay monetary restitution for his act. Domingo and Viernes were the first Asian American activists of their generation to be murdered by a foreign government. The campaign for justice for Domingo and Viernes lasted nearly a decade. The committee disbanded in 1991 after everyone involved directly with the murders was convicted, including the corrupt union leader, Tony Baruso, who supplied the murderers with their weapons.[62]

CONCLUSION: MORE SOPHISTICATED
TACTICS AND TENSIONS

This chapter discusses the Movement's continued growth, particularly among students and working people and its continued role in other areas. It documents how Movement campaigns thus began to reflect the application of multiple tactics, professionalized skills, and mobilized constituencies through more developed community infrastructures and mature strategies. Movement-based activists typically drove the communities' public confrontational campaigns for justice and equity. Efforts like the organizing work to block evictions and development in numerous Chinatowns and Japantowns or protests against labor practices would capture the attention of their cities.

Among the working class, the fusion of new AAM activists with long-time labor organizers and new immigrant workers created a wave of labor organizing that brought attention to the plight of Asian American immigrant workers. Through a number of struggles, the new Asian American labor organizing demonstrated coordinated, complex, and sustained efforts. They could combine public protests and disobedience, conduct negotiations and confrontation with corporations and public entities and, in the case of Domingo and Viernes, even foreign countries. They demonstrated the ability to bring together diverse constituencies of labor, community, and students, utilize media skills, and adapt to working with established unions or developing community based workers organizations with limited resources.

At times labor, community, and student struggles required specialized professional skills related to labor organizing, development, policy, or criminal justice, depending upon particular issues. A more sophisticated movement network could now mobilize these skills.

The AAM had to adjust to changing conditions, paying greater attention to organization building. For a significant segment of the AAM, this meant institutionalizing its work, focusing on funding and other forms of financial support, and finding permanent quarters. For others, it meant developing more conscious strategies, working out differences, clarifying their priorities, and refocusing work.

These difficult choices generated greater tensions within the AAM. Efforts clearly began to diverge. Service agencies, Asian American Studies, women's groups, and art and cultural groups began to seek paths independent of the political organizations. Often, they developed strategies that, while no less activist, were less confrontational and critical of the power structure.

This chapter also discussed some significant weaknesses in the Movement that accompanied its development. Group antagonism and competition heightened and tapped energy and good will from the Movement. And even as the AAM developed more sophisticated frames, its shift toward workers, particularly blue collar workers "at the point of production," reflected shortcomings in its understanding. The U.S. had decisively entered a post-industrial trajectory where corporations increasingly phased out factory jobs. Such a strategy for organizing a base for a new society became increasingly limited.

NOTES

1. Mimi Abramovitz, "Saving Capitalism from Itself: Whither the Welfare State?" *New England Journal of Public Policy* 20, no.1 (2004–2005): 21–32; John Logan and Harvey Molotch, *Urban Fortunes: The Political Economy of Place* (Berkeley, CA: University of California Press 1987); Omatsu, "The Four Prisons."

2. Virgo Lee, interviews.

3. E. San Juan Jr., "The Predicament of the Filipinos in the United States," in *The State of Asian American Activism and Resistance in the 1990s*, ed. Karin Aguilar-San Juan (Boston: South End Press, 1994), 206.

4. Habal, "How I Became a Revolutionary," 205.

5. Samuel Bowles, David Gordon, and Thomas Weisskopf, sect. II and III in *After the Waste Land: A Democratic Economics for the Year 2000* (Armonk, NY: M. E. Sharpe 1990).

6. *INS Annual Report* 1969, *INS Statistical Yearbook* 1985, cited by Hing, *Making and Remaking*, 82.

7. Hing, *Making and Remaking*; Don Mar and Marlene Kim, "Historical Trends," in *The State of Asian America: Economic Diversity, Issues and Policies*, ed. Paul Ong (Los Angeles: LEAP Asian Pacific American Public Policy Institute and UCLA Asian American Studies Center, 1994), 13–30.

8. Lin, *Reconstructing Chinatown.*

9. Though refugee resettlement agencies initially dispersed the Vietnamese (and later other Southeast Asian refugees), lessening their impact on the centers of the AAM, secondary migration after the initial years began to create significant Vietnamese American enclaves that would influence the AAM.

10. Bureau of the Census, *Asian and Pacific Islander Population by State: 1980* (Washington, DC: 1983).

11. Madhulika S Khandelwal, *Becoming American, Being Indian* (Ithaca, NY: Cornell University, 2002).

12. R. Nakano, "Marxist-Leninist Organizing."

13. For a discussion of professionalization and funding, see Espiritu, *Asian American Panethnicity*. Võ, *Mobilizing* also gives an illuminating description of the development of largest Asian American service organization in San Diego from its movement beginnings in chapter 3.

14. In 2000, according to IRS filings, the Health Clinic (now renamed the Charles B. Wang Community Health Center) had $8.7 million in assets.

15. Asian American for Equality, "AAFE history," Asian Americans for Equality, www.aafe.org/timeline.phtml (accessed January 19, 2002).

16. Stephanie Fan, interview, 2004.

17. Regina Lee, telephone interview by Michael Liu, Boston, MA, 12 March, 2004, tape recording.

18. Ho, *Legacy to Liberation,* 396–99.

19. Though overly focused on this aspect, see Wei, *The Asian American Movement.*

20. Wei Min She, Tai Shu and Wei Min Bao, "Asian Contingent Solidarity Statement," *I.W.K. Journal* 1, no. 10 (August 1974), 10.

21. R. Nakano, "Marxist-Leninist Organizing."

22. In the winter of 1979 China and Vietnam fought a seventeen-day border war. China was able to take several provincial capitals in Vietnam but suffered heavy casualties. The war took place against a backdrop that involved tensions among Vietnam, Kampuchea (Cambodia), China, and the Soviet Union.

23. In December of 1978, Vietnam invaded Democratic Kampuchea. Vietnam claimed that the invasion was necessary to protect Cambodians and Cambodians of Vietnamese descent and against border incursions into Vietnam. The toppled Khmer Rouge continued to wage guerilla war against the Vietnamese-supported regime until well in the 1990s.

24. One indication was the proportion of coverage during this period that papers such as *Unity*, the newspaper of the League of Revolutionary Struggle, devoted to international affairs, including pieces on Asia, Africa, the Middle East, and Latin America.

25. Dean Toji, "Hibakusha," *East Wind* 1 no. 2 (Fall/Winter1982): 3–5.

26. This was most graphically documented in Curtis Choy's film, *The Fall of the I-Hotel* (San Francisco: National Asian American Telecommunications Association 1983), videocassette.

27. Bob Nakata, "The Struggles of the Waiahole-Waikane Community Association," *Social Process in Hawai'i* 39 (1999): 60–73.

28. *Ang Katipunan*, August 15–31.

29. Kathy Masaoka, interview by Michael Liu, Los Angeles, 19 June, 2004; "Sun Building Evicted," *Getting Together*, August 1977, 6; Chin, *Seattle's International District.*

30. Sayo Fujioka, "Becoming a Worker: A Matter of Choice," *East Wind* 2, no. 1 (Spring/Summer 1983): 40–41.

31. "Chinese Workers Win Union Contract," "Cannery Workers Fight Unemployment Benefit Cuts," "Chinese Workers Win Contract, Set Precedent," *Getting Together*, April–August 1978.

32. "Horikawa Workers vow to continue unionization fight," *Unity*, 27 July 1979, 6.

33. Lora Jo Foo. "The Role of Asians in the Recent Struggles of the San Francisco Culinary Industry," *Yellow Journal* 1, no. 2 (Spring 1986): 21–38.

34. Foo, "The Role of Asians."

35. Patricia Lee, "Asian Immigrant Women and HERE Local 2," *Labor Research Review* 11 (1988): 29–38

36. Lora Jo Foo, interview by Kim Geron, San Francisco, CA, 15 November, 2006.

37. Kent Wong, "Building an Asian Pacific Labor Alliance: A New Chapter in Our History," in *The State of Asian American Activism and Resistance in the 1990s*, ed. Karin Aguilar-San Juan (Boston: South End Press, 1994), 335–49.

38. Kwong, *The New Chinatown*, 140.

39. Kwong, *The New Chinatown*, 137–47.

40. At the time, Chinese workers were similarly excluded and ignored by most unions. An organization analogous to CSWA formed on the West Coast that established a working relationship with the trade union movement. In 1937, the CWMAA was founded and received support from many different Chinese workers. The CWMAA called for the unity of workers. Workers joined from diverse industries including restaurants, laundries, sewing, farms, seafaring, and longshoremen. The association had close connections with several unions. It assisted workers of all trades—"the association was in the forefront of bringing the Chinese workers into labor unions." It opposed Japanese aggression against China, provided workers' education, and mutual support. Unions were just beginning to take organizing Chinese workers seriously, opening branch offices of the AFL and CIO organized labor federations in San Francisco Chinatown. The CWMAA eventually disbanded after intense government persecution during the Cold War era.

41. Lyle Wing, interview by Michael Liu, Berkeley, CA, 22 June 2004.

42. Asian Pacific Student Union, Southern Cal Region, "Asian/Pacific Students Unite!" (Summer, 1978), Asian Student Union, California State University, photocopy; Francis Wong, "Movement Still Shaky, but Trying," *Winds* 2:1 (March, 1978), Asian American Student Association, Stanford): 1.

43. Christine Chen, interview by Michael Liu, tape recording, Boston, MA, 29 July, 2004; Asian Pacific Student Union Coordinating Committee, "Proposal for the National Link-Up of the East Coast Asian Student Union and the West Coast," authors' collection, 25 October 1978, Photocopy.

44. University of California Regents v. Bakke 438 U.S. 265 (1978), laws.findlaw.com/us/438/265.html (March 10, 2007).

45. At least two national coalitions formed, the Anti-Bakke Decision Coalition and the National Committee to Overturn the Bakke Decision.

46. Laney College Asian Student Union, "The Third World Caucus and the Asian Student," "Divisional Structure—A Threat to Ethnic Studies," in *Asian Horizon* 2: 11 (1974), 5: 3 (1975), Laney College Asian Student Union, Oakland.

47. Todd Lee, interview by Michael Liu, tape recording, Boston, 12 December 2006.

48. Peter Kiang, "Transformation—The Challenge Facing the Asian American Artist in the '80's," *East Wind* 4, no. 1 (Winter/Spring 1985): 31–33.

49. Wes Sensaki, "Wes Sensaki," *East Wind* 1, no. 1 (Spring/Summer 1982): 39–40.

50. Greg Morizumi, "Profile: Mutya Gener," *East Wind* 2, no. 1 (Spring/Summer 1983): 66–67; Susan Hayase, "Taiko," *East Wind* 4, no. 1 (Winter/Spring 1985): 46–47; Norman Jayo and Paul Yamazaki, "Searching for an Asian American Music: Robert Kikuchi-Yngojo," *East Wind* 5, no. 1 (Spring/Summer 1986): 10–12.

51. David Oyama, "Introduction: Asian American Theatre," *Bridge* 5 (1977): 4–5.

52. Fay Chiang, ed., *Basement Yearbook* 1986 (New York: Basement Workshop, 1986).

53. Kearny Street Workshop, "KSW Remembers 30 Years in Acts Activism," Kearny Street Workshop, www.kearnystreet.org/about_ksw/history/index.html (10 April 2005).

54. Bruce Iwasaki, "Hito Hata: Raise the Banner," *Unity*, 21 May 1981.

55. Shiree Teng, "Women, Community and Equality: Three Garment Workers Speak Out," *East Wind* 2 (Spring/Summer 1983): 20–23.

56. Suzanne Lee, interview by Michael Liu, tape recording, Brookline, 2 September, 2002.

57. Ling, "The Mountain Movers," 61; Rita Fujiki and Cathy Gosho, "Modern Day Issues Facing Asian American Women," in *Concerns of Asian American Women*, Washington Commission on Asian American Affairs. Task Force on Asian American Women (Olympia, WA, 1976), 20–27; Esther Ngan-Ling Chow, "The Feminist Movement: Where Are All the Asian American Women?" in *Making Waves: An Anthology of Writings by and about Asian American Women,* ed. Asian Women United of California (Boston: Beacon Press, 1989), 362–76.

58. Juanita Tamayo Lott, "Growing Up, 1968–1985," in *Making Waves: An Anthology of Writings by and about Asian American Women,* ed. Asian Women United of California (Boston: Beacon Press, 1989), 353–61.

59. Miya Iwataki, "The Asian Women's Movement—A Retrospective," and Lydia Lowe and Beth Shironaka, "Asian Sisters in Action," both in *East Wind* 2, no. 1 (Spring/Summer 1983): 33–35; Wei, *The Asian American Movement.*

60. Thomas Churchill, *Triumph Over Marcos* (Seattle: Open Hand Pub. 1995), 26–28, 42–44.

61. Churchill, *Triumph*, 52.

62. Chung-suk Han, Sue Chin, Ron Chew, Robert Shimabukuro, and David Takami, "Unknown Heroes," *Colorlines*, July 20, 2001, www.arc.org/C_Lines / CLArchive/story_web01_02.html (5 October 2004).

Chapter Six

From Vincent Chin to Jesse Jackson (1983–1989): The Horned Snake Rattles

The groups that constituted the core of the AAM had evolved to the point that called into question the identity of the AAM. Did the growing professionalization and institutionalization of major sectors of the AAM and the integration of Asian American political formations into broader groups subvert a recognizable Asian American Movement? Sustained increasingly by the political formations of the AAM, such as the League of Revolutionary Struggle (LRS) and Line of March, large numbers of Asian American activists maintained in large measure the Movement's particular values of structural change, equality for Asian Americans, and valorizing the working class. In every major Asian American enclave, they persisted as "collective efforts to challenge the conditions and assumptions of their lives" and "the boundaries of established institutional rules and routinized roles." This chapter will describe how their work not only continued but became more effective and broader in its collective challenges to the status quo.

The progression of the maturing Movement nevertheless brought it into surprising terrain, where many would have to reevaluate their frameworks. As Eddie Wong recalled:

> One person put it to me in a very distinct way, "We were selling revolution, and no one was buying. After that what's the point?" Perhaps that's an oversimplified way of putting it. You pour in all this effort, time, and energy, and it was really not going very far. You have to change in some way. We didn't know what that change would be.[1]

The infrastructure that the early Movement built and the growing abilities of experienced organizers placed them in a position where they would often juggle short-term and long-term concerns. In more influential positions, activists worked increasingly with those from different classes, sectors, and political orientations. These interactions brought opportunities for both expanding influence and structural assimilation, where the negotiation between these conflicting goals was unclear.

The increasing diversity coincided with a rising right-wing dominance that the administrations of Ronald Reagan facilitated. Under these conditions, the divergence of different sectors within the AAM expanded. The disassociation that began in the previous era only widened, and working for reform was the ascendant form of activism. Only within those arenas—community, labor, and student—where Marxism provided some direction, was structural change factored in and discussed. Yet, it was also this direction that gave the AAM some remaining coherence.

This chapter will describe the simultaneous development of the Movement's increasing scope and increasing stresses it faced.

COMPLEXITY

The effects of globalization were becoming increasingly obvious, altering the environment that activists had to now face. Within labor, changes were particularly dramatic. In the garment industry, for example, Xiaolan Bao observed the rapid changes in that industry's structural conditions during the 1980s. Such changes drove up costs for garment contractors and increased the supply of labor, creating the conditions for greater exploitation of their workers. During this time, imports rose from 6.9 percent in 1959 to 51 percent in 1980. Other effects of globalization included the creation of global cities, accompanied by global capital investment in Asian enclaves, and increased immigration from Asia.[2]

These challenges were heightened by the right-wing campaign of the Reagan administrations. Among his signal acts was a public antagonism toward organized labor, most famously in his 1981 termination of 11,000 airport traffic controllers and their union. In sanctioning an anti-union offensive, the Reagan administration legitimized corporate aggressiveness toward unions—and heralded a trend toward conservative dominance of the U.S. polity.

U.S. corporate interests also rallied around Reagan's dramatic expansion of military budgets at the expense of social service programs and amplified U.S. triumphalism and anti-communism. His White, conservative base supported his attempts to limit affirmative action and civil rights programs. These policies all affected the conditions that challenged activists. They stewarded in the self-indulgence of the "Me decade" of the 1980s.

To the trends of a rapidly increasing and more diverse Asian American population, the rise of "Reaganism" sharpened the need to defend the advances of the previous periods. The right wing's "supply-side economics" implemented a plan of large tax cuts and huge deficits to preclude present and future social service spending. Reagan and conservatives targeted, among other programs, refugee aid that supported services to many Southeast Asians.[3] This public spending had supported the growth of much of the new infrastructure in Asian American communities.

Conservatives also targeted immigrants, leading to the 1986 reform of immigration laws and the constriction of support that immigrants could receive. They conducted campaigns, typically successful, to ban the use of languages other than English in schools and public places.[4] Though many of the essential issues that the rising AAM had identified remained—the tenuousness of enclaves, the conditions for working Asians, widespread poverty—and new ones like hate crimes arose, the community organizations had created means to address these problems. The threatened dismantling of the social welfare system aggravated tensions as the growing number of organizations from diverse communities competed for a diminishing pie.

Nevertheless, as irresistible immigration fed the growing Asian American population and attracted greater notice, community organizations continued to multiply to meet their needs. The Movement was now felt not only in the different areas where they had begun work but also in new areas such as local government and foundations, unions, and the courts. In the areas where they had worked, enclave communities, workplaces, and campuses, they had built up bases of power and positions of influence. However, in the worsening political atmosphere and shriveling of resources, they faced new challenges.

GRIEVANCES, RESOURCES, AND FRAMEWORK

The rise of the AAM had placed on the table many previously disregarded issues concerning Asian Americans. In doing so, organizing around them helped ameliorate a number of them—the slowing of the redevelopment of enclaves, greater attention to wages, unionization, and conditions of workers, creation of Asian American studies programs, and liberalization of community politics and institutional repression. Though far from resolving these issues, the Asian American community's grievances, however, increasingly acquired a defensive tone—defending affirmative action, ethnic studies, unionization and enclave housing. They focused on the preservation of gains made in the earlier decade in an increasingly hostile environment.

Chapter Six

Despite shrinking resources, the communities had established an infrastructure that continued as a base for the AAM. Moreover, the communities continued to expand these infrastructures, creating an increasing number of organizations, primarily service, but also social and culturally oriented ones, to meet a growing population (see figure 6.1). The AAM groups had established themselves as a recognized part of the growing community infrastructure. Some had now been active for over a decade. They were within a dynamic and proliferating spectrum of organizations. The ECASU student network was able to compile what was surely an abbreviated list of more than three hundred student and community groups in New England and the mid-Atlantic region, where the Asian American populations were relatively small. It listed organizations as specific as the Lao Ministry and Fellowship and Japanese American Legal and Technical Translation Institute. The listings also testified to the growing ethnic and class divides; major colleges had begun to organize six to eight ethnic Asian student organizations in addition to an Asian American student association, and professional, electoral, and suburban-based community organizations were listed along with Khmu, Lao, Indian, Hmong, Korean, and Pakistani groups.[5] The setting had developed rapidly from a relatively simple one in the 1960s to a complex and changing environment.

The intellectual climate continued its conservative trajectory. The spontaneous generation of skepticism toward authority and activism had ceased, the

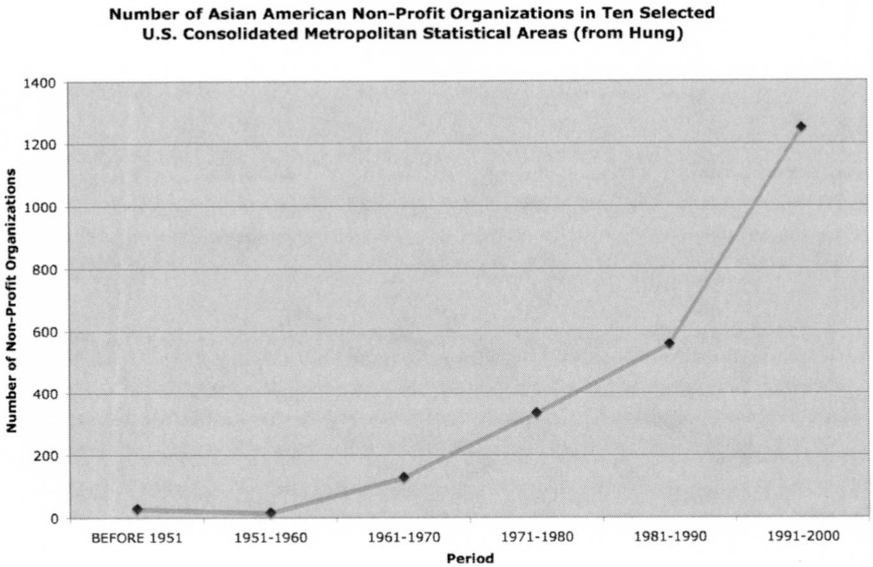

Number of Asian American Non-Profit Organizations in Ten Selected U.S. Consolidated Metropolitan Statistical Areas (from Hung)

Figure 6.1.

demand for full equality for Asian Americans as an oppressed minority was fading, and entrepreneurs and professionals replaced working people as the center of Asian American narratives. Now it was established organizations that drove the expansion of activism through recruitment and activities. Under these circumstances, the more developed and flexible frameworks of the AAM served Movement groups well in enabling their efficacy as well as confronting the difficult terrain.

IMMIGRANT LABOR ACTS

Though the 1980s ushered in a more hostile labor environment, the work of Asian American activists in labor organizing continued to grow. In 1982, two important developments occurred that typified the dilemma and promise of Asian American labor. Asian American and progressive labor activists were forced to combat the continuing anti-Asian aspects of the "Buy America" campaigns of the 1980s. While the ILGWU was the principal offender in the early 1970s, the United Autoworkers Union took up this theme in succeeding years in a manner creating deadly results for Asian Americans. However, the decade also demonstrated new potential in organizing Asian American labor.

In the late 1970s, the bottom fell out of the U.S. auto industry. As the Japanese and German auto industries were rebuilt after the war, they began to squeeze the U.S. auto companies with Japanese economy vehicles and highly engineered German luxury cars. Following the oil embargo by OPEC nations in 1973–1974 that resulted in gas shortages and block-long queues at service stations, U.S. consumers began to look for ways to cut their gas consumption and turned to imported automobiles. Between 1978 and 1981, domestic auto employment shrank from 760,000 to 490,000, and automakers took drastic steps to cut costs.[6] Massive layoffs did not just create a serious, growing unemployment among American workers; they also fueled a rising highly racialized, anti-imports sentiment. Criticism of Japanese imports spread to anti-Asian immigrant attitudes.[7]

Further complicating the growing anti-Asian sentiments was the growing number of refugees from Southeast Asia. Anti-Asian sentiments grew louder and exploded into anti-Asian violence. The murder of Vincent Chin by disgruntled Detroit autoworkers who mistook Chin to be of Japanese descent highlighted the intensity of feelings felt by White autoworkers.[8] Auto corporations and their union leadership repeatedly told these workers that Japanese imports were taking their jobs. Those whose features represented this global threat became a target for racists. Asian American labor activists opposed these efforts in a variety of ways. They explained to their fellow trade unionists that the enemy was really an American auto industry that had failed to adapt to new conditions, but, rather than building solidarity with international autoworkers to stop runaway factories, autoworkers blamed a racial or ethnic group.

A more optimistic aspect of labor organizing was the continuing mobilization of immigrant workers. In New York City, the garment industry contract for the thousands of Chinese garment workers expired in 1982. Since the early 1970s, three-year contract renewals between the ILGWU and the garment manufacturers' Chinatown subcontractors were fairly routine with insignificant input from the workers. However, when this particular contract expired, the Chinese contractors, who felt they were excluded from the ongoing negotiations between the union and the manufacturers, called for the workers to support them and leave the union.[9]

When the workers refused, Chinatown contractors locked them out. While the ILGWU first weakly responded, simply organizing workers to apply for unemployment benefits, the union next mobilized activists and shop floor representatives, going from shop to shop, for a rally near Chinatown to protest the lockout. In two historic rallies, 20,000 workers attended each time, a massive show of solidarity in the Chinese community. This forced the contractors to sign with the union.

Subsequently, the ILGWU became more active in community issues and organized factory workers to oppose building a local jail in the community, support a daycare center in Chinatown, and engage in other issues.[10] This historic strike also created a cadre of grassroots labor activists.[11] Unfortunately, the ILGWU failed to follow up on the potential demonstrated in these rallies by organizing large numbers of Asian American workers, thus weakening the overall garment workers movement.

Asian American workers exhibited a similar organizing potential in Boston. P and L Sportswear, the largest garment shop in Boston, closed its doors in December 1985 and laid off its 300 workers, 60 percent Chinese immigrant women. The shutdown of a factory that once employed 1,000 workers was a reflection of the general decline of the garment industry in the Northeast.

Local media ignored the shutdown, the local leadership of the ILGWU ignored the workers, and the state Division of Employment Security took no action to provide any applicable benefits. Everyone viewed the case as unavoidable "structural unemployment." Three-fourths of all local Chinese women worked in garment industry jobs, and those working in union shops were often the only source of health insurance for their families. Under Massachusetts state law, workers displaced by plant closings were entitled to job retraining. The workers, however, found out about the provisions only when their English-speaking children saw on local news coverage primarily White workers receiving benefits immediately at a closing meatpacking plant.[12]

The P and L workers approached the Chinese Progressive Association of Boston, and a workers support committee formed and framed objectives. The workers and their community supporters organized a series of public demonstrations and confrontations that pressured the state and the city of Boston to agree to the workers' demands. Among these concessions were that workers would determine the guidelines and funding for their retraining programs, monitor the programs' progress, and receive sufficient unemployment and health insurance during their retraining. After an eighteen-month campaign, they had won the first Chinese bilingual retraining program in New England. Developing their own leadership, the workers demonstrated what women workers could accomplish by remaining organized and building strong community ties.

In 1987 the new wave of Asian American labor organizers began to feel strong enough to institutionalize itself. The Alliance of Asian Pacific Labor formed in Los Angeles and brought together Asian union staff and rank and file leaders throughout LA. They met regularly to discuss the specific concerns they shared as Asia Pacific labor activists. This group built a presence in the Asian American community and the labor movement by opposing "Japan Bashing" and anti-Asian sentiments and becoming active in various local campaigns by unions that involved Asian Pacific workers.[13]

PROLIFIC COMMUNITIE(S)

Other advances occurred in the community. Around development issues, activists not only continued to mobilize to preserve their communities, but some moved into community planning. Some of the activists around the I-Hotel joined the Kearny Street Housing Corporation, which tried to find solutions to rebuilding housing on the site. Committee Against *Nihonmachi* Eviction reinvented itself in 1983 as the Japanese Community Progressive Alliance to affect community development and build housing.[14] Similar transformation occurred with other groups like the Asian Americans for Equality in New York, Inter•Im in Seattle, and the Chinatown Housing and Land Development Task Force in Boston. Members of the inactive Little Tokyo People's Rights Organization (LTPRO) became members of the Little Tokyo Service Center Housing Committee and later its Community Development Corpporation (CDC).

Little Tokyo redevelopment became a focus for the local Asian community in 1975, when Little Tokyo People's Rights Organization was formed. Before that there had been a redevelopment committee in Japanese Community Services, Asian Involvement. After 1978, an agreement was reached that suspended evictions until the elderly housing was built and allowed for relocation expenses for tenants and businesses. So the issue was resolved, and people moved on to other things such as workers organizing and redress. LTPRO began to meet infrequently, though newcomer services and other programs continued.

In 1985, former LTPRO members still working in Little Tokyo heard that people from the Alan Hotel and Annex and the Masago Hotel were being evicted, and small businesses on Second Street faced eviction. There was no LTPRO to respond. There was only the Little Tokyo Service Center and a few who remembered the struggle of the 1970s, Judy Ota, Kathy Masaoka, and Bill Watanabe. They saw it as a continuation of LTPRO's fight. The Far East building was city owned but services like hot water were being denied to the tenants. This was a mixed population of three hundred tenants, with elderly Japanese and other non-Japanese in the building, a dangerous place to venture. Mo Nishida, another LTPRO member, who lived in that hotel, formed a housing committee. Judy Ota began to look into what could be done for the tenants and created a housing committee within Little Tokyo Service Center. Judy in particular began to investigate how to affect the city and proposed gaining control of the building to save it. She was a lawyer but left legal services to learn about development. The housing committee then became a CDC, and the Far East building became its first project.[15]

Similarly around education, health, women's and youth issues, and legal rights, the Movement often found itself assuming greater responsibilities. Activists assumed executive directorships in agencies or took professional positions as physicians, teachers, or social workers. Conversely, people of similar professional backgrounds became activists. These activists needed more immediately to improve schools, conditions in workplaces, housing projects, hospitals, or the quality of day care available. Their activities were no longer simply oppositional but took into account organizational and institutional interests, pragmatic concerns, and the immediate living conditions of people.

New activist organizations arose, representing more diverse constituencies and complicating the Asian American equation. Those involved in fighting for Korean democracy had built a new national organization, Young Koreans United (YKU), which beginning in 1983 spread to wherever Korean American communities had sunk roots. While primarily focused on Korea, YKU popularized the broadening of community work to address issues faced by Korean Americans and introduced the possibilities of organization into the Korean American community. The influence of that movement is symbolically manifested in the use of lively Pung-mul drumming and Korean dress as political theater in many demonstrations, adaptations introduced by YKU. The Committee Against Anti-Asian Violence (CAAAV) formed in 1986 in New York, involving Korean Americans, Cambodian Americans, and South Asians as well as Chinese Americans, to combat hate crimes against Asian

Americans. They eventually saw their role as organizing diverse and distinct Asian American communities, changing their name to CAAAV: Organizing Asian Communities, emphasizing the plural in communities. Many new organizations for South Asian women, formed in the late 1980s, such as Sakhi in New York. In Hawai'i an indigenous movement, divergent from Asian American activism, gathered force beginning with the campaign to stop the bombing of Kaho'olawe.[16] Similarly, more activist groups focused on gender and sexual identities within the Asian American community.

REGIONAL STUDENT NETWORKS

Divergences also affected student organizing. While debate on the relation between Asian American studies and the community continued, the space between them increased over time. While this alienation was understandable due to institutional and professional pressures,[17] Asian American Studies' increasing drift from the most disadvantaged in the communities, where Asian American Studies had been rooted in its beginnings, was scarcely defensible. Students felt and noticed the disconnection more than others. New activist students now fought battles not only to win ethnic studies but also to make existing programs relevant to communities. They independently continued to build bridges to the community. Espiritu cited Filipino student support for nurses sanctioned by English-only laws in local hospitals, and ECASU students in the Boston area worked with the Asian American Resource Workshop (AARW), a community group, to undertake a multi-year Asian American Studies campaign.[18]

Another divergence reflected the growth of the immigrant population and diversity in the larger Asian American population. Numerous ethnic-specific student organizations now grew alongside pan-Asian American student organizations. The ethnic-specific organizations also developed regional and even national networks. This diversity complicated and often frustrated common efforts among Asian American students.

However, on the whole, Asian American student organizing demonstrated continued growth and development. Pan-Asian student organizations had long histories and the benefit of the experience of Marxist groups, who worked in the APSU and ECASU networks and supported their efforts in political involvement. True to the Asian American identity's origins as a political expression, the pan-Asian student groups on the whole were the most stable, politically and organizationally sophisticated, and effective in mobilizing. They had active and collective steering committees and standing committees on organizational functioning and the educational issues of the time, admissions, and ethnic studies. They adopted a "broad view of what it meant to fight racism and oppression, and that included valuing the social and cultural life and looking at the experience of Asian Americans on campus overall and whether that was equal to that of White students. It was a comprehensive and encompassing view of what it meant to build the Asian student movement." Over this period, they grew steadily. In 1990 an APSU conference drew a thousand students.[19] The ECASU and APSU student networks were active, vibrant entities.

Within the student movement in this period of cutbacks, the main issues were educational rights around costs and standards. On the West Coast, maintaining ethnic studies was another major issue. In California, the APSU network built coalitions with other student networks. In the face of funding cutbacks for the pubic higher education system, APSU and other Asian American student groups often united with Chicano and African American student networks to better organize. During 1987 and 1989, these Third World coalitions drew tens of thousands of students to march on Sacramento, the state capital. Moreover there were ongoing alliances on various campuses.[20]

Identity and establishing Asian American studies were more relevant on the East Coast's concentration of private schools. Thus ECASU, along with the AARW, mobilized a region-wide effort on Asian American studies. This had limited success. In 1987, however, a University of Connecticut racial harassment incident ignited a community-student campaign that resulted in the eventual creation of the Asian American center.[21] Asian American students and faculty won Asian American studies courses and programs of varying scope on different campuses.

NATIONAL ASIAN AMERICAN ARTS: OPPORTUNITIES AND "CULTURAL ACTIVISM"

For Asian American Arts and culture, this was a watershed period. In an increasing movement away from the political sector of the Asian American Movement, artists, rather than being disoriented by developments in China and Vietnam, looked for inspiration elsewhere, and the increasing interaction with different classes opened up new resources for the arts community. Asian American cultural work also began to integrate a more global perspective. For example, China became more accessible due to the normalization of its state-to-state relations with the United States, and Chinese Americans traveling there became more commonplace.

A major influence was that Asian Americans emerged on the social, political and cultural scene in issues that attracted nation-wide attention. This created a new environment where Asian American artists and arts organizations could achieve recognition. There was the increasing professionalism among artists in both artistic and business aspects of cultural production. The National Endowment for the Arts, state arts agencies, and foundations provided new funding opportunities in an effort to address issues of race of an increasingly diverse society. Theater companies, jazz festivals, and film organizations developed in the major Asian American urban concentrations of San Francisco, New York, Los Angeles, and Seattle. In San Francisco, media arts organizers pioneered a national strategy in creating the National Asian American Telecommunications Association, an organization that lobbied institutions for increased funding and support for Asian American filmmakers.

Media organizations, grassroots organizations such as the Chinese Progressive Associations, and political campaigns such as Asian Americans for Jesse Jackson sought the active participation of artists and arts organizations. This merged an advocacy agenda with the organizing talent of movement activists that led to increases in funding to Asian American organizations.

In many cases, especially among organizations, a spirit of collective advocacy grew toward government and foundation funders. National foundations such as the Ford and Rockefeller Foundations popularized a "multiculturalism" policy to address artists and arts organizations from communities of color. Government agencies like the National Endowment for the Arts or the California Arts Council implemented programs to respond to calls for "cultural equity" in arts funding, which had disproportionately supported Western European cultural forms.

Such development was evident in diverse Asian American cultural fields— film, literature, theater, and music. These opportunities and the growth in both the community and "mainstream" audience for work stressing Asian American themes encouraged a new level of professionalism and spawned a "nonprofit" sector in the arts.

These practices created contradictions in maintaining a community-based mission. The inherent difficulties in sustaining careers in the arts led art and cultural work to be less mission-driven and more oriented toward funding and careers. This was exacerbated by the growth of conservatism in the Reagan era, the AAM's declining presence, and the overall ambiguity in political direction for the arts. Issues in arts advocacy lacked an overall context and were not integrated into any overarching strategy.

"Cultural Activism" however emerged as a new arena of struggle through successful media advocacy campaigns such as the protests against Michael Cimino's film *Year of the Dragon* and the planned re-make of the Charlie Chan detective series. The highly visible Artists Against Apartheid campaign, highlighted by efforts of high-profile artists, also framed Asian American artists' activism. One notable reflection of this cultural activism and an important mobilizing vehicle was the national network around *East Wind* magazine that began publication in 1982. With its tagline of "Politics and Culture of Asians in the U.S.," *East Wind* provided a center of gravity for progressive Asian American cultural activism.

THE MOVEMENT'S NATIONAL AND REGIONAL IMPACT

A case that demonstrated contemporary activists' abilities was the1982 Vincent Chin case in Detroit. The first and one of the best-known national Asian American campaigns, the case, involved the beating death of Vincent Chin, a Chinese-American draftsman. Disgruntled autoworkers Michael Nitz and Bernard Ebens perpetuated the killing because they believed Chin to be "Japanese." The backdrop for the murder was a conservative, chauvinistic, anti-Japanese environment, fanned up by unions and politicians in an auto-industry area suffering from acute unemployment. Unions and corporations and a system that seemed to sanction the violence were symptomatic of the times.[22]

While the community responded slowly to the killing, they reacted rapidly out of outrage at the legal system's treatment of the case. A local judge fined Michael Nitz and Bernard Ebens $3,780, an amount a local writer calculated as "less than the cost of a used car."[23] The court sentenced them to three years' probation while the prosecutors failed to appear at the sentencing.[24]

Throughout the country, the campaign engaged every sector of the Chinese American community and crossed ethnic lines. The American Citizens for Justice (ACJ), a pan-Asian American coalition formed in Detroit specifically around the case, fused activists, mainstream and professional Chinese, Asian American organizations, and ordinary Chinese Americans. They also involved the local JACL, Korean, South Asian, and Filipino groups as well as Jewish and African American ones.[25] The formation of a pan-ethnic vehicle rather than a solely Chinese one, as some of the founders had proposed, suggested the influence of younger activists who had adopted perspectives of the Asian American Movement.

Asian Americans activists were also significant actors in building Vincent Chin support committees that supplied funds, expertise, and political pressure across the country in major areas of Asian American concentrations. The broad community support, which created a flood of letters to the Department of Justice, forced the federal government to file civil rights charges against Nitz and Ebens.

The conduct of a national campaign, involving working class immigrants, traditional family associations, middle class professionals, civil rights organizations, students, and supportive communities with different political orientations and ethnicities, revealed the constraints that attaining broader national influence generates. The issue of race was cautiously introduced into the campaign and with much debate within ACJ. Within the relative success of the organizing efforts,[26] the choice of the name, "American Citizens for Justice," foreshadowed the future drift of activists to struggle within the framework of civil rights circumscribed by the system rather than outside it.[27]

In Hawai'i, activists also demonstrated their new breadth. Across generations and across the islands, they nurtured and built the campaign to stop the U.S. military shelling on the island of Kaho'olawe. Sustaining a three-decade struggle through the Protect Kaho'olawe Ohana (PKO), they organized protests and "illegal" occupations of the island. Love of the land, *aloha 'aina*, was a deeply felt value of Hawai'ians, and two PKO organizers lost their lives crossing to the island to defend it against bombardment. The PKO was able to inspire and motivate thousands of activists from all the islands to participate in the campaign. Using the courts and environmental and cultural regulations, PKO reached a consent decree with the Navy in 1980 allowing limited access to the land. As one in a series of steps that led to ending federal control over Kaho'olawe, in 1982, they persuaded Japan, New Zealand, and Australia to cease shelling during military exercises. In 1990 President George H. W. Bush ordered the end to shelling of the island.[28]

The initial organizing in the Kalama Valley had spread to Niumalu-Nawiliwili and Waiahole-Waikane, Molakai Ranch, Waimanalo Plantation, Ota Camp, Chinatown, and the Stop TH-3 highway campaign through the different parts of Hawai'i and throughout this period. The Ota Camp struggle in the town of Waipahu that began in 1971 against tenant evictions was typical of these widespread struggles against development for tourism and vacation homes. A developer riding the wave of Hawai'ian growth wanted Tatsuichi Ota's land for development of an apartment complex. The mainly working-class Filipino tenants occupied the land as leaseholders, typical of many Hawai'ian arrangements of the time. With the help of activists from Kokua Hawai'i and other groups, the tenants organized the Ota Camp Makibaka (Ota Camp Struggle) Association and fought to stay together as a community. In 1974, the community, with the help of the city, reached a temporary resolution and moved en masse to a nearby site. Pete Tagalog, one of the founders and leaders of the tenants' association, said that they chose the association name to remind themselves of the need to always organize. This proved prescient. The city had enlisted another developer, Jack Ujimori, to develop the new site. While the tenants believed that they were making payments to purchase their new homes, Ujimori abruptly raised what he considered to be their rents in the early 1980s, which precipitated another confrontation. With a continuing combination of rallies, demonstrations, fundraising, and legal strategies, the tenants, with support from University of Hawai'i students, professors, and staff, finally won their right to buy their homes and stay.[29]

ORGANIZING FOR REDRESS AND REPARATIONS

The effort that most dramatically demonstrated an Asian American community's new capacity for organizing was the successful struggle for redress and reparations for the internment of Japanese Americans. Dominant narratives have focused on the legislative process and the work of Japanese American Citizens League (JACL).[30] The critical role of the National Coalition for Redress and Reparations (NCRR), a product of the AAM and the organizing component, has been underdocumented and underestimated in these recountings.

In reflecting back on the redress campaign, Alan Nishio, a former NCRR co-chair, observed, "The end result is a testament to the work of all the parties [in the campaign]. They all played important roles. . . . It was a testament to the willingness of a community to put aside differences to work for a common cause." Even within this acknowledgment, NCRR's history delineated the contributions that the AAM could make. Nishio continued, "NCRR was very important in certain key phases, especially in the early phase. By making clear the community perspective, NCRR pressured the JACL to support community reparations. NCRR's role was two things—making sure that the monetary compensation was part of the demand and mobilizing the larger community."[31] NCRR's protracted and multi-class and -sector work also demonstrated the AAM's matured abilities.

The drive for redress represented a decade of intense work. Some earlier efforts, such as persuading Rep. George Danielson, a Black Democrat, to file the first redress bill in 1974, occurred from local initiatives. Over the 1970s, driven by demands of a restive JACL membership,[32] the JACL national council passed a resolution in 1978 that called for reparations. This news electrified the community. While the JACL eventually backtracked on the call for reparations in favor of a federal study commission on the internment, three different initiatives sprang up to take up redress. The community, particularly JACL, successfully prevailed upon Congress to approve the Commission on Wartime Relocation and Internment of Civilians (CWRIC).

The first phase of the Redress and Reparations campaign revolved around the Commission and its multiple hearings. In 1983, the Commission's work resulted in a compelling report and strong statement of support for redress and monetary reparations. In the second phase encompassing the next six years, activists and elected officials focused on keeping the issue and legislation alive. The final two years during the 100th Congress led to passage of a bill, Reagan's signing of the legislation in 1988, and finally, appropriations.[33] Within this general sweep of the redress campaign saga was the less detectable "dark matter" of Movement organizing.

It was the spirit of resistance in the 1970s that revived proposals about redress, the making of amends for the violations of Japanese American rights, and reparations, compensation for their experiences. Movement activities such as institutionalizing internment camp pilgrimages and Day of Remembrance commemorations brought forward the long-whispered topic of the internment and helped popularize the demands for redress.[34]

The NCRR, established in 1980, begun as a largely *Sansei* or third generation, drew in growing numbers of *Nisei* and *Issei*. Throughout its life, it was strictly volunteer driven, a "coalition of Japanese community organizations, churches, civic and student organizations, progressive groups, and several chapters of the JACL." The NCRR was built initially upon individuals who were also active in the community groups of the Little Tokyo People's Rights Organization in LA, *Nihonmachi* Outreach Committee in San Jose, and Japanese Community Progressive Alliance in San Francisco. It drew upon the personal networks of these organizers as well as local community members. Consciously and openly acknowledging its role as part of the AAM as it developed, it drew support from the Asian Pacific Student Unions, at the time a strong regional network. The League of Revolutionary Struggle (LRS) also played an important role, providing organizers and political leadership to the activists.[35]

Despite NCRR's informality and lack of resources, they could draw upon the resources of these Movement networks and established active grassroots chapters in eight different cities and a network of individual supporters. They spearheaded a grassroots movement that pressed popular demands for redress and reparations on the wavering sectors in the community and ambivalent or hostile sectors of society at large.[36]

NCRR proceeded from Movement ideals about respecting and mobilizing the grassroots. Several surveys, such as one conducted by *Rafu Shimpo*, an LA community newspaper, indicated popular support for redress and monetary reparations. The NCRR took these two goals as their main organizational goals.

This seemed particularly necessary given concern and suspicions that JACL wanted to restrict the goals of the growing redress movement to a commission inquiry. As NCRR, some of whose members belonged to JACL, describes it in the retrospective on the campaign, JACL "seemed torn between its' [sic] more conservative leadership and dissident individuals within the organization. The conservative leadership indicated that they felt more at ease with the idea of a process that might result in some sort of an educational study and a fund." NCRR, driven by its populist perspective, stood consistently for redress and reparations throughout its ten years.[37]

The NCRR also shaped the redress and reparations campaign through a frame of empowerment and deep engagement of community members. Despite the National JACL leadership's hesitations about bringing ordinary internees to testify before the commission, the NCRR prevailed upon the CWRIC to hold hearings in cities with Japanese American communities and to solicit the testimony of ordinary individuals. They organized foot soldiers to do outreach and mobilize people to speak in various cities, arranged for translation and transportation. Many of the elderly *Issei* and *Nisei*, who had experienced the camps, had never spoken about their experience nor spoken publicly. NCRR went door to door to talk to those who were interned and prepared them for public speaking and testimony. Though there was tension between the national JACL, who perceived NCRR as "radicals," the NCRR often worked closely with local JACL chapters in organizing for the hearings. Kathy Masaoka of Los Angeles' NCRR recalled,

> a lot of the regular people we [NCRR] brought out, the people who were truck drivers or worked for DWP or the person who was a foreman on a farm, just a wide variety of people, the women that lost children in the camps. We encouraged those people to speak.[38]

NCRR's huge effort, with support from local JACL chapters, to create a people's hearings around the camps changed U.S. public opinion and restored bonds within the JA community. Todd Lee, who worked on the redress hearings in San Jose as a student, remembers its profound effects:

> In general, that was really a pivotal moment for the Japanese American people in terms of bringing the generations together. That also played out in terms of students organizing for the hearings, being able to broach discussions with their parents as a result of some of the things that came out during that time. Even though I'm a Chinese American, those hearings had a real big impact on deepening my commitment and my understanding of the connection between the struggles of Asians in the past and the kinds of things we're struggling with today.[39]

Mitchell Maki, Harry Kitano, and S. Megan Bethold concluded, "the NCRR began to function as the expressive voice of the redress movement."[40]

The NCRR also brought this grassroots organizing to influence the legislative process, most evident in its 1987 lobbying of congress when hundreds of ordinary Japanese Americans descended on their congressional representatives to have them, many for the first time, confront the injustices committed against their Japanese American constituents. NCRR organized "the largest Asian American lobbying effort ever to descend upon Washington, in such a concentrated period of time."[41] On a shoestring budget but yet highly coordinated, it occurred shortly before the bill H.R. 442 was to come to the floor and influenced many congressional members to support the bill.

Between the hearings and the successful passage of legislation, there were six years of protracted work. After the initial legislation, there were another two years to get the bill signed and money appropriated. The NCRR continued to mobilize ordinary Japanese Americans and to press their two demands, despite misgivings of more established parts of the community and even its elected members of the community. Ronald Reagan led a Republican controlled Congress that was unsympathetic to Japanese American claims.

They coordinated lobbying strategies toward Congress, organized "Days of Remembrance" commemorating the internment camps, conducted mass letter writing and solicited congressional support. They forged an alliance of dozens of national organizations. In certain localities, they or other Japanese Americans were able to win back pay and reinstatements for Japanese Americans dismissed during the war period. Don Misumi, a NCRR member, felt this work was catalytic: "As we built up popular support within the Japanese American community and among the general public, the JACL and the Japanese congressmen moved more strongly in the same direction."[42]

Nisei and *Sansei* activists, who had learned to utilize multiple tactics addressed at multiple layers of social structure, kept the organizing together, and the mass mobilization produced reparations. The NCRR maintained stability and consistency during the campaign to create change amid a complex terrain.

There were three major coalitions that formed around redress and reparations. Along with JACL and NCRR, the National Coalition for Japanese American Redress (NCJAR) included several chapters of the JACL and various individuals. They pursued a legal strategy, and their primary means was a class-action lawsuit.

The NCRR worked to unite the various coalitions and organized the first cross-coalition conference to coordinate efforts for redress. They were the most consistent in maintaining unity within the Japanese American community and among the various forces fighting for redress. While the National JACL considered the other two to be upstarts and NCJAR demanded that NCRR choose between themselves and JACL, NCRR saw that a coordinated effort was necessary to create the best chance for success. For example, despite initial misgivings about the CWRIC, the NCRR decided to support the commission's work.

Throughout this intense period of organizing and coalition building, NCRR used its experience from the Movement to maintain its bearing. As Lillian Nakano, a *Nisei* interned at Heart Mountain, Wyoming, reflected,

> NCRR did a lot, and one thing we did was the united front movement . . . but ultimately for NCRR too there was a lot of people who, and understandably so, who were against the united front. They would say forget JACL, forget Bill Hohri, we'll go on our own, and let's blast them every time they say something, tit for tat, you know. And you can't blame them because JACL was constantly attacking us. They were just deriding us, very condescending, "what is NCRR doing now?" that kind of thing. But Bert [Nakano] as leadership always had to, and Alan [Nishio] too, as chair, and we were always explaining . . . we have to stay united. The government wants to see us fighting among each other. And then when we divide the community to the point where it's too weak, the redress thing is . . . gonna go backward. Those kind of things that we learn from the left . . . to remember keep the goal, the long term goal, always in mind. [43]

It was these ideals and abilities that allowed NCRR, a product of the AAM, to play a critical, influential role in one of the signal campaigns for change in modern U.S. history. It was a campaign that spanned a decade, integrated community, built coalitions, and established politics. Most significantly, it changed the atmosphere in the Japanese American community, so that it was "ok to talk about the camps and stand up for justice." The redress movement went to the heart of the Japanese American experience and transformed it. As Burt Nakano, NCRR national spokesperson, said before a thousand people in the Los Angles victory celebration, "We achieved what we have been fighting for decades. The camps were our nightmare. August 10th marks the beginning of our dream—a dream many of us thought would never come true."[44]

The NCRR demonstrated that the AAM was not a marginal force. It was still an insurgent one, but one that was deeply integrated into the community. It relied on the people and held together a "united front." It signified the lasting ability of the mature movement. Based on ideals, the maturity to work from the grassroots community level to the corridors of decision-makers, and the infrastructure and experience to sustain a years long movement, the NCRR was an effective and significant voice at the national level for Asian Americans.

THE JESSE JACKSON PRESIDENTIAL
CAMPAIGNS AND ELECTORAL POLITICS

African American civil rights leader Reverend Jesse Jackson's two campaigns for president in the 1980s were other experiences that demonstrated Asian

American activists' capacities. It also confronted them with the reliability of their assumptions. The catalytic effect of the Jackson campaigns pulled activists who had earlier rejected the electoral system into the electoral arena. The maturation of the AAM's perspective opened them to embracing the Jackson candidacy.

In 1984, and then again in 1988, Jesse Jackson's historic bids for the presidency of the United States caught the country by storm. His message of the possibility of change, inclusion, social and economic justice, and for "peace with justice" internationally, mobilized a literal Rainbow Coalition of African Americans, Native Americans, Latinos, Asian Americans, labor, farmers, students, gays and lesbians, environmentalists, and peace activists.

A grassroots campaign that grew to serious contention, Jackson's crusade won the second highest number of votes in the 1988 primary season. March 8, 1988 was known as "Super Tuesday" because nineteen primaries and caucuses (including most of the southern states) were scheduled on that day. Southern Dixiecrats had high hopes that Super Tuesday would favor conservative Democrats and thus shift the party to the right. With virtually no paid staff and a shoestring budget (for example, its one hundred thousand dollars for media buys paled compared to the other campaigns' millions), Jesse Jackson electrified the country when he garnered the greatest number of votes on Super Tuesday. That day, he won 95 percent of the African American vote, 59 percent of lowest income group, 42 percent of those with high school education or less; and 60 percent of the unemployed.[45]

Asian Americans, long excluded from any significant political participation, responded strongly to Jackson's movement. Though some Asian Americans had been previously active in traditional electoral politics, Jesse Jackson reached into the AAM and deep into the communities. Up until the 1984 Jackson campaign, the AAM had not seen electoral politics as an avenue for advancing the agenda, except in specific local races.[46]

The Jesse Jackson for President campaigns were movements and thus engaged those animated by the same anti-establishment politics that bred the AAM. These insurgencies challenged business-as-usual and the existing distribution of power, first by putting forward an agenda that embraced the disenfranchised. The "Rainbow" inspired heretofore non-participants and expanded the political system through voter registration, get-out-the-vote campaigns, as well as removing structural barriers to participation. In Hawai'i alone, two thousand out of the three thousand new voters registered in the lead-up to the March 8, 1988, caucuses were attributed to Rainbow initiatives.[47]

Asian American movement activists embraced the Jackson for President campaigns as opportunities to build the people's movements, to "move from the background to the political foreground."[48] With a more mature perspective on how change could be achieved, most were able to fully enter into this arena without a perceived compromise of their principles. They saw Jackson's success as success for the causes to which they had dedicated their lives. For example, Jackson became the first presidential candidate to ever speak in Little Tokyo, Los Angeles, and issued the invitation, "to join me as equal partners in our crusade to change the whole direction of American politics."[49] Jackson learned about and became an advocate for Asian American issues, including redress and reparations, immigrant rights, and anti-Asian violence. His campaign incorporated these issues as part of its platform, and educated Americans throughout the nation.

In many cases, Jackson and his political allies supported Asian Americans around specific issues. For instance, Jackson and his New York State Chair, Manhattan Borough President David Dinkins, joined NY Chinatown in opposing the building of a jail in Chinatown. Though Mayor Ed Koch built the jail in spite of the opposition, Dinkins helped the community negotiate important concessions.

Asian American activists were also more open to entering this arena in 1984 because of a sense of urgency that four years of Ronald Reagan's presidency had wrought. Other conditions also made electoral work more attractive. The hoped-for revolution in the 1960s and 1970s turned out to be more a distant objective than many had imagined. Electoral victories, particularly for those unrepresented and underrepresented racial groups in the power structure, offered some limited change. The increase of people of color in the demographics of the country also made plausible the possibility of successes in this arena, a possibility that activists could not previously contemplate. The Asian American population was growing, with concentrations that could be developed into voting blocks. From 1970 to 1990, Asian Americans had risen from 0.7 percent to nearly 3 percent of the population. Similar growth characterized Latinos, while the Black population had grown more slowly, though faster than the White population. Jesse Jackson's campaigns offered message, movement-building opportunity, and significant allies.

Jesse Jackson's under-financed Rainbow Coalition, like the AAM, relied on organizing, political networks, mobilized people, hard work, and passion as its resource base. As AAM activists stepped up to organize for Jesse Jackson, they brought years of experience and movement organizing skills that fit well with the campaign's needs and style. May Louie, who was the New England Coordinator and later became Jackson's executive assistant, specified that connection:

> Through the work that a lot of activists did in the Asian American Movement, we developed skills, discipline, and an analysis that were very effective in the

Jackson campaign. The campaign didn't have a lot of money. It wasn't about making the right media buys. It was about grassroots organizing, which was also at the center of building the Asian American Movement. So Asian American activists brought an appreciation for the role of people and skills in movement organizing. Secondly, in the Asian American Movement, we applied the concept of "united front" that was similar to Jackson's Rainbow Coalition. By analyzing what was going on, and what people's interests were, we were able to "unite all that can be united" and bring together very unlikely coalitions.[50]

Asian Americans, including Movement activists, came to play significant roles in Asian Americans for Jesse Jackson activities, but also in nationwide and campaign-wide roles. Whether it was on a local, regional, or national level, Asian Americans engaged in complex, sophisticated organizing, contributing their experience and networks, but learning more and making new allies. Eddie Wong, who became the National Field Director, recalled,

I was really sensitive to building the broadest coalition possible, but I don't know if that came from our work in the Asian American Movement. That was just good organizing. That was just common sense, and it was a balance because Jackson had a very broad coalition. You couldn't have the Black ministers dominate the State steering committees. You had to make sure that everything had its place.[51]

Seventy-five chapters comprised a national network of Asian American Jesse Jackson committees. While the Asian American Jesse Jackson Campaign was not free from the tensions between political groupings, it also brought various Asian ethnic groups together under one umbrella. Thus New York's Asian Americans for Jackson's steering committee included Japanese and Korean ministers, Filipino federal government workers, and AAM activists from Chinatown.[52] Through this work, AAM activists worked on a national scale and stage and worked effectively with a broad cross-section of U.S. society.

As a consequence of this campaign, Asian American activists began to be significant actors in local urban areas. May Louie observed,

He treated Asian Americans as full members of the Coalition. His platform included an Asian American agenda, and he rallied other parts of the Rainbow around those issues. He created a setting in which Asians were treated as equal partners, everyone moving forward together around a progressive platform. He helped instill pride and a sense of power within the Asian American communities.[53]

After the relative success of the Rainbow Coalition, activists participated in other electoral campaigns. Many of these were clearly alternative, grassroots efforts. Quite often they were focused around energizing campaigns of progressive Black politicians such as Harold Washington. In New York City, Asian Americans were appointed to top levels in the David Dinkins mayoral administration, while others became influential at the state level. Asian Americans were also among those who won office because of the groundwork laid by the Jackson campaigns. Mabel Teng, co-chair of Jesse Jackson's California presidential campaign, won a county supervisor office in San Francisco, and Velma Veloria, a Seattle-based Jackson activist, won and held a Washington State Assembly seat for eighteen years. Eric Mar was elected to the San Francisco Board of Education. The election of progressive activists signaled that the political power structure within Asian American communities had shifted to incorporate new voices.

In effectively engaging in the electoral arena, activists confounded the avenues through which radical social change was expected to course. In deciding to contest for electoral power, the positive rationales for engagement overshadowed any concerns about the limits of change through established structures. In participating in this arena, the Rainbow demonstrated to AAM activists the potential of institutionalized avenues for change as well as the popular distance from revolution. Upon election, however, several Asian American activists found themselves in positions where the structural limitations of under-funded government services and resources for workers would pose difficult challenges to represent those historically underrepresented.

AN EFFECTIVE BUT CHANGING MOVEMENT

In the fifteen years from 1975 to 1990, environmental, demographic, and internal changes complicated and matured the Movement. No longer young or isolated, the Movement now operated in many different sectors and in diverse ways. The ability to mobilize business owners alongside workers, youth along with the elderly, social service workers as well as entrepreneurs, and activists next to traditional organization leaders were demonstrations of the new organizational skills and resources within the Movement. Yet, dangerous tensions had developed, and to the stream of the arriving immigrant community who constituted an increasing segment of the population, the Movement was little known. There were more and different resources and interests to nurture and maintain. Planning needed to become more long term and broad.

For the service organizations, maturation proved the soundness of their decisions to work within the system. Building upon the growth in numbers of immigrants and their own increasing institutionalization, they were able to build larger, more sophisticated organizations that provided a greater range of services.

This chapter described how the political movement activists responded by adopting more developed worldviews, playing diverse roles, and becoming more flexible in their tactics. They engaged in a tenser but closer relationship to the system that they sought to change. In doing so, they proved themselves capable of accomplishing larger-scale and more sustained effects. However, they also had begun to blur the boundaries between reform and revolutionary change that grounded their past direction. Their growing elevated position in the community, academic, and labor infrastructure and the need for professionalization generated conflicting goals between immediate needs and long-term change. Their framework had begun to shift under the weight of the length of struggle. Tensions strained the persistence of the AAM; both exhaustion and the appeal of institutionalization had undermined this sector of the movement. Since the political movement was the sector most deliberately building the AAM, such strains were potentially fatal for the Movement.

Organizing efforts were led by community activists, some of whom were influenced by revolutionary ideas and viewed these immediate struggles as part of an overall organizing project for fundamental change in the country. Many individuals joined in specific issue campaigns, became committed community activists, and remained active, as other issues arose, in new organizing efforts. Most individuals, however, would become active in one issue and participate in a more limited fashion.

The self-conscious Movement had narrowed. Though they would intervene in broad mobilizations, service agencies no longer spoke to changing the system. Art and culture organizations continued to professionalize. Dedicated women's organizations sprang up to focus on women's issues. Even the more recent activist organizations had a weak sense of a broader, collective project. Nevertheless, the AAM had deepened its impact. Veterans of the AAM were the core leadership of many of these movements that flourished in the Asian community in the 1970s and into the 1980s. Precisely because these more mature organizing efforts had experienced leadership, they understood the importance of strategy and tactics and of building a "united front" of various classes against a specific target, attempted to apply political theory to practical issues, and built grassroots organizations with strong community support. They were effective, and their organizing efforts became national in their scope. However, the strength of such resources would be unable to withstand further deterioration of the conditions necessary for a social movement.

NOTES

1. Eddie Wong, telephone interview by Michael Liu, tape recording, Boston: 23 March 2005.

2. Saskia Sassen, *The Global City* (Princeton, NJ: Princeton University Press, 1992); Lin, *Reconstructing Chinatown*; Xiaolan Bao, *Holding Up More than Half the Sky: Chinese Women Garment Workers in New York City, 1948–1992* (Urbana, IL: University of Illinois, 2001).

3. *Asian Week*, May 30, 1986 7: 40 p.1; May 26, 1983 4: 39, p. 7.

4. Peter Kiang, "When Know-Nothings Speak English-Only: Analyzing Irish and Cambodian Struggles for Community Development and Educational Equity," in *The State of Asian America: Activism and Resistance in the 1990s,* ed. Karin Aguilar-San Juan (Boston: South End Press, 1994), 125–46.

5. East Coast Asian Student Union, "Asian American Resource Directory," *Asian American Spirit* 3 (1988), East Coast Asian Student Union, Boston; 30–35.

6. Frank, *Buy America*.

7. Similar to distinctions made during World War II, when Japanese Americans but not German Americans were interned in camps, labor unions and the general public targeted Japanese but not increasingly popular German vehicles during this period.

8. Helen Zia, *Asian American Dreams, The Emergence of an American People* (New York: Farrar, Straus and Giroux, 2000).

9. Kwong, *The New Chinatown*.

10. Kent Wong, "May Chen," in *Voices for Justice: Asian Pacific American Organizers and the New Labor Movement* (Los Angeles: Center for Labor Research and Education, UCLA, 2001).

11. Bao, *Holding Up More than Half the Sky*. In her study, Bao distinguishes a number of major organizers of the strike who later became active in the union ILGWU (later to become UNITE) either through staff positions, local executive board members, or members of Asian labor organizations. A minority became more active in the Chinese Workers and Staff Association, which has often been at odds with the union.

12. Therese Feng and Shirley Mark Yuen, "Through Strength and Struggle—A Victory for Garment Workers in Boston," *East Wind* 6, no. 1 (Spring/Summer 1987): 31–32.

13. Wong, "Building an Asian Pacific Labor Alliance."

14. David B. Okita, "Redevelopment of San Francisco Japantown," Master's thesis, California State University Hayward, 1980.

15. Evelyn Yoshimura, Mark Masaoka and Kathy Masaoka, interviews by Michael Liu, Los Angeles, 17–19 June 2004

16. Ibrahim Aoude, "Strategic Considerations for Social Struggles," *Social Process in Hawai'i* 39 (1999): 291.

17. Kenyon S. Chan, "Rethinking the Asian American Studies Project: Bridging the Divide between 'Campus' and 'Community'," *Journal of Asian American Studies* 3, no. 1 (2000): 17–36.

18. Suzanne Pan and Ellen Lam, "ECASU: Education for Action." *East Wind*. 6, no. 1 (Spring/Summer 1987): 27–28; Clement Tsao, "Transgressing Institutional Boundaries in Asian American Studies: A Student Intervention," authors' collection,

2003, photocopy; Augusto Espiritu, "Twenty Years of Struggle towards the Decade of Empowerment," in *Gidra: The XXth Anniversary Edition*, ed. Gidra Staff (Los Angeles: Gidra 1990), 38; Asian American Resource Workshop "AARW Workshop on Building a Campaign for Asian American Studies" Boston: 2 (13 April 1985).

19. Todd Lee, interview; A. Espiritu, "Twenty Years of Struggle," 38.

20. Christine Kaneshige and Sheri Miyashiro, "Racism at Cal Poly Pomona," and Valerie Mih and Judy Wu, "Stanford Sit-In," both in *Gidra: The XXth Anniversary Edition*, ed. Gidra Staff (Los Angeles: Gidra 1990), 39–40.

21. Hei Wai Chan and Marta Ho, "The UConn Incident: Responding to Racism," *East Wind* 7, no. 1 (Spring/Summer 1989): 16–20.

22. Espiritu, *Asian American Panethnicity*, Zia, Asian *American Dreams*.

23. Nickie McWhirter, *Detroit Free Press*, 25 March 1983.

24. American Citizens for Justice, "The Case for Vincent Chin: A Tragedy in American Justice," authors' collection, 1983, photocopy.

25. Citizens for Justice, "Case for Vincent Chin"; Zia, *Asian American Dreams*.

26. Ebens and Nitz were first convicted but eventually acquitted of civil rights violations.

27. Tomio Geron, "Vincent Chin and Asian American Politics in the 'Ambiguous' 1980's," (paper presented at the 17th National Conference of the Association for Asian American Studies, Scottsdale, Arizona, 2000).

28. Mary Choy, Mililani Trask, "Mary Choy" "Mililani Trask," both in *Autobiography of Protest in Hawai'i*, by Robert H. Mast and Anne B. Mast (Honolulu: University of Hawai'i Press, 1996), 402–50, 426; Tracy Takano, "Aloha Aina (Love of the Land): The Struggle for Land and Power in Hawai'i," *East Wind* 1, no. 1 (Spring/Summer 1982): 18–21; Daviana P. McGregor, "'Au'a 'ia' to 'Mele o Kaho'olawe': Voices of Power and Vision," in *New Visions in Asian American Studies: Diversity, Community, Power*, eds. Franklin Ng et al. (Seattle: Washington State Press, 1994), 253–70.

29. Mast, *Autobiography of Protest in Hawai'i*, 181–84; Takano, "Aloha Aina," Aoude, "Introduction to the Ethnic Studies Story: The Political Economic Environment," *Social Processes in Hawai'i*, 39. (1999): xxvii; Gordon Y.K. Pang, "Ota Camp." *Honolulu Star-Bulletin Online Edition*, 15 April 2001 starbulletin.com/ 2001/04/15/news /story4.html (20 November 2004).

30. The most comprehensive account of the campaign for redress and reparations is Maki, Kitano, and Berthold, *Achieving the Impossible Dream*.

31. Alan Nishio, telephone interview by Michael Liu, tape recording, Boston, 26 September 2006.

32. Particularly in the Seattle chapter, but also Southern California.

33. Much of the details of this section are derived from Nikkei for Civil Rights and Redress, *NCRR Reader*, www.ncrr-la.org/reader/index (accessed on October 1, 2006).

34. Kathy Masaoka, telephone interview by Michael Liu, tape recording, Boston, 24 September 2006.

35. Don Misumi, interview by Shauna Lo, Boston, 18 August 2002 in the *Asian American Movement Ezine*, www.aamovement.net/narratives/don_misumi.html (27 November 2003).

36. K. Masaoka, telephone interview. The cities where NCRR operated were Los Angeles, San Jose, San Francisco, Seattle, New York, Denver, Sacramento, and San Diego.

37. Nikkei for Civil Rights and Redress, *NCRR Reader*, "Breaking the Wall of Silence . . . Redress Now."

38. K. Masaoka, telephone interview.

39. Todd Lee, interview.

40. Maki et al., *Achieving the Impossible*, 91.

41. Maki et al., *Achieving the Impossible,* 173.

42. Don Misumi, interview by Michael Liu, Lexington, MA, 12 February, 2002.

43. Bert and Lillian Nakano, interview by Jan Yen, audio cassette; Nikkei for Civil Rights and Redress, Los Angeles, 24 August 2001.

44. Bert Nakano, "Reparations: Our Historic Victory," *East Wind* 7, no. 1 (Spring/Summer 1989): 26–29.

45. Frank Clemente and Frank Watkins, eds., *Keep Hope Alive: Jesse Jackson's 1988 Presidential Campaign* (Boston: South End Press and Keep Hope Alive PAC, 1989).

46. For example, Mel King's bid for the Boston mayoralty in 1983.

47. Clemente and Watkins, *Keep Hope Alive*.

48. Eddie Wong, "Asian Empowerment and Jackson," *East Wind* 7, no. 1 (Spring/Summer 1989): 7–11.

49. Jesse Jackson, "The Rainbow Coalition: An End to Racial Division," *East Wind* 3, no. 1 (Spring/Summer 1984): 21.

50. May Louie, interview by Michael Liu, Brookline, 29 December, 2006

51. Wong, interview.

52. Sasha Hohri and Penny Fujiko Willgerodt, "Jackson Culminates Campaign in Asian Communities at Chinatown Rally," authors' collection, April 14, 1988, photocopy.

53. Louie, interview.

Chapter Seven

Last Dance and a New Motion in a Tube of Bamboo (Post–1990)

The 1990s began with Republican presidential administrations that managed over the decimation of government support for urban programs, fierce attacks on workers, reduction of taxes for the most wealthy, and a massive buildup of the Defense Department and the military industrial complex. Numbers skyrocketed in the prison population, most of whom were people of color. The international picture continued to dramatically change, which was to have a critical influence on global politics.

Where the other legs that supported the AAM as a social movement had become tenuous, the AAM's ideological frame assumed a particular importance. The political opportunity structure of course continued to close on the ideals of the Movement. The community infrastructure, which had been a source of strength, threatened to fragment among the different Asian American ethnicities and classes and had become more problematic to mobilize. These strains created a potential tipping point for the AAM. The collapse of international models then undermined the ideological framework of the political Asian American Movement; a vulnerable AAM went into a dramatic free fall. In this chapter, we describe that ebb and the AAM's legacy to ongoing work.

FRAMES: THE FALL OF SOCIALISM, RISE OF MARKET FORCES IN ASIA, AND IDEOLOGICAL DISORIENTATION

In the late 1980s, Mikhail Gorbachev initiated the policies of *perestroika* (restructuring) and *glasnost* (openness) in the Soviet Union but could not prevent its eventual breakup in 1989. In the latter half of the decade, the deterioration of the Soviet Union and the Soviet bloc became undeniable.

While the Communist Party of China retained a more stable hand, China, once an icon for the Asian American Movement, had continued to incorporate a market-based economy. In 1989, millions of urban Chinese participated in demonstrations airing concerns with China's state of affairs. The protests, sparked by student protesters, culminated in the People's Liberation Army's deadly attack on student squatters on Tiananmen Square. This sight turned many progressives against the Chinese Communist regime.[1] For the radical sector of the Movement, these developments undermined ideological frameworks and visible alternatives to the capitalist system.

Meanwhile capitalism in various forms had taken hold in Asia with spectacular and increasingly obvious material success. The "Four Tigers," "Japan Inc," and the "Asian Century" have all at various times and stages described the ascent of Asian economies during the prior decades.[2] While the decade-old recession in Japan and the "Asian Contagion" in the mid-1990s, which saw the collapse of several models of Asian capitalism, took the edge off this success, capitalism had raised the living standards in much of the Pacific Rim, transforming former hotbeds of rebellion into ones of money chasing.[3] The triumph of global capitalism, opening the decade as it did with "the end of history,"[4] in Fukayama's terms, continued the consolidation of conservative trends that began after 1975.

The international environment, which had done so much to inspire young Asian Americans, eventually contributed to the social movement's decline. The situation only continued to worsen for the Asian American Movement. It hastened the natural tendencies of the social movement cycle, one component of the weaknesses that crippled it. The political organizations that relied the most on these movement frames were the ones most affected.

CLOSING POLITICAL OPPORTUNITIES: THE CONTINUED RETREAT FROM LIBERAL GOVERNMENT

The decade's internet bubble marshaled in a seeming period of prosperity[5] and a new capitalist vision that competed with one for a different, progressive society. The Asian American managerial and professional strata occupied disproportionate space in the engines of the new economy. Culture and frames were filled with "new economy" get-rich-quick discourse, pushing aside concerns for social justice and inequality.

While the Democrats, under the Clinton administrations, regained the White House, they practiced a calculated and modulated conservatism, including passing an anti-immigrant welfare reform plan, support for globalized trade and wealthy elites, and implementing fiscal austerity.[6] Traditional liberalism yielded to the leadership of the centrist New Democratic wing in the Democratic Party, who advocated a compromised response to a resurgent conservatism, leaving little doubt that the American electorate merely chose between the two wings of a ruling class. The New Democrats continued to reduce funding to many of the programs that Asian American Movement activists built and worked in. The work of movement activists remained on the defensive under increasingly successful and aggressive conservative attack. The Clinton administration not only continued but also solidified the closure of political opportunities for social movements.

The combination of a disorienting framing vacuum along with a continued inhospitable political opportunity structure wrought havoc on the remaining revolutionary organizations, the bulwarks of the Movement. The long decades of increasing political hostility had created a growing exhaustion among these organizations' leaderships, and the bureaucracy of deepening resources were insufficient to support them. The alternative models to capitalism toppled or metamorphosed, removing the ideological underpinnings of the Asian American Movement and leaving a vacuum that remains unfilled. With an unstable foundation and under attack, the AAM's strategies, values, and alternatives to capitalism were unconvincing.

With surprising suddenness, many of the Marxist and revolutionary organizations disbanded. Within the span of two years, the successor groups to I Wor Kuen/Red Guard, KDP, and Asian Study Group had all dissolved.[7] Without this framework or a reconstruction of community leadership, diversity and dissonance in the community would assert themselves.

Those parts of the activist movement, the Korean American and Filipino American cohorts, that more closely focused on the situations in their ancestral countries insulated themselves to a limited degree. By partially detaching themselves from general Asian American activism and connecting to the continued vitality of activism overseas, they deflected some of the effects of the Movement's ebb.

In Sidney Tarrow's conception, the following considerations necessarily apply for a social movement to develop:

> Contentious politics is triggered when changing political opportunities and constraints creates incentives for social actors who lack resources on their own. They contend through known repertoires of contention and expand them by creating innovations at their margins, people with limited resources can act contentiously—if only sporadically. When backed by dense social networks and galvanized by culturally resonant, action-oriented symbols, contentious politics leads to sustained interaction with opponents. The result is the social movement.[8]

Few incentives existed for contentious social actors. While denser social networks had evolved, few of those organizations any longer rallied to movement symbols, and their support was questionable. Movement symbols and ideas only occasionally resonated with their communities. Did the Asian American

Table 7.1. The Asian American Movement Cycle

Cycle	Grievances	Resource Mobilization	Ideological Framing	Political Opportunity Structure
1968 to 1975: Rapid Rise in Movement	Working class and poverty issues, Identity, Ethnic enclaves	Creation of organizations and leadership	Creation of symbols and basic ideas; eclectic radicalism or alternative ideals	Favorable, divisions and vacillation among elites
1976 to 1982: Matured growth	New immigration issues, fighting anti-Asian campaigns, Poverty and labor issues	Experienced Leadership, Continued increase in number and sophistication in organizations	Adoption of Marxism or professionalization	Unfavorable, conservative reaction beginning with Carter administration
1983 to 1989: Regional influence, Growing Strains	Defense of past gains, global economic effects, Ethnic enclaves, Diverse class grievances,	Experienced Leadership, Expanding but fragmenting infrastructure	Weakening of Marxist framework; professionalization and institutionalization	Antagonistic; "Reagan Revolution"
1990: Collapse	More complex, bifurcated community grievances	Fragmented, newer leadership, Expanding but fragmenting infrastructure	Policy change	Antagonistic

Movement continue? For those who participated in the Movement who had those shared experiences, the AAM's values persisted in their continued activities, but for the Asian American community overall, the original AAM ended with the dissolution of the political organizations. Despite its wide-ranging effects, the AAM, in an increasingly conservative environment, had lost its cultural resonance for any significant part of the community and its ability to mobilize social networks.

In our social movement framework, the trajectory of the AAM could therefore be summarized in table 7.1 on page 150.

It was a social movement that, despite a more complex and difficult environment, continued to grow based on the new resources and ideas accumulated in its early stages. In the late 1980s, a closed political opportunity and dissipating framework overcame the AAM's resources, a dialectic of great tension that led to its rapid collapse.

GRIEVANCES: THE BIFURCATED COMMUNITY

The AAM receded against the backdrop of a transformed Asian American community. There were new complex challenges. Community-based, service-oriented, and reform organizations continued to build on a growing Asian American community. The Asian or Pacific Islander population was 3 percent of the national population in 1990, a 95 percent increase from the previous census. At the same time, these groups faced the countervailing gravity of falling public and institutional support for social services and immigrants, who made up more than three out of five persons in the API population.[9]

A confounding factor was the 1965 immigration reform's evident effects on community demographics.[10] Comparing the occupational profile of the Asian Americans in 1960 and 2000, there is nearly a reversal of proportions between higher socioeconomic and lower socioeconomic status occupations (see table 7.2). Whereas less than one in five were professionals and managers in 1960, now over two in five in 2000 were. Conversely, where over two in five were laborers, operatives, and service occupations (lower laboring and service categories) in 1960, less than one in four were in 2000.[11]

Table 7.2. Percent of Asian Americans' Defined Occupational Categories, 1960 and 2000

Year	Professional Occupations and Managers	Clerical and Crafts Occupations	Laborers, Operatives, and Service Occupations
1960	19.8%	26.6%	43.4%
2000	42.9%	23.9%	24.5%

The Asian American Movement had built their concept of community on the primarily working class population of Chinese, Japanese, and Filipino descent, who populated the Asian American communities of the day. In contrast, the new middle class stratum assumed different roles within capitalist reproduction.[12] These new roles often clashed with the welfare of the disadvantaged sector of the established Asian communities.

Koreans, South Asians, and Southeast Asians were major parts of the new population. Chinese, Filipino, and Japanese, who had constituted virtually all of the Asian American population, were now only a little over a half of it.[13] The new groups' and classes' social roles and grievances were different. Southeast Asians, for example, resuscitated a visible role for Asians in farming and fishing.

Claims to grievances grew more complex. Census figures, though acknowledging larger family size and number of wage earners in an Asian American household, now indicated a higher median household income than Whites.[14] This certainly reflected immigration policies favoring populations with managerial and professional skills and resources. As Paul Ong and Suzanne Hee observed, "This 'success' is rooted in a policy of selective immigration that has attracted some of the most highly-educated and economically mobile in Asia."[15] The high tech economy also enhanced this sector. Many, particularly in the larger society, perceived that Asian Americans no longer had legitimate claims and grievances.

Despite their economically privileged positions, the sector faced a series of shocks that shook their confidence. Professionals had constantly complained about glass ceilings in employment and the lack of access to mainstream political, social, and cultural institutions. Even on the West Coast, the number of Asian American office-holders was relatively small.[16] Scandals around political contributions, small business relations with minority neighborhoods, and the perceived loyalties of Asian American professionals put the standing of this sector in question within the larger society.

Overshadowed in the ascendancy of the professional and managerial sector was the still-growing Asian American working class. Garment, restaurant, and light industry workers still employed large sectors of the population, also primarily driven by immigration. Many were undocumented.[17] The Asian American poverty rate, particularly those of Southeast Asians, exceeded that of the population as a whole.

The developments over the two decades, moreover, had not resolved many of the grievances that had inspired the Asian American Movement—the declining conditions of working class Asians, community-based political power, the destruction of ethnic enclaves, poor housing and services, discrimination, and violence against Asian Americans. Contemporary trends in cutting of social service and public funds threatened gains and programs from previous periods.[18]

We will look at how, in this environment with the end of the AAM, API communities have organized. In evaluating these changes, we will incorporate voices reflecting a range of contemporary activists. Based in Boston, Los Angeles, New York, Oakland, Seattle, Providence, San Francisco, and Washington, D.C., the voices are largely community-based but organize in diverse arenas—anti-war, art and culture, civil rights, community development, students, immigrant rights, international support, and workers' rights.

SHIFTING RESOURCES AND FRAMES: EFFECTS OF THE MOVEMENT'S EBB AND NINETIES ACTIVISM

The loss of leadership within the self-identified Asian American Movement led to its complete retrenchment. Asian American voices that were more systematic and structural in their critique, calling for the fundamental redistribution of power and the elimination of social inequalities and systemic racial oppression, became infrequent. A unity around a broad community vision and the activist focus on solidarity for people of color, grand coalition building, and the working class faded with the diminishing voices. Moreover, it had been these activist forces that had more broadly coordinated their organizing and that provided the continuity and coherence to the Asian American Movement.

Activism among Asian Americans took diverse forms and for a broad range of issues within its communities during the 1990s. Asian Americans worked in various identity-based issues, electoral access in voter registration, appointments, and representation, sexual orientation, media representation and access, glass ceilings, and educational equity,[19] as well as in broader issues such as globalization and the environment. Most often these issues focused on achieving equity within the contemporary social structure. Activism also adopted the mainstream conventions of competitive, pluralistic interest groups and an agnostic perspective toward classes within the Asian American communities. On the one hand, the politics of identity became widespread within the communities, but that framework lacked the resonance that could passionately animate large segments of the population.

Without a left progressive axis in the Asian American communities and other communities of color, the center of gravity both moved toward the confines of the status quo and became less defined. Representation in the electoral arena reinforced and was supported by this shift. An increasing number of Asian Americans were elected to political office, primarily at the local and state level. Sectors tended to curb their efforts to their immediate and proximate spheres. In the

Asian American community, with the exception of labor organizing, initiative shifted from the urban, working class constituencies to the professional, managerial ones and established power centers. This shift was reflected in arts and culture, which became personal.

> When we had a highly politicized time period like the late 60s and mid 70s, it more naturally infused people's lives. For artists, it was a big source of inspiration. Today, you don't have that so people find their inspiration from other things—MTV, the mass culture. I see it best in filmmaking because there are so many more Asian American filmmakers doing really high quality work. It's personal drama, documentary, thrillers, lots of genre pictures, nicely done. A lot of stuff has a cultural subtext; there's something going on there. You know that they're conscious of the politics, but they don't want to make it the central part of what they're doing. That's the difference. It's the time period.[20]

Elected office holders and national advocacy groups such as Organization of Chinese Americans and National Asian Pacific American Legal Consortium led the major campaigns in the Asian American community.[21] These were more limited in their scope and largely confined to educated professionals and wealthy elites. One such campaign in 1996 opposed the targeting of Asian American donors to presidential campaigns. Republican charges of a foreign hand behind Asian American donations to the Clinton-Gore ticket led to a wholesale investigation of Asian American donors by the Democratic Party.[22] Another major campaign defended Wen Ho Lee, a physicist at Los Alamos Nuclear Laboratories, accused of passing secrets to China in the late 1990s and early 2000s. The effort, primarily led by an emerging professional class of Asian Americans, used the Internet and fundraising efforts to mobilize the Asian American community to defend Lee. Cecilia Chang, a businesswoman from Fremont, California, joined veteran AAM activists such as Ling Chi Wang at UC–Berkeley and became instrumental in this nationwide and international organizing effort to support the Lee family's efforts to win justice for him. These and other various mobilizations of the Asian American community operated under the concepts of equal rights and utilized the methods of nonviolent confrontation, interracial coalition building, and public protest that the AAM had introduced.

Yet, while these mobilizations adopted the forms and methods of organizing of the Movement, their content revolved around liberal notions of the rights of citizenship. Asian Americans in the 1990s, accepting established channels of change, called for equitable access to the seats of power, changes in policies, and a more color-sensitive functioning of social institutions.

These more modest goals were accompanied by a lost discourse of how to achieve and characterize the contours of structural change. There was also a retreat from systematic movement building and the mobilization of growing circles of individual activists. Without a means of reproducing activists for social justice, the efforts of the Asian American community to advance broad goals suffered a significant setback.

Another effect was the collapse of "third world unity." The 1992 Los Angeles unrest, Sa-i-gu, and the conflicts between Korean storeowners and African Americans in poor neighborhoods, most dramatically in New York, testified to fraying coalition building between communities. At the same time, the rise of cultural nationalism, a diasporic redefinition of Asian ethnic communities—Chinese, Korean, and Indian—distanced Asians from other U.S. communities of color.[23] Other entities in the communities failed to replace the AAM's grassroots work of inter-racial community building, which held such work as one of its principles.

The effects of activism transformed could be seen in one of its former strongholds, the campuses. They mirrored the changes in Asian American activism. Without the dedicated leadership of AAM revolutionaries, left to the influences of the era, the infrastructure of regional student organizations hollowed out. Rather than contributing to a larger campaign or project, conferences became ends in themselves. Corporate colorization crept in. Adopting what they saw around them, East Coast Asian Student Union (ECASU) students sought Asian dot-com companies and other pillars of capitalism to sponsor their conferences, as their website proudly attested. APSU disappeared after a few years. On individual campuses, idealistic student-based formations, sometimes ephemeral, would organize to question these assumptions. The Asian Revolutionary Circle was one such formation.[24] But without a larger effort to anchor their work, students by themselves could sustain little momentum.

Absent viable options to work for structural change, many who developed their skills and views within the radical sector of the Movement applied this experience to building the service, advocacy, labor, and reform infrastructure. Many former activists took for granted participation in electoral efforts as the avenue for change. While various branches of the AAM had overlapped since 1975, the migration of movement radicals to the reform sector became wholesale in the 1990s, and some of the most effective leaders of reform organizations shared this movement history.[25]

NEW IMMIGRATION/NEW COMMUNITY NON-PROFIT ORGANIZATIONS AND RESOURCES

Overall, the Asian American organizational infrastructure continued to expand. Service organizations became institutionalized in the community and the fabric of mainstream society. As community-based organizations routinely adopted the norm to become tax-exempt 501(c)3 organizations, they also accepted significant limits on their political activity. Service organizations became part of the growing private non-profit sector, integrating into networks like the United Way. For those who had worked within the system, they had become more integrated into it. In becoming a central part of the mainstream, they rarely associated with the Movement's alternative principles and its social critique.

Asian Americans were often, though not typically, considered in the civic discourse. This integration of the participants of the 1960s and 1970s protests led to the nominal adoption of certain less challenging movement values as norms within the larger society. New concepts were trafficked in foundations and education and even in the businesses world. "Black, Brown, and Yellow Power" morphed into "diversity." "Power to the people" and "community control" led to "empowerment" and local advisory input into municipal services. Pride in identity became "multiculturalism" and "assets-based community development." Institutional acceptance of movement conventions has circumscribed these organizing conventions, defusing much of its vitality and creativity. The conduct of mobilization was eased, but these easements were permitted only as long as they distanced themselves from structural issues and power relations.

CAAAV: Organizing Asian Communities in New York is an organization that has struggled with these contradictions. Hyun Lee, a staff person, in a critique extending beyond community non-profits, recognized this:

> It's very challenging to maintain a radical vision and also be a good non-profit manager at the same. It's all based on values that we all try to fight against in trying to develop a different kind of culture in our organization.[26]

Based on her involvement with Nodutdol, a Korean community-based organization in New York, Yul-San Liem echoed these sentiments:

> The whole 501(3)c has had a de-radicalizing effect on some really radical organizations and puts constraints. The service work is what's funded so organizations will tend toward doing the service work rather than the organizing work because you can't get money for that.[27]

Organizations were more numerous, varied, and interconnected. Some new organizations such as South Asian Youth Action (SAYA!), founded in 1996 in New York, continued the creation of activist groups. Nearly 2,500 Asian American organizations in the ten largest metropolitan areas in the country had developed by the year 2000.[28] Even grassroots and action-oriented organizations had become more institutionalized and grounded in their constituencies, and these organizations' constituencies continue to grow.

Immigration has continued to drive up the numbers of Asian Americans. New populations built new enclave communities. Among the most well known of these are the Vietnamese enclave in Westminster, California, the Cambodian enclaves in Long Beach, California, and Lowell, Massachusetts, the Hmong in St. Paul, and the various Asian American enclaves, Chinese, Korean, and South Asian, in the New York/New Jersey area and parts of Los Angeles. There was also the first Asian American city, Monterey Park, outside of Los Angeles, primarily Chinese from Taiwan and Hong Kong.[29] It was the first of a number of cities where Asian Americans constituted the largest racial group. Other growing populations such as Asian Indians developed primarily dispersed populations; their numbers became evident only at community social and cultural gatherings. South and Southeast Asians were a visible and significant proportion of Asian Americans.

These newer communities developed their own layers of organizational infrastructure. Many of the Southeast Asians built their community infrastructure out of the refugee resettlement network that first hosted them. They regenerated variants of their traditional organizations and added their own service, cultural, and social groups. South Asians, often more professional and dispersed, initially formed professional and cultural organizations and later, political and women's and youth advocacy organizations.[30]

The shifts in immigration laws that brought in large, well-educated and well-off strata also led to their own distinct organizations. This newer professional and business strata have formed groups such as the Committee of 100, National Asian Pacific American Bar Association, or the Silicon Valley Indian Professional Association.

These growing class differences influenced community infrastructure and organizing. Sarath Suong attended Brown University and organized working class Southeast Asian youth in Providence. He noticed the disconnect between Asian American college students organizing and working class Southeast Asian youths and concluded that "One of the biggest issues in the broader Asian American body is that we're unable to address issues of class and issues of struggle and our responsibilities to Southeast Asians."[31]

Hyun Lee pointed out that this issue played itself out in the history of CAAAV when they tried to take up the issues of domestic workers, gentrification in Chinatown, and Southeast Asian youth:

A lot of the membership was middle class, college, young activists, and a lot of people felt that we really needed to recommit to working class struggles, relearn things. It actually took years of struggle to get to the point where it decided that it was going to organize different projects in different communities.[32]

Meeting the competing demands of sustaining 501(c)3 tax-exempt organizations and service needs, outreach priorities and resource building may often be influenced by unintended class biases. The creation of a community infrastructure is one of the primary achievements of the original Asian American Movement, but the level and direction of funding, as well as the community's relatively impotent political influence today, reveals inherent limitations.

These organizational networks nevertheless became one of the main refuges for those, particularly the young, who were interested in social justice and activism. Their ubiquity as well as developed structures generally channeled such energy along established routines to address community issues.[33] Community-based organizations, with all their limits, are the primary sites and resources to contest the inequalities, exploitation, and discrimination against Asian American communities. Sites of "contentious politics" thus shifted to localized pockets of activism.

There were, however, potential hints for a new Movement. These have concerned direct inheritors of the original Movement, rooted in the early Movement, organizations such as the Chinese Progressive Associations in San Francisco and Boston, J-town Voice in Los Angeles, Chinese Staff and Workers' Association in New York, Asian Immigrant Workers Association (AIWA) in Oakland, and Asian Americans United in Philadelphia. Most are 501(c)3 institutionalized groups but have tried to maintain a mobilizing and militant tradition within that status's confines.[34] Consistent with their beginnings, they are closely associated with ethnic enclaves and are heavily involved with workers' issues and the defense of the enclaves as well as other issues.

CPA–Boston and the Asian American Resource Workshop waged a prototypical contemporary struggle. They fought the proposed construction of a 455-car hospital garage in residential Chinatown. Their campaign endured for over a year and a half and energized hundreds of community residents. Despite being opposed by the city, a medical center-developer, and a segment of the community, they organized a successful and popular grassroots campaign. They applied a multiplicity of methods, including protest politics involving a series of public demonstrations and a community referendum, and mounting a relentless media campaign to defeat the project. Allied with a cohort of public interest group lawyers, they also used interest group lobbying—mobilizing for and legally fighting the approval process at procedural and regulatory hearings and building a citywide coalition against the city's redevelopment authority. More importantly, the campaign's organizing of community residents ushered in a more civically engaged neighborhood in Boston Chinatown.[35]

Community-based labor formations were among these rooted groups, and they accomplished significant advances in organizing Asian workers. One important nationwide campaign that involved Chinese women garment workers and Asian American activists began in 1992. The Lucky Sewing Company, a subcontractor to fashion designer Jessica McClintock, laid off their workers without paying them their owed back wages. The workers worked with AIWA on a campaign that targeted the Jessica McClintock Company for their wages. They launched a grass-roots campaign, holding demonstrations at McClintock stores that focused media attention on the plight of the workers. Four years later, a settlement was reached that included payment of back wages, an education and scholarship fund for workers and their children, and a hotline to report labor rights violations in garment shops associated with McClintock.[36]

There were also newer social justice groups. Among the oldest in this cohort is CAAAV, mentioned above. Founded in 1986, CAAAV sought to counter a wave of anti-Asian violence and initially carried out its work on this terrain. CAAAV expanded its focus to structural issues, on "institutional violence that affects immigrant, poor and working-class communities such as worker exploitation, concentrated urban poverty, police brutality, Immigration Naturalization Service detention and deportation, and criminalization of youth and workers."[37]

On a more recent horizon, Oakland's Chin Jurn Wor Ping (CJWP), translated as "Moving Forward for Peace," established itself with four points of unity. The unity, while reflecting more contemporary concerns of consciousness, sustainability, and culture, spoke to a broader structural vision of "self-determination of all oppressed peoples, and those engaged in resistance against unjust regimes of rule, terror and oppression." They also see themselves as part of a global resistance but have consciously looked back to the early Movement. One of its main fundraising devices is T-shirts and sweatshirts proclaiming "Our roots in Revolution" with the logo of I Wor Kuen.

Another newer group is DRUM (Desis Rising Up and Moving) in New York, which arose from one of the more recent Asian American communities, the South Asian Americans. Their description on their Web site describes the group as a community-based social justice organization that focuses on working class and poor South Asian immigrants. DRUM envisioned coalition building "through joint work with progressive forces in other people of color and oppressed communities." It sought leadership from the poor and working class. Other mobilizing critical examples include the Asian Pacific Environmental Network (APEN), which formed in 1993 to address the concerns of Asian Pacific Islander communities about environmental injustices that they were exposed to in urban areas. This organizing effort grew out of a national summit of environmental justice activists among communities of color and engages API communities around environmental and social justice issues.

Lydia Lowe of Boston's Chinese Progressive Association believes that the activists from the 1970s could share analytical methods and long-term strategies, while younger activists offer fresh approaches:

> The older generation, especially people who were Marxist-influenced, were trained in thinking about things very concretely and analyzing the social forces the material impact of things and doing that in a systematic and disciplined way. The younger generation in a lot of ways are much more creative. They make a lot of different kinds of connections more easily and are less constrained by traditional ideas of what's right or wrong, what fits into a strategy or doesn't fit.[38]

Illustrative of this creativity is a more recent aggregation of resistance that has arisen in the art and culture sphere through the spoken word community. Among the best-known pioneers was the spoken word group I Was Born with Two Tongues, from Chicago. With a yellow fist logo that echoed the symbols of an earlier period, Two Tongues offered a militant attitude and organized a campaign against anti-Asian lyrics by rappers. In an interview with *Asian-Week*, Anida Esguerra, a member of Two Tongues, placed spoken word within the political spectrum:

> I think people underestimate the power of art as activism. We are political poetry. We are just telling the shit we feel and telling our stories. Actively participating in trying to create a better world and trying to create change, which starts within yourself.[39]

Spoken word artists articulate issues of the day as well as provide the means for youths to develop skills and stay connected instead of dropping out of school. These cultural activists have resonated with many youth. In Seattle, Isangmahal, a performance art collective, blends art and politics through workshops on internalized oppression and neo-colonialism in the Philippines and creating a project on API workers' history, while the Blue Scholars perform to encourage voter registration. While the connection to a larger political project is unclear, they have created a national network that bases itself on a radical critique of the status quo. In the view of one Boston spoken-word artist, Giles Li, however, as spoken word grew, the connection between this creative political space and direct political organizing grew more tenuous:

> When I first started seriously about ten years ago, I would say the majority if not all the Asian American spoken word performers that I knew or knew of were all politically involved beyond just the creation of art, but also involved in something, whether it was service or education or organizing. Now within the past ten years, it has changed a little in that, when it used to go hand in hand, now a lot of people who are spoken word performers may be political but may not be as

involved aside from being political in their art. Now, there's an assumption among some young people, and I hear it, both from friends of mine who are performers as well as people who are critical of it, there's an assumption that being political in one's art leads to real change, but I think it's the opposite.[40]

Li and others have tried to institutionalize the connection between the community and art through a storefront organization, Boston Progress.

Some of these many groups were capable of conducting significant community campaigns such as opposing the placing of a hospital garage or a baseball stadium in Chinatowns.[41] They were also capable of dramatic immigrant workplace organizing such as the taxi drivers' campaign in New York in the late 1990s or various workers' demands for back pay, health, or against plant closings in different cities. At various times, they built tentative alliances with other communities in their area. There were efforts to transcend localized effects through networks. The Asian Left Forum formed in 1998 but, without grounding in specific work, proved transitory.[42]

These sites, however, remained spontaneous, discrete and unarticulated. The need for sorting out the grievances of a more complex community, a new culturally resonant framework, and new methods of mobilizing remained. Political opportunity remained closed. Until these actors successfully answered these questions and the political environment changed, the possibilities for transforming contentious politics to a new movement were stunted.

ASIAN PACIFIC AMERICAN
LABOR ORGANIZING AND RIGHTS

As Americans progressed in the community non-profit sector, they continued to expand in the labor movement. The continuing presence of Asian American (AA) organizers that matured in the AAM gave Asian American labor organizing momentum. Asian Pacific American (APA) labor institutionalized itself into a national structure as part of the American Federation of Labor–Congress of Industrial Organizations (AFL-CIO). With advances in institutionalization, support from labor unions, a new generation of labor activists, and growing resistance among Asian Pacific American workers,[43] APA workers fought a number of notable struggles.

The pan-ethnic organizing efforts of Asian Americans in several local areas throughout the 1980s culminated in the formation of the Asian Pacific American Labor Alliance (APALA). The idea of an Asian Pacific American labor committee won the support of the AFL-CIO Executive Council and led to the first national convention of Asian Pacific union activists in May 1992. Becoming a formal part of the mainstream labor structure, APALA became very effective as a national vehicle to highlight the concerns and needs of Asian Pacific workers and establish a program to recruit and train new APA organizers. From less than twelve Asian Pacific American union organizers nationally in 1992, more than one hundred were recruited to various unions in a few years.

In the 1990s, there was growth in the breadth and diversity of organizing of Asian Pacific American workers. Asian immigrant workers were heavily concentrated in services and light manufacturing industries—meatpacking, domestic work, casinos, tourism, food, government, health and home care, and warehousing. As unions desperately sought to turn around decades of declining membership, they began organizing in these lower paid sectors of the working class, where large numbers of Asian and immigrant workers were employed and, particularly in the private sector, unorganized.

A significant development was the organizing of numerous sustained campaigns involving APA workers. Though the numbers of APA unionists had grown to 580,000, they were still less than 5 percent of all unionized workers. Labor unions in partnerships with Asian community supporters led some of these campaigns, while workers' centers rooted in specific ethnic enclaves led others.

In Los Angeles, the Hotel Employees and Restaurant Employees (HERE) Union, Local 11, faced numerous struggles involving unionization of hotel workers, many of Asian descent. Two campaigns were significant for the support work that was built within the Asian communities.

One campaign was the New Otani Hotel organizing drive, the second attempt by HERE to organize the luxury hotel located in L.A.'s historic Little Tokyo. In 1993, the union launched a full-scale organizing drive of Latino and Asian workers at the hotel, which involved broad Japanese American community support and the internationalization of a boycott campaign. The union took the boycott campaign directly to Japan where they met with trade unionists and human rights organizations.

The second campaign involved the Koreana Hotel. In 1991, Koreana Hotel Co. Ltd., a Korean corporation, took over the Wilshire Hyatt. The change in ownership left 175 workers without jobs. Though the workers had hoped to be rehired by the new ownership, only a few were, amid charges that Koreana arranged the rehiring process to exclude unionized workers. HERE began to picket the hotel.

Los Angeles had just seen rioting after the Rodney King verdict in 1992,[44] so there was the potential for the campaign to transform itself into an anti-Korean campaign. To avoid this, the union enlisted the help of Asian community activists. They recognized the critical role that the local Korean American community could play; the community was expected to be a major source of business for the hotel. The union sought out APALA and representatives from twenty other Asian Pacific American, African American, and Latino groups who signed a letter to the hotel's president. They warned that Koreana's labor polices around rehiring workers and the union would not help racial trust in Los Angeles. In particular, the work of Korean Immigrant Workers Advocates was critical in building support for the boycott and persuading Korean American leaders to talk with hotel management to settle the dispute.[45]

After ten months of a union-led boycott, protests including sit-ins at the Korean Consulate, the hotel reached a contract agreement with the union in late 1992. This campaign demonstrated the importance of Asian American community activists allying with unions to build broad campaigns.

Labor networks had become another refuge for social justice activists. This was an arena of increased activity, but like the community, this expansion, securely limited to trade-union issues, remained divorced from a larger social movement project. Union work, however, allowed activists to work on concrete issues with disadvantaged populations.

One couldn't speak then of an Asian American Movement in the 1990s. Splinters survived, or new clusters contesting for social justice arose in isolated sites. To a broadly perceived Asian American Movement, Giles Li comments, "There's no really cohesive 'everybody's working for the same thing' nationally. A lot of different people work on different things, care about different things."[46] But in the interstices of the new labor and community organizational networks, activists seeking social change still persisted.

ACTIVISM TRANSFORMED

Reflecting the end of the original AAM, the campaigns that activists carried out in the 1990s marked a change from those of the early movement. A close examination reveals the increased sophistication of organizing tactics and tools but also narrower, more localized goals and focus.

With growing diversity of resources and skills within the community and the adoption of more diverse methods, campaigns now made a greater use of lobbying, media, corporate campaigns, transnational alliances, technology-based methods, and legal tactics as well as the protest mobilizations and coalition building that were the core of the AAM's tactics. These allowed campaigns to use more specialized skills and choose from a broader range of tools. At times, the continued progress in labor and community demonstrated the power of collective action when broad coalitions of labor, community, students, and others concerned with social justice achieved victories against immense odds.

Yet these greater tactics were focused more narrowly. Whereas in an earlier period, the grassroots efforts for Japanese American redress and reparations might include a commentary on "A revolutionary view of the reparations/ redress movement,"[47] contemporary campaigns limited their claims. For example, during a the Parcel C redevelopment struggle in Boston Chinatown, eighteen months of literature focused on the themes of municipal commitments to the neighborhood, a democratic and representative decision-making process in the city, and quality-of-life neighborhood issues. These were local concerns within the existing structure. While mobilizing Chinatown residents, the campaign did not expand concerns beyond structural bounds to question the role of the state or of capital. Nor did the groups emerge from the campaign with a clearer direction or greater resources for future organizing. In fact, some of the groups so exhausted themselves as to refrain from other, imminent struggles.[48]

Similarly, the unionization of the Koreana Hotel in Los Angeles as well as other labor issues remained within trade-union lines around working conditions and wages. These battles were fought for entry into a traditional labor movement that had served well U.S. capitalism but that had haltingly begun to question itself. Despite grimly declining union enrollments, the union movement had not expanded its role into social and structural issues. During the 1990s, despite Asian American activists' orientation toward workers, labor organizing still retained a narrow focus.

The maturation of the AAM over the previous two decades had led to grassroots participatory community campaigns that spanned large regions and challenged the social structure. These were now absent. The organizing leadership and broader vision that once strove to provide direction to a larger movement has in recent years succumbed to lowered expectations and a more limited vision for the AAM.

THE "BATTLE OF SEATTLE" AND POST–SEPTEMBER 11 REACTION IN THE NEW MILLENNIUM

Two events created an agitation for a new vision. An ideological Republican administration reclaimed the U.S. presidency to begin the new century. The new Bush administration's first signal accomplishment was to cut taxes once again, part of the conservative campaign to "starve the beast" of government of its ability to fund social programs. In doing so, it placed greater strains on the extensive Asian American infrastructure built over the preceding several decades. A number of Southeast Asian mutual aid associations, for example, collapsed during this period as refugee assistance funds dried up.[49] The administration of George W. Bush dismantled regulatory restraints on corporations in regard to worker safety and the environment and continued to promote the neoliberal global economic regime.

Yet, there were signs that this trend would not go unopposed. From November 29 to December 3, 1999, tens of thousands of people mobilized against the World Trade Organization (WTO) meetings in Seattle. Beginning in February through mid-December, over 500 events critiqued the WTO's role and impact on the environment, trade, and democratic process.[50] An alliance of labor, human rights, environmental, and political activist communities protested the manifold effects of global capitalism and successfully frustrated the WTO talks. While primarily White, the mobilization was a diverse amalgam of organizations and networks, and they presented an evolving and eclectic set of ideas. The appearance of a dynamic center of resistance to the institutions of global capitalism inspired hope and action. Both the new ideas and a counter-hegemonic pole to the rightward gravitation stimulated new activism. The Seattle mobilization was followed by a series of global protests against the Republican National Convention, the International Monetary Fund, and Asian Pacific Economic Cooperation conferences.[51]

Two years later, the terrain for activism shifted again. On September 11, 2001, terrorist attacks killed nearly three thousand people in New York and Washington. These attacks gave the Bush administration the mandate to announce a global "War on Terrorism." It proceeded to limit civil liberties, flout international norms, ratchet up militarism, initiate war against other countries, and "create our own reality."[52]

A different form of domestic terrorism swept over the United States as hate crimes against those perceived to be Arabs or Muslims increased dramatically. In the weeks after 9/11, the American Arab Anti-Discrimination Committee cited over 200 incidents of hate crimes and harassment against Arab Americans and Muslims. The Council of American-Islamic relations received some 1,700 reports of anti-Muslim incidents, including eleven deaths, in the months following the attacks.[53] In addition to widespread hate crimes and racial violence, more than 1,200 persons were detained for months at a time, many on minor immigration violations. Eleven months after the terrorist attacks, none of the detained had been charged with a crime related to September 11th. In Orwellian fashion, the Bush administration refused to reveal the names of those being held, making a state secret the identities and the charges against these individuals.

ASIAN AMERICAN MOBILIZATION

These two currents, particularly 9/11, agitated the environment for social justice activism. The Seattle events against the WTO highlighted the anti-globalization movement for the American public. For Asian American activists, it demonstrated unrecognized possibilities. Moreover, the anti-globalization movement was embedded within an international movement, with models that argued for alternatives to existing structures. The movement coupled disadvantaged constituencies—small farmers, workers, immigrants, and animals—with grievances. The movement developed potent symbols, such as martyred farmers and innovative repertoires of contention, blockades, and decentralized affinity groups.

But holding all this activity together was an oppositional, amorphous framework. Factions opposed to globalization knew what they didn't like about it but found it difficult to converge on positive alternatives to galvanize a social movement. Moreover, resources to support anti-globalization trends were scarce or fleeting.

Nevertheless, growing numbers of Asian American activists and groups joined or linked their activities to the anti-globalization movement. Particularly for sectors of the community who focused much of their work on transnational concerns, it was a natural connection. Other mobilizations continued both internationally and locally, catalyzed by periodic World Social Forum events.

If the Seattle mobilization gave hope to Asian American activists, the country's path after 9/11 jolted many others into action. Japanese Americans particularly responded quickly to the racial violence and government actions. Many in the Asian American community saw parallels between events after 9/11 and after the 1941 attack on Pearl Harbor. In both cases, individuals were rounded up and held in isolation from their families and friends for long periods of time. In both cases, racial violence took place with little government protection for the targeted group's civil rights. Also, in both cases, the established Asian community leadership professed support for the American government at the same time as civil rights violations were occurring.

However, in contrast to the 1940s, there was in place an organized, fairly sophisticated network of community and civil rights organizations, both pan-Asian American and ethnic specific groups. Asian American groups nationally and locally participated in ceremonies to mourn the loss of life on 9/11 and condemn the hate crimes and mass roundup of Arab and Muslims. Asian American Legal Defense and Education Fund's Stan Mark characterized the abuses as "a form of profiling that is really racial, ethnic, and religious profiling, against Muslims, Middle Eastern and South Asian people."[54]

The Asian American community responded with multiple voices reflecting the South Asian community and a new generation of community activists. There were generally two types of responses. One came from the vast majority of civil rights and social service organizations such as the National Asian Pacific American Legal Consortium, the JACL, the Organization of Chinese Americans, and

Asian American Congressional members. Through press releases and rallies, they condemned the racial violence against South and Central Asians, Muslims, and Arabs and the actions of the Department of Justice. Similarly, most civil rights groups have questioned the potential civil rights violations to these communities. Related actions have come from relatively new organizations such as the Sikh Media ART; they have aggressively sought to educate U.S. society and institutions about their religion, customs, and practices.

A second type of response by Asian American groups and individuals has been to more broadly condemn the U.S. "war on terrorism," the invasions and occupations of Afghanistan and Iraq, and the subsequent roundup of Arab and Muslim immigrants in the United States. This eclectic mix includes veteran peace, young anti-war, and immigrant rights activists and people concerned with the curbing of civil rights. This response has encompassed peace vigils, marches, and protests to oppose the U.S. government's international military actions and domestic attacks on immigrants under the guise of "fighting the war on terrorism." These groups and individuals tend to view the U.S. government's actions as a continuation of its global and military dominance. Some of the groups involved with this trend include Asian Pacific Islander Coalition Against the War in the San Francisco Bay Area, and Nikkei for Civil Rights and Redress (NCRR). Many immigrant rights organizations that include Asian Americans, such as the National Network for Immigrant and Refugee Rights, have also spoken out forcefully or organized around specific abuses, such as the deportation of Khmer youth[55] and South Asians.

In Los Angeles, the NCRR initiated several events that reached out to the Muslim community and linked the WWII internment of Japanese Americans to the events following September 11. NCRR activist and former internee Lillian Nakano said the situation recalled how Japanese Americans "were rounded up and herded into concentration camps, all on the basis of our skin color, because we looked like the enemy." An important lesson learned from the Nikkei redress campaign, Nakano said, was to "speak out against the singling out of any group of people."[56]

These two types of broad community responses are significant. With support from traditional civil liberties communities and the growing numbers of Muslim and Arab American organizations, they helped deter even greater abuses. One Arab American activist noted, "We can only do it if we work together. . . . Precisely because we're the targeted group, we cannot go at this alone."[57] In July 2002, a U.S. District Court judge ruled that the administration improperly withheld the identities of more than 1,000 detainees and ordered it to release the names.

The post–September 11th actions of Asian Americans were unique in their 150-year history in the United States. Faced with a global crisis, they acted as one. Instead of disidentifying, Asians united to oppose racial profiling. This achievement was a legacy of many years' hard work by Asian American community activists, social service, civil rights, and legal advocacy organizations to overcome historical cultural and political differences.

Thus, two streams, the anti-globalization movement and the "war on terror," have sparked widespread policy opposition within the overall Asian American community and spurred renewed activist mobilization against broader and more structural issues. Moreover, the Asian American response to 9/11 signaled that this organizing would start at a new point while incorporating aspects of past organizing, including many of those of the AAM.

ACTIVISM IN TRANSITION: EMERGING FROM LOCALIZED STRUGGLES

There has been a resurgence of activism, primarily among the young who have identified the hypocrisies and failures of the American system and its effects on the people of the world. Some have looked back toward the early Movement. The "Serve the People" conference in Los Angeles in 1998 and subsequent local forums in various cities featuring veterans from the early AAM have tried to divine that period's lessons that are applicable today.

While contemporary Asian American activism remains focused on local community, student, and labor sites, they have also begun to overcome their fragmentation by building various networks. Activists that these authors interviewed have helped build Southeast Asian American, transnational Korean, immigrant rights, spoken word, anti-war, and API networks, as well as national scale organizations. Most of these are still active, and new ones, such as the API Movement network, have emerged.

There has also been some self-reflection, a re-evaluation of how activism is situated. Specifically, questioning of the non-profit framework as the primary vehicle for change has been widespread and even the subject of a national conference in 2004, but viable alternatives have yet to be developed.

Furthermore, there has been some coalescence on broader themes. In recognition of the more interconnected world, activists often focus on global solidarity. They also have given particular importance to youth and immigrant workers. Many of the activist organizations described in this manuscript work with one or both constituencies.

The development of the AAM may inform contemporary conditions. In looking at the elements that contributed to the AAM's emergence, the political conditions, or "political opportunity" structure in social movement terms, were critical. Though this is an element outside the control of social justice activists, they can determine others in building a social movement.

The fundamental issue—full equality—remains. Grievances—hate crimes, poverty, the targeting of immigrants, workplace issues—persist though they had been complicated by a change in the Asian American class structure. Moreover, in the context of more global perspectives, the grievances against the consequences of the behavior of U.S. corporations and the U.S. military abound. That is evident in how and the conditions under which profit is generated and secured.

Resources are no longer the barriers that they posed in the past. This text described the growth of the infrastructure in the community and labor, areas generally supportive of movement building. The campuses, having played at times a tempestuous role for Asian American activism, also contribute. Daphne Kwok, formerly of the Asian Pacific American Institute for Congressional Studies, characterized the contributions from the growth of Asian American studies as "huge factor," and Emily Porcincula Lawsin, poet and lecturer at the University of Michigan, notes that Asian American studies programs support the community today through mechanisms like service learning and mentorship.[58]

There are now a greater diversity of mobilizing conventions, including many from the AAM that were popularized within old and new Asian American communities. Public demonstrations, voter drives, and other mobilization efforts, once unusual practices, are now pedestrian and ritualized acts of protest, drawing in greater numbers of people.

FRAMES

Certainly a different frame of reference is necessary for revitalizing an Asian American social movement. The first AAM did not anticipate contemporary conditions. The knowledge-based society enables spontaneous, decentralized planning and instantaneous and universal information, at least among the Internet-connected. Organizing methods that were established from the civil rights and Black Power periods have become ritualized and devitalized. A de-industrialized, de-personalized society complicates solidarity and community, and actual alternative models are not apparent.

Within intellectual circles, the dominant progressive school influencing recent cohorts of activist students has been post-modernism, but this offers little direction. As E. San Juan observed, post-modernism's emphasis on the "'metaphysics of textualism' and 'language games' only reinforces the unequal division of labor and the unjust hierarchy of power in U.S. society and in international relations."[59] At the same time, Marxism, historically influential among revolutionaries, has been widely discredited among masses of people and has yet to prove that it can transcend the failures of the past decades.

Asian American political awareness has also advanced to some further understanding. The unity of the leadership of the Asian American communities after 9/11 was an unprecedented development. The anti-globalization movement has also presented a set of ideas—decentralization, democracy, environmentalism, and diversity among them.[60] While worthy of consideration, they lack a guiding, cohesive analysis to chart a new direction. Those working to build organized resistance in communities and workplaces as well as the cross-linkages that gird a movement need a more fully formed, material, and resonant set of ideas.

Such a set of ideas is primarily the responsibility of contemporary activists. At the same time, the experience and resources of those steeled in the early AAM should be applied to these issues. If this new synthesis is to come, it will arise from those who daily struggle for change and out of the ferment of their ideas and intersections.

Some groups are committing themselves to this unifying process that would be necessary for a movement today. CAAAV challenges others to take up this responsibility.

> It's a conscious decision that organizations make [participating in developing a vision]. They're either going to put some time into that, or they're not. CAAAV is making a conscious decision to be able to do that but still staying grounded in terms of the local organizing work but trying to cut out any inefficiencies in the way that we operate so that we can actually participate in some more of that theorizing or strategizing or reflection with allied organizations from other parts of the country.[61]

The API Movement national network has also made efforts to develop more analysis based upon the work and experience of local groups. These efforts are ongoing.

Finally, that history tells us that movement building requires a systematic and long-term constructive effort. While conditions for rapid change have occurred in history, movement building that is contingent on a burst of activity opens the door for some of the weaknesses of the Asian American Movement activism. These weaknesses stemmed from short horizons that begat unnecessary in fighting, deflated expectations, and the lack of systematic infrastructure building that would have sustained movement for the longer term.

NOTES

1. Jon Jang and Francis Wong, "A Conversation with Jon Jang and Francis Wong," interview by Nic Paget-Clarke, *In Motion Magazine,* 1997, www.inmotion magazine.com /jjfw1.html (24 November 2004).

2. The Four Tigers refers four Asian areas, Korea, Taiwan, Hong Kong, and Singapore, which underwent rapid development in the post–World War II era. Japan Inc. refers to Japan's challenge to U.S. economic supremacy in the 1980s. Some consider the twenty-first century to be the "Asian Century," where the economies of Asia will dominate globally.

3. Paul Ong, Edna Bonacich, and Lucie Cheng, "Introduction: The Political Economy of Capitalist Restructuring and the New Asian Immigration," in *The New Asian Immigration in Los Angeles and Global Restructuring*, eds. Paul Ong, Edna Bonacich, and Lucie Cheng (Philadelphia: Temple University Press, 1994), Liu and Cheng, "Pacific Rim Development;" Johnson, *Blowback*.

4. In his influential article in the "National Interest," Fukuyama speculated that capitalism's liberal democracy may constitute the "end point of mankind's ideological evolution" and hence the "final form of human government."

5. Kevin Phillips, *Wealth and Democracy: A Political History of the American Rich* (New York: Broadway Books, 2002).

6. Grace Yoo, "The Fight to Save Welfare for Low-Income Older Asian Immigrants," *AAPI Nexus* 1, no.1 (2003): 85–100; Skip Thurman, "Clinton Puts Free Trade First this Fall," *Christian Science Monitor*, 9 September 1997; Phillips, *Wealth and Democracy*; Robert L. Borosage, "The Politics of Austerity," *The Nation* 262 (May 1996): 22–24.

7. Ho, ed., *Legacy to Liberation*, 396–98.

8. Tarrow, *Power in Movement*.

9. Bureau of the Census, *1990 Census STF-3*.

10. Hing, *Making and Remaking*; Mar and Kim, "Historical Trends"; Paul Ong, Bonacich and Cheng, "Introduction."

11. IPUMS, Minnesota Population Center.

12. Lucie Cheng, "Chinese Americans in the Formation of the Pacific Regional Economy"; Arif Dirlik, "Asians on the Rim: Transnational Capital and Local Community in the Making of Contemporary Asian America," both in *Across the Pacific: Asian Americans and Globalization*, ed. Evelyn Hu-DeHart (New York: Asia Society, 2000), 29-60, 61-78.

13. Bureau of the Census, *1990 Census STF-3*.

14. Bureau of the Census, *Asian and Pacific Islander Americans: A Profile* (Washington, DC, 1993).

15. Paul Ong and Suzanne Hee, "Economic Diversity," in *Economic Diversity, Issues and Policies*, ed. Paul Ong (Los Angeles: LEAP Asian Pacific American Public Policy Institute and UCLA Asian American Studies Center, 1994), 31–56.

16. L. Ling-chi Wang, "The Politics of Ethnic Identity and Empowerment: Asian American Community Since the 1960s," *Asian American Policy Review* 2 (1991): 43–56.

17. Liu and Cheng, "Pacific Rim Development"; Mar and Kim, "Historical Trends"; Ong, Bonacich, Cheng, "Political Economy"; Jeffrey S. Passel, *The Size and Characteristics of the Unauthorized Migrant Population in the U.S.; Estimates Based upon the 2005 Current Population Survey* (Washington, DC: Pew Hispanic Center, 2006).

18. Mimi Abramovitz, "Saving Capitalism from Itself," *New England Journal of Public Policy* 20 no.1 (Fall/Winter 2004–2005): 21–32.

19. Zia, *Asian American Dreams.*

20. Wong, interview.

21. There has developed a tension in the terms Asian American and Asian Pacific American or Asian Pacific Islander. Many Pacific Islanders seek their distinct identity. Yet many organizations retain this blended identity. We will continue to use Asian American, aware of all its issues for consistency, and use Asian Pacific American in proper names or classifications that use them.

22. Frank H. Wu and Francey Lim Youngberg, "People From China Crossing the River: Asian American Political Empowerment and Foreign Influence," in *Asian Americans and Politics: Perspectives, Experiences, Prospects,* ed. Gordon H. Chang (Stanford: Stanford University Pres. 2000): 311–53.

23. Dirlik, "Asians on the Rim."

24. Diane C. Fujino and Kye Leung, "Radical Resistance in Conservative Times: New Asian American Organizations in the 1990s," in *Legacy to Liberation,* ed. Fred Ho (San Francisco: AK Press, 2000): 141–58.

25. For example, in addition to community health and legal services, former radical activists have contributed significantly to community development corporations such as Little Tokyo Service Center CDC and Asian Americans for Equality.

26. Sung E. Bai and Hyun Lee, interviews by Michael Liu, tape recording, New York, 14 December, 2004.

27. Yul-san Liem, interview by Michael Liu, tape recording, Brookline, MA, 16 August 2004.

28. Hung, "Asian American Participation in Civil Society." This is a lower bound since reporting is voluntary and requested only of those groups with annual revenues exceeding $25,000. It also excludes groups which choose not to incorporate as tax-exempt 501(c)3 organizations.

29. Timothy P. Fong, *The First Suburban Chinatown: The Remaking of Monterey Park, California* (Philadelphia: Temple University, 1994).

30. Khandelwal, *Becoming American.*

31. Sarath Suong, interview by Michael Liu, tape recording, Providence, RI, 28 December 2004.

32. Bai and Lee, interviews.

33. Dennis Hayashi and Daphne Kwok, "Wards Cove Packing vs. Antonio," *Asian American Policy Review* 3 (1993): 5–16; Aden Kun, "An Interview with Angela Oh," *Asian American Policy Review* 3 (1993): 55–63; Peter Kiang, "Southeast Asian Empowerment: The Challenge of Changing Demographics in Lowell, Massachusetts," *Asian American Policy Review* 1 (1990): 29–38.

34. Omatsu, "The Four Prisons"; Scott Kurashige, "Pan-Ethnicity and Community Organizing," *Journal of Asian American Studies* 3, no. 2 (2000): 163–90.

35. M. Liu, "Neighborhood Mobilization"; Zenobia Lai, Andrew Leong, and Chi Chi Wu, *The Lessons of the Parcel C Struggle: Reflections on Community Lawyering,* Los Angeles: LEAP Asian Pacific American Public Policy Institute and UCLA Asian American Studies Center, 2001.

36. Miriam Ching Louie, *Sweatshop Warriors: Immigrant Women Workers Take on the Global Factory* (Cambridge, MA: South End Press, 2001).

37. CAAAV: Organizing Asian Communities, "On the Occasion of CAAAV's 15th Anniversary," *CAAAV Voice* 11, no. 1 (Spring 2002), New York: CAAAV, 3.

38. Lydia Lowe, interview by Michael Liu, tape recording, Cambridge, MA, 11 August 2004.

39. Neela Banerjee, "Spoken Word," *AsianWeek* (1–7 June 2001).

40. Giles Li, interviews by Michael Liu, tape recording, Boston, 23 November 2004, 6 December 2006.

41. M. Liu, "Neighborhood Mobilization"; Lai, Leong, and Wu, *Community Lawyering*.

42. Fujino and Leung, "Radical Resistance."

43. More recent terms to designate those formerly referred to as "Asian Americans" include "Asian Pacific Americans" and "Asian Pacific Islanders." These designations are controversial, and Pacific Islanders in the U.S. themselves have debated whether to be associated with or separated from Asian Americans. The Asian American term itself has become an issue of whether it is too inclusive and conflates differences among Asian sub-groups.

44. Los Angeles police officers were acquitted of beating an African American motorist, Rodney King. The savage assault had been captured on a home videotape. The acquittal set off days of rioting that included armed confrontations between Korean shop owners and rioters, most of whom were African American and Latino.

45. Jake Doherty, "Hotel Labor Pact: Room for Everyone," *Los Angeles Times*. 1 November 1992, City Times Section, p. 1.

46. Giles Li, interviews.

47. National Coalition for Redress/Reparations, *National Coalition for Redress and Reparations,* authors' collection, circa 1980, photocopy.

48. M. Liu, "Neighborhood Mobilization."

49. Long Nguyen, conversation with Michael Liu, 14 May 2003; Vong Ros, conversation with Michael Liu, 15 March 2007.

50. Harry Bridges Center for Labor Studies, "Introduction to the Protests," *The WTO History Project*, depts.washington.edu/wtohist/intro.htm (June 3, 2005).

51. Eddie Yuen, George Katsiaficas, and Daniel Burton Rose, eds., *The Battle of Seattle: The New Challenge to Capitalist Globalization* (New York: Soft Skull Press, 2001): 237–300.

52. Ron Susskind, "Without a Doubt," *New York Times Magazine*, 17 October 2004.

53. Other reports of hate crimes in the months following came from the Sikh coalition, who reported 251 incidents of hate crimes directed at Sikh Americans, and the National Asian Pacific American Legal Consortium documented nearly 250 bias motivated incidents targeting Asian Pacific Americans and South Asians.

54. Stan Mark, "An Interview with the Movement: Reasserting the Immigrant Rights Agenda after 9/11," *Network News* (Spring 2002), National Network for Immigrant and Refugee Rights, Oakland, CA, 10.

55. API and Khmer organizations formed a national network opposing the roundup of Cambodian non-citizens being deported. Post 9/11 statutes mandated these deportations for past crimes. Young adults who had committed crimes, some relatively

minor, in their youth became targets for immigration authorities. See the film *Sentenced Home* by Nicole Newham and David Grabias, 2006 and SEARAC, 2002, "Issue Area: Deportation," www.searac.org/cambrepbak6_02.html (7 December 2006)

56. Taksehi Nakayama, "Little Tokyo Ceremony Honors Terrorist victims with Candlelight Ceremony," Los Angeles *Rafu Shimpo*, 2001, www.ncrr-la.org/news/candle light.html (5 March 2005).

57. Thomas Ginsberg, "Ethnic Groups and Lawyers Will Examine the Cases of Immigrants Detained in PA during the Last Year," *Philadelphia Inquirer*, 2002, pp. 6–8.

58. Daphne Kwok, interview by Michael Liu, tape recording, Washington, DC, 15 December 2004.

59. E. San Juan Jr., "Interrogations and Interventions: Who Speaks for Whom?" In *Beyond Postcolonial Theory* (New York: St. Martin's Press, 1998).

60. International Forum on Globalization, "Ten Principles for Sustainable Societies," in *Alternatives to Economic Globalization*, ed. International Forum on Globalization (San Francisco: Berrett-Koehler Publishers, 2002), 54–80.

61. Sung E. Bai and Hyun Lee, interview.

Chapter Eight

Conclusion

In 1960, a weary worker, perhaps a World War II veteran, would rise on a Saturday and sit in his small kitchen to join his wife. He would have his customary morning cigarette. As he sat or squatted in his vinyl-covered chair, the eddies and curls of smoke rising from his mouth reached around the room to his native-born children doing chores or preparing for the day. That worker, Filipino, Chinese, Japanese, or Korean, may have toiled in a restaurant, in other people's gardens or fields or factories. The grinding, drab, daily routine encoded in that smoke imprinted the unspoken issues of the history of Asian Americans upon a generation. That generation would build upon those learned grievances, slights, inequities, or daily violence of American life, either personally witnessed or absorbed through the new miracle medium of television. They would build a new, social movement that would transform the circumstances that future Asian American parents woke up to. In doing so, that generation, perhaps the first to go to college or alternatively roaming the streets, built upon past struggles and reproduced the dynamics of social movements that arise when sufficient factors of resources, framing visions, and political opportunities converged.

What most scholars weakly and the generation of AAM participants more deeply know is that the Asian American Movement resulted from deep-seated currents in the contemporary Asian American communities. In the late 1960s, a new, more assertive generation coupled with numbers driven by a baby boom and immigration reform came of age in a time of political turmoil but also of inspiration. These inspirations incited an alternative interpretation of the world and introduced them to methods of contention. The generation was situated in college and community environments that allowed them to utilize a network of institutional resources and social networks of activists indigenous to Asian

American communities. Finally, divisions in the country created an opportunity for mobilization, an opportunity of which this cohort took full advantage.

The three tenets that introduced this text were a reassessment of the Asian American Movement's length, breadth, and effects, its vision for structural change, and the appropriateness of social movement theory to ground this reassessment.

The AAM began in the late 1960s and evolved with the succeeding decades. While the insurgencies of the time informed the AAM, the AAM didn't simply act as their pale imitation. As a product of their communities, it derived a particular character. This character gave it a practicality, collectivity, and persistence. From their initial base, the AAM created community infrastructures and a growing resource base for mobilization. They developed increasingly sophisticated visions and strategies and tactics. They conducted increasingly influential campaigns, moving from campus-specific and enclave-specific struggles to the national campaigns of Redress and Reparations and Vincent Chin. This evolution accounted for their lengthy persistence into the 1980s, despite the increasingly difficult political environments. It continued as a social movement that remained vital beyond the Black Liberation Movement and other parallel movements that had been such a significant source of inspiration to them.

Moreover, it had broad involvement and effects. The AAM engaged most of a generation—those in service, those seeking reform, and those envisioning radical change—and pervaded the different corners of Asian American life. While this text looked at the areas of community, student, labor, art and culture, and feminism, parallel histories could have been written about electoral equity, sexual identity, immigration, media, and civil rights.

In its effects the AAM, among other things, created a new, modern framework of Asian community infrastructure, achieved more democratic governance in their communities, and changed the essential curriculum in the academy. The AAM also shaped more accommodating public policies affecting a range of issues from preserving ethnic enclaves and the conditions of Asian American workers to Japanese American reparations. Reformers alone did not address these issues, until militant revolutionaries made them major issues in the community, and the structures of power had to respond to them.

The AAM also triggered a wave of new leaders streaming throughout the Asian American civic life. They populated the new institutions this text has described, the service, advocacy, and grassroots organizations that they had built or re-energized. On this infrastructure, they negotiated new roles and processes engaging a more extroverted community.

Most importantly, AAM activists re-imagined and conceptualized their role and identity in the U.S. society and, by insisting on full equality for their people, interjected the Asian American communities into the public discourse. They created the paradigm for modern Asian American political participation. To an extent, the changing demographics, brought about by the new immigration and the growing dominance of professional and managerial classes within the Asian American communities, has amended this paradigm, but its essential contours arose from the AAM's work.

Second, the AAM grounded its vision in structural change that would provide their communities and the people in the United States with peace, equality, justice, and necessary basic services. The AAM repeatedly challenged the U.S. social and power structure through numerous and myriad campaigns — basic health, decent schools, employment, education that served and reflected their communities, redress for historic wrongs, preservation of enclaves, workers' rights, democratic and inclusive politics, and humanitarian values. The remoteness of achieving this vision led to additional efforts for realization through self-reliant efforts like volunteer services and then the shunting of efforts into more practical and immediate reform and service projects. This text documented some of those who consciously carried forward the AAM's legacy in the succeeding decades and was increasingly focused on those committed to visions for systemic change. In this passage, as the AAM more sharply represented this vision, fewer individuals represented the AAM. Nevertheless, this vision vitalized activists with the boldness to undertake intimidating challenges such as the campaigns for Justice for Domingo and Viernes, Japanese American redress and reparations, and Jesse Jackson for President.

Third, examining the AAM through a social movement lens, this text identified factors that contributed to its rapid development and led to its ultimate ebb. We looked at the AAM within the context of social movement cycles. The AAM didn't achieve its initial objectives. Its "snake dance" of activism struggled to adjust to changing conditions. As a product of a changing U.S. society, AAM activists accelerated that change and eventually became change's victims. The transformation of the United States into a post-industrial, globalized society and the success of the ruling class to stifle dissent and manage the transition of its hegemonic position in the post-colonial (though not post-imperialist) world undermined the bases of the Movement. The AAM's framing did not factor in and accommodate sufficiently these transitions. Many who had entered into the industrial workplaces to persuade the perceived primary constituency of social change organized in vain amid growing job losses and dwindling numbers of industrial workers.

The AAM was unable to develop a more realistic and sustainable long-term strategy. If, as Eddie Wong has suggested, they had built up institutions to sustain them, then they might have persisted to the present.[1] Certainly, there was unnecessary competition among groups that sapped their energy. However, the fundamental drain on their energies was the receding horizon of change and the exhaustion of those who had kept moving toward it. In the end, most conceded to drifting with the prevailing currents in society.

This text documented the end of the AAM but not the end of Asian American activism. The grievances and conditions that fed the AAM continued but were transformed. We looked at how these new globalized, knowledge-based activists and forms of organizing are beginning to regenerate a potential new social movement cycle. What has emerged, after a period of drift, is a new post-1990s gathering of forces. While standing on shoulders of the past AAM, this new emergent activism does not inherit the preceding movement cycle's dynamics. It creates its own and occupies a different terrain.

Today, a typical parent may more likely be a highly educated professional worker, who visits the enclaves for lunch rather than lives in its tenements. In this new environment she passes the immigrant workers smoking outside storefronts. The whorls of smoke from these workers cannot cover the growing distance between the purposeful stride of the corporate "salaryman (or woman)"on a business lunch and the slumping postures of immigrant workers on a break, the inconsistently documented and legitimated. Instead, the smoke dissipates into the atmosphere.

The legacy of the Asian American Movement pervades the contemporary institutional environment from the language that mainstream institutions use to the community services and advocacy groups that serve the population and the political alliances, tactics, and dialogue that they enter into.

One of the most positive consequences was evident in the pan-Asian opposition to the targeting of South Asians and Middle Easterners after 9/11. Another emerging legacy is a strong API presence in the labor movement and in Asian community-based labor organizing among immigrant workers. The plight of these workers, historically ignored by the organized trade union movement, has been brought to light, highlighted, and organized around by today's activists in conjunction with AAM activists from the 1960s and 1970s. Efforts to join together with immigrant workers in other minority communities, such as Multi-ethnic Immigrant Worker Organizing Network in Los Angeles, have the potential to educate and mobilize in the Asian American (and perhaps Pacific Islander) communities of the twenty-first century.

Despite these connections, the leadership that consciously pioneered the contemporary environment is, with a few notable exceptions, secluded and inaccessible to most of today's activists. It is a presence that is recollected and aspired to but can't be drawn from readily. Except for episodic instances of 1960s forums and partial, academic allusions and interpretations, contemporary activists are left to decode today's issues themselves. The absence is considerable. While today's organizers are creative in pursuing their work, they are relegated to repeat many of history's mistakes. An objective legacy is a poor substitute for a consciously mediated one. The 1960s generation of AAM activists worked with an older generation of labor and community activists, drawing from their understanding and experiences in challenging the power structure. Such interactivity needs to continue with today's activists.

In the voices presented, a vision for a new movement to resolve continuing injustice in this country and globally struggles to emerge. That vision needs to be a synthesis that builds upon the past storehouse of experience of Asian Americans yet recognizes the present, dynamic environment and its unique conditions. Finally it needs to envision a compelling, equitable, humane future.

Social movements arise when injustice, inequality, and exploitation exist. Yet these grievances do not guarantee mass upsurges; the action must be deliberately constructed through popularizing alternative frameworks and mobilizing resources. Asian Americans have shown that they have been capable of such constructions. How the past Movement informs the present remains a project in progress. The dance goes on.

NOTE

1. Eddie Wong, interview, by Michael Liu, Boxton, 23 March 2005.

Bibliography

Abramovitz, Mimi. "Saving Capitalism from Itself: Whither the Welfare State?" *New England Journal of Public Policy* 20, no. 1 (Fall/Winter 2004–2005): 21–32.

Aguilar-San Juan, Karin. *The State of Asian America: Activism and Resistance in the 1990s*. Boston: South End Press, 1994.

Almaguer, Tomás. *Racial Fault Lines: The Historical Origins of White Supremacy in California*. Berkeley, CA: University of California Press, 1994.

American Citizens for Justice. "The Case for Vincent Chin: A Tragedy in American Justice." Authors' collection, photocopy, 1983.

Ang Katipunan: National Newspaper of the Union of Democratic Filipinos (Oakland), 28 June 1976–15 September 1977.

Aoude, Ibrahim G. "Introduction to the Ethnic Studies Story: Political and Economic Environment." *Social Processes in Hawai'i* 39 (1999): xv–xxxvi.

———. "No Jam Da Program! Ethnic Studies Highlights: 1969–1998: Our History, Our Way." *Social Processes in Hawai'i* 39 (1999): 1–7.

———. "Strategic Considerations in Social Struggles" *Social Process in Hawai'i* 39 (1999): 284–300.

Ariyoshi, Koji. *From Kona to Yenan: The Political Memoirs of Koji Ariyoshi*. Honolulu: University of Hawai'i Press, 2000.

Asian Alliance. "Today's Hiroshimas." Authors' collection, mimeographed, 1970.

Asian American Political Alliance. "Asian American Political Alliance Statement." In *To Serve the Devil*, edited by Paul Jacobs and Saul Landau. New York: Vintage, 1971.

Asian American Resource Workshop. "AARW Workshop on Building a Campaign for Asian American Studies." Boston: 13 April 1985, 2.

Asian Americans for Action Newsletter 2: 1 (February 1970). Asian Americans for Action, New York: 3.

Asian Family Affair (Seattle). February 1972–October 1982. Seattle: University of Washington Suzzallo Library, microfilm.

Asian Legal Services Committee to Defend Harry Wong. "American Justice and Harry Wong." Authors' collection, 1972.

Asian Pacific Student Union Coordinating Committee. "Proposal for the National Link-Up of the East Coast Asian Student Union and the West Coast Asian/Pacific Student Union:" Authors' collection, 25 October 1978.

Asian Pacific Student Union, Southern Cal Region. "Asian/Pacific Students Unite!" (Summer, 1978) Asian Student Union, California State University–Los Angeles: 10.

Asian Student Union. *Asian Students Unite* 4:1 (Fall 1975). Asian Student Union, University of California–Berkeley: 2–10.

Azuma, Eiichiro. "Racial Struggle, Immigrant Nationalism, and Ethnic Identity: Japanese and Filipinos in the California Delta." *Pacific Historical Review* 67, no. 2 (May 1998): 163–99.

Bacevic, Andrew J. *American Empire: The Reality and Consequences of U.S. Diplomacy*. Boston: Harvard University Press, 2002.

Bai, Sung E. Interview by Michael Liu. Tape recording. New York: 14 December 2004.

Banerjee, Neela. "Spoken Word," *AsianWeek*. 1–7 June 2001.

Bao, Xiaolan. *Holding Up More than Half the Sky: Chinese Women Garment Workers in New York City 1948–1992*. Urbana, IL: University of Illinois, 2001.

Blair, R. Jeffrey. "Fighting the Japanese Internment in Federal Court: The A.C.L.U. During World War II." *The Faculty Journal of the Junior College Division of Aichi Gakuin University* 8, 84–105. Nagoya, Japan: 2000.

Blauner, Robert. *Racial Oppression in America*. New York: HarperCollins, 1992.

Boggs, Grace Lee. *Living for Change*. Minneapolis: University of Minnesota Press, 1998.

Bonus, Rick. *Locating Filipino Americans*. Philadelphia: Temple University Press, 2000.

Borosage, Robert L. "The Politics of Austerity." *The Nation* 262 (May 1996): 22–24.

Bowles, Samuel, David Gordon, and Thomas Weisskopf. *After the Wasteland: A Democratic Economics for the Year 2000*. Armonk, NY: M. E. Sharpe, 1990.

Brandeis Asian American Student Association. "Asian American Views on the War." Authors' collection, 1971.

Buechler, Steven M. *Social Movements in Advanced Capitalism: The Political Economy and Cultural Construction of Social Activism*. New York: Oxford University Press, 1999.

Bulosan, Carlos. *America Is in the Heart, A Personal History*. Seattle: University of Washington Press, 1974.

Bureau of the Census. *Asian and Pacific Islander Population by State: 1980*. Washington, DC: 1983.

Burtless, G. "Public Spending on the Poor." In *Confronting Poverty: Prescriptions for Change*, edited by S. H. Danzinger. Cambridge, MA: Harvard University Press, 1994.

CAAAV: Organizing Asian Communities. "On the Occasion of CAAAV's 15th Anniversary." *CAAAV Voice 11*, no. 1 (Spring 2002). New York: CAAAV, 3.

Chan, Hei Wai, and Marta Ho. "The UConn Incident: Responding to Racism." *East Wind* 7, no. 1 (Spring/Summer 1989): 16–20.

Chan, Kenyon S. "Rethinking the Asian American Studies Project: Bridging the Divide between 'Campus' and 'Community'." *Journal of Asian American Studies* 3, no. 1 (2000): 17–36.

Chan, Sucheng. *Asian Americans: An Interpretive History.* New York: Twayne Publishers, 1991.

Chen, Ching-In. Interview by Michael Liu. Tape recording. Boston, MA: 29 July 2004.

Chen, Christine. Interview by Michael Liu. Tape recording. Boston, MA: 29 July 2004.

Cheng, Lucie. "Chinese Americans in the Formation of the Pacific Regional Economy." In *Across the Pacific: Asian Americans and Globalization*, edited by Evelyn Hu-DeHart. Philadelphia: Temple University, 2000.

Chiang, Fay, ed. *Basement Yearbook 1986.* New York: Basement Workshop, 1986.

Chin, Doug. *Seattle's International District.* Seattle: International Examiner Press, 2001.

Chin, Frank, Jeffery Paul Chan, Lawson Fusao Inada, and Shawn Wong, eds. *Aiieeeee!: An Anthology of Asian American Writers.* Washington, DC: Howard University Press, 1974.

Chin, Rocky. "New York Chinatown Today: Community in Crisis." *Amerasia Journal* 1, no. 1 (March 1971): 1–24.

——. "The House that JACS Built." *Bridge* 2, no. 6 (August 1973): 5–10.

——. Interview by Michael Liu. New York: 21 July, 2002.

Chinatown Study Group. "Chinatown Report 1969." New York: Columbia University's Urban Center, 1970.

Chinese Awareness (Los Angeles), July 1971–July 1976.

Cho, Milyoung. "Overcoming Our Legacy as Cheap Labor, Scabs, and Model Minorities: Asian Americans Fight for Community Empowerment." In *The State of Asian America: Activism and Resistance in the 1990s,* edited by Karin Aguilar-San Juan. Boston: South End Press, 1994.

Cho, Peggy Myo-Young. "Return the Islands Back to the People: A Legacy of Struggle and Resistance in Ka Pae'aina." In *Legacy to Liberation,* edited by Fred Ho. San Francisco: AK Press, 2000.

Chow, Esther Ngan-Ling. "The Feminist Movement: Where Are All the Asian American Women?" In *Making Waves: An Anthology of Writings by and about Asian American Women,* edited by Asian Women United of California. Boston: Beacon Press, 1989.

Chow, Peter. "More Media Guerillas." *Bridge* 7, no. 4 (Winter 1981–1982): 34.

Choy, Catherine Ceniza. *Empire of Care: Nursing and Migration in Filipino American History.* Durham, NC: Duke University Press, 2003.

Chu, Bernice. "Media Guerillas Revisited." *Bridge* 7, no. 4 (Winter 1981–1982): 35.

Chu, Hiep. Interview by Michael Liu. Boston, MA: October 2, 2003.

Chu, Marilyn. "Metamorphosis of a Chinatown, International District, Seattle." Master's thesis, University of Washington, 1977.

Chung, Sue Fawn. "Fighting for Their American Rights: A History of the Chinese American Citizens Alliance." In *Claiming American: Constructing Chinese American Identities During the Exclusion Era*, edited by K. Scott Wong and Sucheng Chan. Philadelphia: Temple University Press, 1998.

Churchill, Thomas. *Triumph Over Marcos.* Seattle: Open Hand Publishers, 1995.

Clemente, Frank, and Frank Watkins, eds. *Keep Hope Alive: Jesse Jackson's 1988 Presidential Campaign*. Boston: South End Press and Keep Hope Alive PAC, 1989.

Conlon, Timothy. *New Federalism: Intergovernmental Reform from Nixon to Reagan*. Washington, DC: Brookings Institution, 1988.

Daniels, Roger. *Asian America: Chinese and Japanese in the United States since 1850*. Seattle: University of Washington Press, 1988.

Darnovsky, Marcy, Barbara Epstein, and Richard Flacks, eds. *Cultural Politics and Social Movements*. Philadelphia: Temple University Press, 1995.

De la Cruz, Enrique. "The Opposition Movement in the Filipino American Community." California State University Northridge, n.d.

De Vera, Arleen. "Without Parallel: The Local 7 Deportation Cases." *Amerasia Journal* 20, no. 2 (1994): 20–25.

Dirlik, Arif. "Asians on the Rim: Transnational Capital and Local Community in the Making of Contemporary Asian America." In *Across the Pacific: Asian Americans and Globalization*, edited by Evelyn Hu-DeHart. New York: Asia Society, 2000.

The District Design Group. *The International District Seattle—an Action Program for Physical Development*. Seattle: International District Improvement Association, 1973.

Doherty, Jack. "Hotel Labor Pact: Room for Everyone," *Los Angeles Times*, City Times section, page 1. 1 November 1992.

Dong, Harvey C. "The Origins and Trajectory of Asian American Political Activism in the San Francisco Bay Area 1968–1978." Ph. D. diss., University of California–Berkeley, 2002.

Dubrow, Gail, et al. "Asian/Pacific Americans in Washington State: Historic Context Document." Department of Community Development, Office of Archaeology and Historic Preservation. Olympia, WA: February 1992.

East Coast Asian Student Union. "Asian American Resource Directory." *Asian American Spirit* 3 (1988). East Coast Asian Student Union, Boston: 30–35.

Elbaum, Max. *Revolution in the Air*. New York: Verso, 2002.

Eng, Tom. "Telling it like it is in Seattle." *East Wind* 4, no. 1 (Winter/Spring 1985): 56–58.

Espiritu, Augusto. "Twenty Years of Struggle towards the Decade of Empowerment." In *Gidra: The XXth Anniversary Edition*, edited by Gidra Staff. Los Angeles: Gidra, 1990.

Espiritu, Yen Le. *Asian American Panethnicity: Bridging Institutions and Identities*. Philadelphia: Temple University Press, 1992.

———. *Asian American Women and Men: Labor, Laws, and Love*. Thousand Oaks, CA: Sage Publications, 1996.

Espiritu, Yen Le, and Paul Ong. "Class Constraints on Racial Solidarity among Asian Americans." In *The New Asian Immigration in Los Angeles and Global Restructuring*, edited by Paul Ong, Edna Bonacich, and Lucie Cheng. Philadelphia: Temple University, 1994.

Fan, Stephanie. Interview by Michael Liu. Tape recording. Brookline, MA: 17 February 2004.

Feng, Therese, and Shirley Mark Yuen. "Through Strength and Struggle—A Victory for Garment Workers in Boston." *East Wind* 6, no. 1 (Spring/Summer 1987): 31–32.

Fong, Timothy P. *The First Suburban Chinatown: The Remaking of Monterey Park, California.* Philadelphia: Temple University Press, 1994.

——. *The Contemporary Asian American Experience.* Upper Saddle River, NJ: Prentice-Hall, 1998.

Foo, Lora Jo. "The Role of Asians in the Recent Struggles of the San Francisco Culinary Industry." *Yellow Journal* 1, no. 2 (Spring 1986): 21–38.

——. Interview by Kim Geron. San Francisco: 15 November 2006.

Frank, Dana. *Buy America: The Untold Story of Economic Nationalism.* Boston: Beacon Press, 1999.

Freeman, Jo, ed. *Social Movements of the Sixties and Seventies.* New York: Longman Inc., 1982.

Friday, Chris. *Organizing Asian American Labor: The Pacific Coast Canned-Salmon Industry, 1870–1942.* Philadelphia: Temple University Press, 1994.

Fu, May Chuan. "Keeping Close to the Ground: Politics and Coalition in Asian American Community Organizing, 1969–1977." Ph. D. diss., University of California–San Diego, 2005.

Fujikane, Candace. "Asian Settler Colonialism in Hawai'i." *Amerasia Journal* 26, no. 2 (2000): xvi–xxii.

Fujiki, Rita, and Cathy Gosho. "Modern Day Issues Facing Asian American Women." In *Concerns of Asian American Women.* Washington Commission on Asian American Affairs. Task Force on Asian American Women. Olympia, 1976.

Fujino, Diane C. *Heartbeat of Struggle: The Revolutionary Life of Yuri Kochiyama.* Minneapolis: University of Minnesota Press, 2005.

Fujino, Diane C., and Kye Leung. "Radical Resistance in Conservative Times: New Asian American Organizations in the 1990s." In *Legacy to Liberation*, edited by Fred Ho. San Francisco: AK Press, 2000.

Fujioka, Sayo. "Becoming a Worker: A Matter of Choice." *East Wind* 2, no. 1 (Spring/Summer 1983): 40–41.

Garcia, Arnoldo. "No Nation of Immigrants would treat Immigrants this Way." *Network News* (Spring 2002). National Network for Immigrant and Refugee Rights, Oakland: 2.

Gee, Emma, ed. *Counterpoint: Perspectives on Asian America.* Los Angeles: UCLA Asian American Studies Center, 1976.

Gee, Shannon. "A Look Back at Seattle's Asian Activism." *ColorsNW Magazine* (May 2001): 10–13, 17, 23.

Geron, Kim. "Asian Pacific Americans' Social Movements and Interest Groups." *PS: Political Science and Politics* 34, no. 3 (September 2001): 619–24.

Geron, Tomio. The Asian American Movement in New York City, 1968–1975. Authors' collection, 1996. Photocopy.

——. "Vincent Chin and Asian American Politics in the 'Ambiguous' 1980s." Paper presented at the annual meeting of the Association for Asian American Studies. Scottsdale, Arizona, 2000.

Getting Together (New York and San Francisco), Feb. 1970–August 1978.

Getting Together. *Chinese-American Workers: Past and Present: An Anthology of Getting Together.* San Francisco: Getting Together, 1973.

Gidra (Los Angeles). April 1969–June 1971.

Gimpel, James G., and James R. Edwards, Jr. *The Congressional Politics of Immigration Reform*. Boston: Allyn and Bacon, 1999.

Gitlin, Todd. *The Sixties: Years of Hope, Days of Rage*. New York: Bantam Books, 1987.

Goodwin, Jeff, and James M. Jasper, eds. *Rethinking Social Movements: Structure, Meaning, and Emotion*. Lanham, MD: Rowman and Littlefield, 2004.

Gupta, Anu. "At the Crossroads: College Activism and Its Impact on Asian American Identity Formation." In *A Part Yet Apart*, edited by Lavina Dhingra and Rajini Srikanth. Philadelphia: Temple University Press, 1998.

Gurr, Ted. *Why Men Rebel*. Princeton: Princeton University Press, 1969.

Habal, Estella. "How I Became a Revolutionary." In *Legacy to Liberation*, edited by Fred Ho. San Francisco: AK Press, 2000.

———. *San Francisco's International Hotel: Mobilizing the Filipino American Community in the Anti-Eviction Movement*. Philadelphia: Temple University, 2007.

Han, Chung-suk, Sue Chin, Ron Chew, Robert Shimabukuro, and David Takami. "Unknown Heroes." *Colorlines*, July 20, 2001. www.arc.org/C_Lines/CLArchive /story_web01_02.html (5 October 2004).

Harry Bridges Center for Labor Studies. "Introduction to the Protests." *The WTO History Project*, depts.washington.edu/wtohist/intro.htm (June 3, 2005).

Hayano, David M. "Ethnic Identification and Disidentification: Japanese American Views towards Chinese Americans." *Ethnic Groups* 3, no. 2 (1981): 157–71.

Hayase, Susan. "Taiko." *East Wind* 4, no. 1 (Winter/Spring 1985): 46–47.

Hayashi, Dennis, and Daphne Kwok. "Wards Cove Packing vs. Antonio." *Asian American Policy Review* 3 (1993): 5–16.

Hess, Gary R. "The Forgotten Asian Americans: The East Indian Community in the United States." In *The History and Immigration of Asian Americans*, edited by Franklin Ng. New York: Garland Publishing, 1998.

Hing, Alex. "Alex Hing: Former Minister of Information Red Guard Party and Founding Member of IWK." Interview by Fred Ho and Steve Yip. In *Legacy to Liberation: Politics and Culture of Revolutionary Asian Pacific America*, edited by Fred Ho. San Francisco: Big Red Media and AK Press, 2000.

Hing, Bill Ong. *Making and Remaking Asian America Through Immigration Policy, 1850–1990*. Stanford: Stanford University Press, 1993.

Hing, Ray. Interview by Michael Liu. San Francisco: 1 March, 2006.

Hitchens, Christopher. "The Case against Henry Kissinger," in *Harper's Magazine*, February 2001: 49–71, March 2001: 33–58.

Ho, Fred, ed. *Legacy to Liberation*. San Francisco: AK Press, 2000.

Hohri, Sasha, and Penny Fujiko Willgerodt. "Jackson Culminates Campaign in Asian Communities at Chinatown Rally." Authors' collection, April 14, 1988.

Hou, Jeffrey. "Preserving for Multiple Publics: Contesting Views of Urban Conservation in Seattle's International District." *City and Time* 1, no. 1, 20 October 2004. www.ceci-br.org/novo/revista/viewarticle.php?id=8 (6 July 2006).

Hsiao, Andrew. "The Hidden History of Asian American Activism in New York City." *Social Policy* 28, no. 4 (Summer 1998): 23–31.

Hsu, Huei-Hsi. "Passage to Chinatown, Managing the Sense of Place—Chinatown–International District, Seattle." Master's thesis, University of Washington, 1987.

Hung, Richard. "Asian American Participation in Civil Society in U.S. Metropolitan Areas." Paper presented at the annual meeting of the Association for Research on Nonprofit Organization and Voluntary Action, Montreal, Canada, November 2002.

I Wor Kuen. "Political Summation of the Jung Sai Strike." *I.W.K. Journal* 2 (May 1975).

Ichioka, Yujii. *The Issei: The World of the First Generation Japanese Immigrants, 1885–1924.* New York: The Free Press, 1988.

Ijima, Chris, and Nobuko Miyamoto. "We are the Children." New York: Paredon Records, 1973.

International Examiner (Seattle), 19 April 1994–19 February 2002.

International Forum on Globalization. "Ten Principles for Sustainable Societies." In *Alternatives to Economic Globalization*, edited by International Forum on Globalization. San Francisco: Berrett-Koehler Publishers, 2002.

Iwataki, Miya. "The Asian Women's Movement—A Retrospective." *East Wind* 2, no. 1 (Spring/Summer 1983): 35.

——. Interview by Sherna Gluck and Angela McCracken. 8 March 2004. "Women's History: Asian American Women's Movement Activists." *The Virtual Oral/Aural History Archive, California State University, Long Beach.* www.csulb.edu/voaha (January 24, 2007).

Jackson, Jesse "The Rainbow Coalition: An End to Racial Division." *East Wind* 3, no. 1 (Spring/Summer 1984): 21.

Jang, Jon, and Francis Wong. "A Conversation with Jon Jang and Francis Wong," interview by Nic Paget-Clarke. *In Motion Magazine,* 1997. www.inmotionmagazine.com/jjfw1.html (24 November 2004).

Jayo, Norman, and Paul Yamazaki. "Searching for an Asian American Music: Robert Kikuchi-Yngojo." *East Wind* 5, no. 1 (Spring/Summer 1986): 10–12.

Jensen, Joan M. *Passage from India: Asian Indian Immigration in North America.* New Haven: Yale University Press, 1988.

Johnson, Chalmers. *Blowback*. New York: Henry Holt and Company, 2000.

Jung, Kenwood. "The Forces of Revolution were on the Rise." *Amerasia Journal* 15, no. 1 (1989): 135–37.

Kalayaan (San Francisco), 1971–1972.

Kaneshige, Christine, and Sheri Miyashiro. "Racism at Cal Poly Pomona." In *Gidra: The XXth Anniversary Edition*, edited by Gidra Staff. Los Angeles: Gidra, 1990.

Khandelwal, Madhulika S. *Becoming American, Being Indian*. Ithaca, NY: Cornell University Press, 2002.

Kiang, Peter. "Transformation—The Challenge Facing the Asian American Artist in the '80's." *East Wind* 4, no. 1 (Winter/Spring 1985): 31–33.

——. "Southeast Asian Empowerment: The Challenge of Changing Demographics in Lowell, Massachusetts." *Asian American Policy Review* 1 (1990): 29–38.

——. "When Know-Nothings Speak English-Only: Analyzing Irish and Cambodian Struggles for Community Development and Educational Equity." In *The State of Asian America: Activism and Resistance in the 1990s*, edited by Karin Aguilar-San Juan. Boston: South End Press, 1994.

Kim, Woon-Ha. "The Activities of the South Korean Central Intelligence Agency in the United States." In *Counterpoint: Perspectives on Asian America*, edited by E. Gee. Los Angeles: UCLA Asian American Studies Center, 1976.

King, Harriet, and Terry King. "The International District." *View Northwest* (August 1977): 37–40, 52–54.

Kun, Aden. "An Interview with Angela Oh." *Asian American Policy Review* 3 (1993): 55–63.

Kurashige, Scott. "Pan-Ethnicity and Community Organizing." *Journal of Asian American Studies* 3, no. 2 (2000): 163–90.

Kwok, Daphne. Interview by Michael Liu. Tape recording. Washington, DC: 15 December, 2004.

Kwong, Peter. *The New Chinatown*. New York: Hill and Wang, 1987.

Kwong, Peter, and Dusanka Miscevic. *Chinese America: the Untold Story of America's Oldest New Community*. New York: The New Press, 2005.

Lai, Eric, and Dennis Arguelles, eds. *The New Face of Asian Pacific America: Numbers, Diversity and Change in the 21st Century*. San Francisco: Asian Week, 2003.

Lai, Him Mark. "To Bring Forth a New China, to Build a Better America." *Chinese America: History and Perspectives* 6 (1992): 3–82.

———. "Roles Played by Chinese in America during China's Resistance to Japanese Aggression and during World War II." *Chinese America: History and Perspectives* 11 (1997).

———. *Becoming Chinese American: A History of Communities and Institutions*. Walnut Creek, CA: Alta Mira Press, 2004.

Lai, Him M., Joe Huang, and Don Wong. *The Chinese of America 1785–1980: An Illustrated Catalog of the Exhibit*. San Francisco: Chinese Cultural Foundation, 1980.

Lai, Zenobia, Andrew Leong, and Chi Chi Wu. *The Lessons of the Parcel C Struggle: Reflections on Community Lawyering*. Los Angeles: LEAP Asian Pacific American Public Policy Institute and UCLA Asian American Studies Center, 2001.

Lan, Dean. "The Chinatown Sweatshops: Oppression and an Alternative," *Amerasia Journal* 1, no. 3 (1971): 40–57.

Laney College Asian Student Union. "The Third World Caucus and the Asian Student." *Asian Horizon* 2:2 (1974). Laney College Asian Student Union, Oakland: 11.

———. "Divisional Structure—A Threat to Ethnic Studies." *Asian Horizon* 5:1 (1975). Laney College Asian Student Union, Oakland: 3.

League of Revolutionary Struggle. *Statements on the Founding of the League of Revolutionary Struggle (Marxist-Leninist)*. San Francisco: Getting Together Publications, 1978.

Lee, Ben. Interview by Michael Liu. San Francisco: 28 February 2006.

Lee, Hyun. Interview by Michael Liu. Tape recording. New York: 14 December 2004.

Lee, Mae. Interview by Michael Liu. New York: 21 July 2002.

Lee, Pam Tau. "Community and Union Organizing, and Environmental Justice in the San Francisco Bay Area, 1967–2000." Interview by Carl Wilmsen. Regional Oral History Office of the Bancroft Library, University of California–Berkeley, 2003.

Lee, Patricia. "Asian Immigrant Women and HERE Local 2." *Labor Research Review* 11 (1988): 29–38.

Lee, Regina. Interview by Michael Liu. Tape recording. Boston: 12 March, 2004.

Lee, Robert G. *Orientals: Asian Americans in Popular Culture.* Philadelphia: Temple University Press, 1999.

Lee, Suzanne. Interview by Michael Liu. Tape recording. Brookline, MA: 2 September 2002.

Lee, Todd. Interview by Michael Liu. Tape recording. Boston: 12 December 2006.

Lee, Virgo. Interview by Michael Liu. Tape recording. New York: 23 December 2001, 14 September 2003.

Leong, A. "The Struggle over Parcel C: How Boston's Chinatown Won a Victory in the Fight against Institutional Expansion and Environmental Racism." *Amerasia Journal* 21, no. 3 (1995–1996): 99–119.

Li, Giles. Interviews by Michael Liu. Tape recording. Boston: 23 November 2004, 6 December 2006.

Liem, Ramsay. Interview by Michael Liu. Boston: 20 June 2002.

Liem, Yul-san. Interview by Michael Liu. Tape recording. Brookline, MA: 16 August 2004.

Lin, Jan. *Reconstructing Chinatown: Ethnic Enclave, Global Change.* Minneapolis: University of Minnesota, 1998.

Ling, Susie. "The Mountain Movers: Asian American Women's Movement in Los Angeles." *Amerasia Journal* 15, no. 1 (1989): 51–67.

Liu, John M., and Lucie Cheng. "Pacific Rim Development and the Duality of Post-1965 Asian Immigration to the United States." In *The New Asian Immigration in Los Angeles and Global Restructuring*, edited by Paul Ong, Edna Bonacich, and Lucie Cheng. Philadelphia: Temple University, 1994.

Liu, Michael. "Chinatown's Neighborhood Mobilization and Urban Development in Boston." Ph. D. diss., University of Massachusetts–Boston, 1999.

Lo, Sauna. Interview of Don Misumi. *Asian American Movement Ezine.* Boston: 18 August 2002. www.aamovement.net/narratives/don_misumi.html (27 November 2003).

Logan, John, and Harvey Molotch. *Urban Fortunes: The Political Economy of Place.* Berkeley, CA: University of California Press, 1987.

Lott, Juanita Tamayo. "Growing Up, 1968–1985." In *Making Waves: An Anthology of Writings by and about Asian American Women*, edited by Asian Women United of California. Boston: Beacon Press, 1989.

Louie, May. Interview by Michael Liu. Brookline, MA: 29 December, 2006.

Louie, Miriam Ching. "'Yellow, Brown and Red': Towards an Appraisal of Marxist Influences on the Asian American Movement." Pacific And Asian American Center For Theology And Strategies Collection. Graduate Theology Union. Berkeley, 1991.

——. *Sweatshop Warriors: Immigrant Women Workers Take on the Global Factory.* Cambridge, MA: South End Press, 2001.

Louie, Steve, and Glenn Omatsu, eds. *Asian Americans: The Movement and the Moment.* Los Angeles: UCLA Asian American Studies Center Press, 2001.

Low, Ron. "A Brief Biographical Sketch of a Newly Found Asian Male." In *Roots: An Asian American Reader*, edited by Amy Tachiki, Eddie Wong, and Franklin Odo. Los Angeles: UCLA Asian American Studies Center, 1971.

Lowe, Lydia. Interview by Michael Liu. Tape recording. Cambridge, MA: 11 August 2004.

Lowe, Lydia, and Beth Shironaka. "Asian Sisters in Action." *East Wind* 2, no. 1 (Spring/Summer 1983): 33–34.

Lum, Sadie. "Asian American Women and Revolution: A Personal View." *East Wind* 2, no. 1 (Spring/Summer 1983): 46–50.

Ma, L. Eve Armentrout. *Hometown Chinatown: The History of Oakland's Chinese Community*. New York: Garland Publishing, 2000.

Maeda, Daryl J. "Black Panthers, Red Guards, and Chinamen: Constructing Asian American Identity through Performing Blackness, 1969–1972." *American Quarterly* 57, no. 4 (2005): 1079–1103

Maeshiro, Sandy. "It Ain't All Smiles and Sukiyaki." In *Counterpoint: Perspectives on Asian America*, edited by E. Gee. Los Angeles: UCLA Asian American Studies Center 1976.

Maki, Mitchell T., Harry Kitano, and S. Megan Berthold. *Achieving the Impossible Dream: How Japanese Americans Obtained Redress*. Urbana, IL: University of Illinois Press, 1999.

Mar, Don, and Marlene Kim. "Historical Trends." In *The State of Asian America: Economic Diversity, Issues and Policies,* edited by Paul Ong. Los Angeles: LEAP Asian Pacific American Public Policy Institute and UCLA Asian American Studies Center, 1994.

Mar, Warren. "From Pool Halls to Building Workers' Organizations: Lessons for Today's Activists." In *Asian Americans: The Movement and the Moment*, edited by Steve Louie and Glenn Omatsu. Los Angeles: UCLA Asian American Studies Center Press, 2001.

Mark, Stan. "An Interview with the Movement: Reasserting the Immigrant Rights Agenda after 9/11." *Network News* (Spring 2002). National Network for Immigrant and Refugee Rights, Oakland, CA: 10.

Masaoka, Kathy Nishimoto, "Big Bold Steps: The San Pedro Firm Building: the Legacy of Judy Nishimoto Ota." In *Little Tokyo: Changing Times, Changing Faces*, edited by Brian Niiya. Los Angeles: Japanese American Historical Society of Southern California, 2004.

———. Interviews by Michael Liu. Tape recording. Los Angeles: 19 June, 2004; Boston, 24 September 2006.

Masaoka, Mark. Interview by Michael Liu: Los Angeles, 17 June 2004.

Mast, Robert H., and Anne B. Mast. *Autobiography of Protest in Hawai'i*. Honolulu: University of Hawai'i Press, 1996.

Matsuda, Mari J. "Here on Planet Asian America." Speech delivered at the Asian Law Caucus' annual celebration (San Francisco, 31 March 2000). Reprinted in the *Asian Law Caucus Newsletter: The Reporter* 22, no. 1 (July 2000).

Matsusaka, Yoshiro. Interview by Michael Liu. Brookline, MA: 23 August 2002.

McAdam, Douglas. *The Political Process and the Development of Black Insurgency*. Chicago: University of Chicago Press, 1982.

McAdam, Douglas, J. D. McCarthy, and M. N. Zald. "Introduction: Opportunities, Mobilizing Structures, and Framing Process—Toward A Synthetic, Comparative Perspective on Social Movements." In *Comparative Perspectives on Social Movements: Political Opportunities, Mobilizing Structures, and Cultural Framings*, edited by Douglas McAdam, J. D. McCarthy, and M. N. Zald. Cambridge, England: Cambridge University Press, 1996.

McClain, Charles J. *In Search of Equality: The Chinese Struggle against Discrimination in Nineteenth-Century America*. Berkeley, CA: University of California Press, 1994.

McGregor, Daviana P. "'Au'a 'ia' to 'Mele o Kaho'olawe': Voices of Power and Vision." In *New Visions in Asian American Studies: Diversity, Community, Power*, edited by Franklin Ng, Judy Yung, Stephen S. Fujita, and Elaine H. Kim. Seattle: Washington State Press, 1994.

McWhirter, Nickie. *Detroit Free Press*, 25 March 1983.

Mih, Valerie, and Judy Wu. "Stanford Sit-In." In *Gidra: The XXth Anniversary Edition*, edited by Gidra Staff. Los Angeles: Gidra, 1990.

Minami, Dale. "Asian Law Caucus: Experiment in an Alternative." *Amerasia Journal* 3, no. 1 (1975): 28–39.

Misumi, Don, and Jean Hibino. Interview by Michael Liu. Tape recording. Lexington, MA: 12 February 2002.

Miyashiro, Sheri. "Yellow Brotherhood." In *Gidra: the XXth Anniversary Edition,* edited by Gidra Staff. Los Angeles: Gidra, 1990.

Moran, Rachel F. *Interracial Intimacy: the Regulation of Race and Romance*. Chicago: University of Chicago Press, 2001.

Morizumi, Greg. "Profile: Mutya Gener." *East Wind* 2, no. 1 (Spring/Summer 1983): 66–67.

Morris, Aldon D. "Black Southern Student Sit-In Movement: An Analysis of Internal Organization." *American Sociological Review* 46 (December 1981): 755–67.

———. *The Origins of the Civil Rights Movement: Black Communities Organizing for Change*. New York: The Free Press, 1984.

———. "Political Consciousness and Collective Action." In *Frontiers in Social Movement Theory*, edited by Aldon D. Morris and Carol McClurg Mueller. New Haven: Yale University Press, 1992.

Munoz, Carlos, Jr. *Youth, Identity, Power: The Chicano Movement*. New York: Verso Press, 1989.

Murase, Mike. "Why an Asian Contingent?" *Gidra* 4:5 May 1972, 13.

———. "Toward Barefoot Journalism." In *Counterpoint: Perspectives on Asian America,* edited by E. Gee. Los Angeles: UCLA Asian American Studies Center, 1976.

———. "Ethnic Studies and Higher Education for Asian Americans." In *Counterpoint: Perspectives on Asian America*, edited by E. Gee. Los Angeles: UCLA Asian American Studies Center, 1976.

Nagai, Nelson. "Yellow Seed." In *Gidra: The XXth Anniversary Edition*, edited by Gidra Staff. Los Angeles: Gidra, 1990.

———. "I Come from a Yellow Seed (for Bobby)." In *Asian Americans: The Movement and the Moment*, edited by Steve Louie and Glenn Omatsu. Los Angeles: UCLA Asian American Studies Center, 2001.

Nagatani, Nick. "'Action Talks and the Bullshit Walks': From the Founders of the Yellow Brotherhood to the Present." In *Asian Americans: The Movement and the Moment*, edited by Steve Louie and Glenn Omatsu. Los Angeles: UCLA Asian American Studies Center Press, 2001.

Nakano, Bert. "Reparations: Our Historic Victory." *East Wind* 7, no. 1 (Spring/Summer 1989): 26–29.

Nakano, Roy. "Marxist-Leninist Organizing in the Asian American Community: Los Angeles, 1969–1979." Los Angeles: UCLA Asian American Studies Center, 1984.

Nakata, Bob. "The Struggles of the Waiahole-Waikane Community Association." *Social Process in Hawai'i* 39 (1999): 60–73.

Nakayama, Mike. "Winter Soldiers." Authors' collection, 1971. Mimeographed.

National Coalition for Redress/Reparations. *National Coalition for Redress and Reparations*. Authors' collection, 1980.

Nee, Victor, and Brett de Bary Nee. *Longtime Californ': A Documentary Study of an American Chinatown*. New York: Pantheon Books, 1972.

New Youth Center, *Chicago Chinatown Newsletter* 1:1 (May 1972). New Youth Center: Chicago, IL.

Ng, Franklin, ed. *The Asian American Encyclopedia*. 6 vols. North Bellmore, NY: Marshall Cavendish Corporation, 1995.

Ngai, Mai M. "Legacies of Exclusion: Illegal Chinese Immigration during the Cold War Years." *Journal of American Ethnic History* 18, no. 1 (Fall 1998): 3–35.

Nguyen, Long. Conversation with Michael Liu. 14 May 2003.

Niheu, Soli Kihei. "Huli: Community Struggles and Ethnic Studies." *Social Process in Hawai'i* 39 (1999): 43–59.

Nikkei for Civil Rights and Redress. "NCRR Reader: A Reader on the History of the NCRR." 17 April 2006. www.ncrr-la.org/reader/index.html (October 1, 2006).

Nishio, Alan. "Personal Reflections on the Asian National Movements: Alan Nishio." *East Wind* 1, no. 1 (Spring/Summer 1982): 36–38.

———. Interview by Michael Liu. Tape recording. Boston, MA: 26 September 2006.

Okihiro, Gary Y. *Cane Fires: The Anti-Japanese Movement in Hawai'i, 1865–1945*. Philadelphia: Temple University Press, 1992.

Okita, David B. "Redevelopment of San Francisco Japantown." Master's thesis, California State University–Hayward, 1980.

Omatsu, Glenn. "The 'Four Prisons' and the Movements of Liberation: Asian American Activism from the 1960s to the 1990s." In *The State of Asian American Activism and Resistance in the 1990s*, edited by Karin Aguilar-San Juan. Boston: South End Press, 1994.

Omi, Michael, and Howard Winant. *Racial Formation in the United States: From the 1960s to the 1980s*. New York: Routledge Press, 1986.

Ong, Paul, Edna Bonacich, and Lucie Cheng, eds. *The New Asian Immigration in Los Angeles and Global Restructuring*. Philadelphia: Temple University Press, 1994.

———. "Introduction: The Political Economy of Capitalist Restructuring and the New Asian Immigration." In *The New Asian Immigration in Los Angeles and Global Restructuring*, edited by Paul Ong, Edna Bonacich, and Lucie Cheng. Philadelphia: Temple University Press, 1994.

Ong, Paul, and Tania Azores. "The Migration and Incorporation of Filipino Nurses." In *The New Asian Immigration in Los Angeles and Global Restructuring*, edited by Paul Ong, Edna Bonacich, and Lucie Cheng. Philadelphia: Temple University Press, 1994.

Ong, Paul, and Suzanne Hee. "Economic Diversity." In *Economic Diversity, Issues and Policies*, edited by Paul Ong. Los Angeles: LEAP Asian Pacific American Public Policy Institute and UCLA Asian American Studies Center, 1994.

Oyama, David. "Introduction: Asian American Theatre." *Bridge* 5 (1977): 4–5.

Pan, Suzanne, and Ellen Lam. "ECASU: Education for Action." *East Wind* 6, no. 1 (Spring/Summer 1987): 27–28.

Pang, Gordon Y. K. "Ota Camp," *Honolulu Star-Bulletin Online Edition*, 15 April 2001. www.starbulletin.com/2001/04/15 /news/story4.html (20 November 2004).

Passel, Jeffrey S. *The Size and Characteristics of the Unauthorized Migrant Population in the U.S.; Estimates Based upon the 2005 Current Population Survey*. Washington, DC: Pew Hispanic Center, 2006.

Peñaranda, Oscar, Serafin Syquia, and Sam Tagatac. "An Introduction to Filipino-American Literature." In *Aiiieeeee! An Anthology of Asian-American Writers*, edited by F. Chin, Jeffery Paul Chan, Lawson Fusao Inada, and Shawn Wong. Washington, DC: Howard University Press, 1974.

Phillips, Kevin. *Wealth and Democracy: A Political History of the American Rich*. New York: Broadway Books, 2002.

Prashad, Vijay. "Crafting Solidarities." In *A Part Yet Apart*, edited by Lavina Dhingra and Rajini Srikanth. Philadelphia: Temple University Press, 1998.

Pulido, Laura. *Black, Brown, Yellow and Left in LA: Radical Activism in Los Angeles*. Berkeley, CA: University of California Press, 2006.

Quon, Merilynne Hamano. Conversation with Michael Liu, 13 May 2003.

Reimers, David M. *Still the Golden Door: The Third World Comes to America*. 2nd ed. New York: Columbia University Press, 1992.

Ros, Vong. Conversation with Michael Liu. 15 March 2007.

Sagara, Carlton. Interview by Michael Liu. Honolulu, Hawai'i: January, 2002.

Salyer, Lucy E. *Laws Harsh as Tigers: Chinese Immigrants and the Shaping of Modern Immigration Law*. Chapel Hill, NC: University of North Carolina Press, 1995.

Sampan. September 1975. Boston, pages 1–4.

San Juan, E., Jr. "The Predicament of the Filipinos in the United States." In *The State of Asian American Activism and Resistance in the 1990s*, edited by Karin Aguilar-San Juan. Boston: South End Press, 1994.

———. *Beyond Postcolonial Theory*. New York: St. Martin's Press, 1998.

Santos, Bob. "Rebuilding Seattle's I.D.—The Story of Inter•Im." *East Wind* 2, no. 1 (Spring/Summer 1983): 3–7.

———. *Hum Bows, Not Hot Dogs*. Seattle: International Examiner Press, 2002.

———. Interview by Tracy Lai. Tape recording. Seattle, 30 August, 2006.

Sassen, Saskia. *The Global City*. Princeton: Princeton University Press, 1992.

Schrecker, Ellen. *Many are the Crimes*. Princeton: Princeton University Press, 1999.

Senzaki, Wes. "Wes Senzaki." *East Wind* 1, no. 1 (Spring/Summer 1982): 39–40.

Sharma, Miriam. "Ethnic Studies and Ethnic Identity: Challenges and Issues, 1970–1998." *Social Processes in Hawai'i* 39 (1999): 19–42.

Shikuma, Stan. "The Making of a Modern Folk Art: Taiko in the Pacific Northwest/ Canadian Southwest Region." Paper presented at the annual meeting of the Association for Asian American Studies, Toronto, Canada, March 2001.

Smelser, Neil J. *Theory of Collective Behavior*. New York: Free Press, 1962.

Sodetani, Naomi. "Janice Mirikitani: Words from the Third World." *East Wind* 4, no. 1 (Winter/Spring 1985): 28–30.

Soriano-Hewitt, Ester. "The Bayanihan Spirit: The Search to Involve Filipino Americans." In *Gidra: The XXth Anniversary Edition*, edited by Gidra Staff. Los Angeles: Gidra, 1990.

Spickard, Paul R. *Japanese Americans: The Formation and Transformations of an Ethnic Group*. New York: Twayne Publishers, 1996.

Suong, Sarath. Interview by Michael Liu. Tape recording. Providence, RI: 28 December 2004.

Susskind, Ron. "Without a Doubt," *New York Times Magazine*, 17 October 2004.

Tachiki, Amy, Eddie Wong, and Franklin Odo, eds. *Roots: An Asian American Reader*. Los Angeles: UCLA Asian American Studies Center, 1971.

Takahashi, Jere. *Nisei/Sansei: Shifting Japanese American Identities and Politics*. Philadelphia: Temple University Press, 1997.

Takaki, Ronald. *Strangers From a Different Shore: A History of Asian Americans*. Boston: Little, Brown, 1989.

Takano, Tracy. "Aloha 'Aina (Love of the Land): The Struggle for Land and Power in Hawai'i." *East Wind* 1, no. 1 (Spring/Summer 1982): 18–21.

Tanaka, Ron. "I Hate My Wife for Her Flat Yellow Face." In *Roots: An Asian American Reader,* edited by Amy Tachiki, Eddie Wong, and Franklin Odo. Los Angeles: UCLA Asian American Studies Center, 1971.

Tarrow, Sidney. *The Power in Movement: Social Movements and Contentious Politics*. 2nd ed. Cambridge, England: Cambridge University Press, 1998.

Tasaki, Ray. "Wherever There is Oppression." In *Asian Americans: The Movement and the Moment,* edited by Steve Louie and Glenn Omatsu. Los Angeles: UCLA Asian American Studies Center, 2001.

Taylor, Verta. "Emotions and Identity in Women's Self-Help Movements." In *Self, Identity, and Social Movements*, edited by Sheldon Stryker, Timothy J. Owens, and Robert W. White. Minneapolis: University of Minnesota Press, 2000: 271–99.

Teng, Shiree. "Women, Community and Equality: Three Garment Workers Speak Out." *East Wind* 2, no. 1 (Spring/Summer 1983): 20–23.

Thurman, Skip. "Clinton Puts Free Trade First this Fall," *Christian Science Monitor*, 9 September 1997.

Tilly, Charles, and Sidney Tarrow. *Contentious Politics*. Boulder, CO: Paradigm Publishers, 2007.

Toji, Dean. "Hibakusha." *East Wind* 1, no. 2 (Fall/Winter 1982): 3–5.

Toribio, Helen. "Dare to Struggle: the KDP and Filipino American Politics." In *Legacy to Liberation,* edited by Fred Ho. San Francisco: AK Press, 2000.

Trask, Haunani-Kay. *From a Native Daughter: Colonialism and Sovereignty in Hawai'i*. Honolulu: University of Hawai'i Press, 1999.

Tsai, Shih-Shan Henry. *The Chinese Experience in America*. Bloomington, IN: Indiana University Press, 1986.

Tsao, Clement. "Transgressing Institutional Boundaries in Asian American Studies: A Student Intervention." Authors' collection, 2003.

Ture, Kwame (formerly Stokely Carmichael), and Charles V. Hamilton. *Black Power: The Politics of Liberation*. New York: Vintage Books, 1992.

Umemoto, Karen. "On Strike! San Francisco State College Strike, 1968–1969, The Role of Asian American Studies." *Amerasia Journal* 15, no. 1 (1989): 3–41.

U.S. Bureau of the Census. *Statistical Abstract of the United States*. Washington, DC: GPO, 1962.

——. *Asian and Pacific Islander Population by State: 1980*. Washington, DC: GPO, 1983.

——. *Asian and Pacific Islander Americans: A Profile*. Washington, DC: GPO, 1993.

——. *The Asian and Pacific Islander Population in the United States March 2002*, by Terrance Reeves and Claudette Bennett. Washington, DC: GPO, 2003.

Unity Newspaper (Oakland). Feb 1978–May1981.

Virata, Joe. "Memories of America: A Conversation with Philip Vera Cruz." In *Gidra: the XXth Anniversary Edition*. Los Angeles: Gidra, 1990.

Võ, Linda Trinh. *Mobilizing an Asian American Community*. Philadelphia: Temple University Press, 2004.

Wang, L. Ling-chi. "Chinatown in Transition." Paper presented at the Asian American Concern Conference, University of California–Davis, 1969.

——. "The Politics of Ethnic Identity and Empowerment: Asian American Community Since the 1960s." *Asian American Policy Review* 2 (1991): 43–56.

Washington State Commission on Asian American Affairs. Task Force on Asian American Women. *Concerns of Asian American Women*. Olympia, June 1976.

Wei Min She, Tai Shu, and Wei Min Bao. "Asian Contingent Solidarity Statement." *I.W.K. Journal* 1: 10 (August 1974).

Wei, William. *The Asian American Movement*. Philadelphia: Temple University Press, 1993.

Wing, Jean Yonemura. Interview by Michael Liu. Tape recording. Berkeley, CA: 24 October, 2003.

Wing, Lyle. Interview by Michael Liu. Berkeley, CA: 22 June 2004.

Witeck, John. "The Rise of Ethnic Studies at the University of Hawai'i: Anti-war, Student and Early Community Struggles." *Social Processes in Hawai'i* 39 (1999): 10–18.

Wong, Bernard. *Patronage, Brokerage, Entrepreneurship and the Chinese Community of New York*. New York: AMS Press, 1988.

Wong, Buck. "Public Record, 1989." *Amerasia Journal* 15, no. 1 (1989): 119.

Wong, Eddie. "Asian Empowerment and Jackson." *East Wind* 7, no. 1 (Spring/Summer 1989): 7–11.

——. Interview by Michael Liu. Tape recording. Boston: 23 March 2005.

Wong, Francis. "Movement Still Shaky, but Trying." *Winds* 2:1 (March 1978). Asian American Student Association, Stanford: 1.

Wong, Kent. "Building an Asian Pacific Labor Alliance: A New Chapter in our History." In *The State of Asian American Activism and Resistance in the 1990s*, edited by Karin Aguilar-San Juan. Boston: South End Press, 1994.

———. *Voices for Justice: Asian Pacific American Organizers and the New Labor Movement*. Los Angeles: Center for Labor Research and Education, UCLA, 2001.

Wong, Larry Jack. "Poverty Conditions in Chinatown 1964." In *To Serve the Devil, Volume 2: Colonials and Sojourners*, edited by Paul Jacobs and Saul Landau. New York: Vintage Books, 1964.

Wong, Paul. "The Emergence of the Asian-American Movement." *Bridge* 2, no. 1. (1972): 33–39.

Wu, Frank H., and Francey Lim Youngberg. "People From China Crossing the River: Asian American Political Empowerment and Foreign Influence." In *Asian Americans and Politics: Perspectives, Experiences, Prospects*, edited by Gordon H. Chang. Stanford: Stanford University Press, 2000.

Yamamato, Eric K., and Susan K. Serrano. "The Loaded Weapon." *Amerasia Journal* 27, no. 3 (2001); 28, no. 1 (2002) (double issue): 51–62.

Yanagida, R. Takashi. "Asian Students vs. University Control: The Confrontation at C.C.N.Y." *Bridge* 1, no. 5 (May/June 1972): 11–12.

Yen, Jan. Interview of Bert and Lillian Nakano, Nikkei for Civil Rights and Redress, Los Angeles, 24 August 2001. Audio cassette.

Yoneda, Karl. "One Hundred Years of Japanese Labor History in the USA." In *Roots: An Asian American Reader*, edited by Amy Tachiki, Eddie Wong, Franklin Odo. Los Angeles: UCLA Asian American Studies Center, 1971.

———. *Ganbatte: Sixty-Year Struggle of a Kibei Worker*. Los Angeles: UCLA Asian American Studies Center, 1983.

———. A Partial History of California Japanese Farm Workers." In *Racism, Dissent and Asian Americans from 1850 to the Present: A Documentary History*, edited by Philip S. Foner and Daniel Rosenberg. Westport, CT: Greenwood Publishing, 1993.

Yoo, Grace. "The Fight to Save Welfare for Low-Income Older Asian Immigrants." *AAPI Nexus* 1, no.1 (2003): 85–100.

Yoshimura, Evelyn. "How I Became an Activist and What It Means to Me." *Amerasia Journal* 15, no. 1 (1989): 106–09.

———. Interview by Michael Liu. Los Angeles: 19 June 2004.

———. Interview by Julie Bartolotto. 1 May 1995. "Women's History: Asian American Women's Movement Activists." *The Virtual Oral/Aural History Archive, California State University, Long Beach*. www.csulb.edu/voaha (January 24, 2007).

Yuen, Eddie, George Katsiaficas, and Daniel Burton Rose, eds. *The Battle of Seattle: The New Challenge to Capitalist Globalization*. New York: Soft Skull Press, 2001.

Yung, Judy. *Unbound Voices: A Documentary History of Chinese Women in San Francisco*. Berkeley: University of California Press, 1999.

Zia, Helen. *Asian American Dreams: The Emergence of an American People*. New York: Farrar, Straus and Giroux, 2000.

Index

activism: and anti-globalization
movement, 166; and community
organizations, 4, 25, 84–86, 88,164;
and labor, 72–76, 164; and Nisei, 48;
and September 11th, 166; and
students, 71; and youth, 3, 38, 69,
168; and women, 10, 78–81
affirmative action, 38, 110, 122, 123
Agricultural Workers Industrial Union,
22
Agricultural Workers Organizing
Committee, 21
Alan Hotel, 128
Alcantra v. Boyd, 26
Alliance of Asian Pacific Labor, 127
American Citizens for Justice (ACJ),
132–33
American Civil Liberties Union, 24
American Friends Service Committee,
24
American Legion, 23
Anti-Asian violence, 17, 125, 140, 159;
anti-Asian immigrant attitudes, 18,
125; anti-Bakke decision coalitions,
110, 119n45; anti-globalization
movement, 165, 166, 168–70; anti-
Marcos, 77
Anti-Imperialist Women's Conference, 80
anti-imperialist struggles, 4, 68, 80, 93

Anti-Martial Law Alliance, 68, 101
anti-miscegenation laws, 18
anti-nuclear movement:
and Asian Americans, 101–02; and
Asian Americans for Nuclear
Disarmament, 102; Hibakusha, 102
API Movement Network, 168
Ariyoshi, Koji 26
Ark, Wong Kim, 16
Asian Ad-hoc Committee, 72
Asian American agency, xv
Asian American art and culture
movement, 76–78, 111–13, arts and
culture, 84, 87, 130–32, 154; film,
62, 83, 111, 113, 118n26, 131,
174n55; jazz, 85, 111, 131;
kulintang, 112; spoken word,
160–61; taiko, 78, 111, 112; theatre,
68, 78, 84, 131
Asian American Dance Collective, 78
Asian American demographics, 96, 151,
140
Asian American Federation of Union
Members, 108
Asian Americans for Action (Triple A),
39
Asian Americans for Equal Employment
(AAFEE), later Asian Americans for
Equality (AAFE) 74, 98, 100, 127

Minh, Ho Chi, 44
Mirikitani, Janice, 77
Misumi, Don, 137
Miyamoto, Joanne, 64, 77
Mochizuki, Carol, 81
Model Cities, 53, 84, 93
model minority, 10, 31, 45, 62
Molokai Ranch, 133
Morgan v. Hennigan, xiii, xixn1
Morris, Aldon D., 6–7, 9
movement center, 7, 49, 67, 85
Multi-ethnic Immigrant Worker
    Organizing Network, 178
multi-racial coalition building, 5, 62, 83,
    153, 155
Murase, Mike, 60, 71

Nakano, Bert, 138
Nakano, Lillian, 138, 167
Nakayama, Mike, 60
National Asian Pacific American Legal
    Consortium, 154, 166, 173n53
National Association for the
    Advancement of Colored People
    (NAACP), 21, 28
National Coalition for Redress and
    Reparations (NCRR, later National
    Committee for the Restoration of
    Civil Liberties in the Philippines), 68
National Endowment for the Arts, 131
National Lawyers Guild, 95
Nee, Victor and Brett de Bary, 39
neo-liberalism, 93
New Federalism, 93
New People's Army (Philippines), 44, 61
New York City, 4, 10, 21, 22, 29, 40,
    42, 43, 52, 53, 57n44, 63, 68, 71, 73,
    74, 75, 77, 81, 84, 89n13, 90n30,
    109, 111, 112, 114, 126, 127, 128,
    129, 131, 140, 141, 142, 153, 155,
    156, 158, 159, 161, 165
New Youth Center (Chicago), 52
Nihonmachi, 29, 39, 52, 84
Nihonmachi Outreach Committee (San
    Jose), 134

Nikkei for Civil Rights and Redress,
    134–38, 146n36, 166, 167
nisei, 19, 21, 23, 25, 28, 30, 135, 136,
    138; activists, 47–48; nisei and
    sansei activists, 135, 137
Nisei Voters League 21
Nishio, Alan, 134, 138
Niumalu-Nawiliwili, 133
Nodutdol (New York City), 156
Non-Aligned Movement, 43, 56n17
non-profit: organizations, xvi, 53, 112,
    155–56; sector, 131, 155–56, 168
North Beach Youth Council (San
    Francisco), 51
November 4th Coalition, 83

Oakland, 29, 69, 84, 109, 153, 158, 159
Omatsu, Glenn, 4
Omi, Michael, 3
Organization of Chinese Americans,
    154, 166
Organization of Asian American Women
    (New York), 114
Organization of Pan Asian Women
    (Washington, D.C.), 114
Ota Camp, 133
Ota, Judy, 128
Ota, Tatsuichi, 133

P and L Sportswear, 126–27
pan-Asian cooperation, 42, 47
pan-Asian student organizations, 70–71,
    72, 129
pan-Asian unity, xvi, 3, 4, 47, 85, 132,
    166–68, 178
pan-ethnic movement, 3, 39, 63, 161
People Against Chinatown Evictions
    (Honolulu), 88
People's Republic of China, 26, 27,
    48, 49, 101, 113, 130; cultural
    revolution, 43, 44; normalization
    of relations with U.S. 48, 61, 130,
    154; and struggle with Soviet
    Union, 101; support for, 27, 39,
    43–44, 48, 49, 61, 83, 101, 113,

About the Authors

Michael Liu is senior research associate at the Institute for Asian American Studies at University of Massachusetts–Boston. He also participated in a number of the groups described in this book, particularly in the Boston area, including the Asian American Resource Workshop, Chinese Progressive Association, and I Wor Kuen.

Kim Geron is associate professor of political science at California State University–East Bay. He is a scholar activist who has participated in API organizing efforts in California since the late 1960s. He is currently active in the American Political Science Association, Asian Pacific American Labor Alliance, California Faculty Association, and the API Movement Building Network.

Tracy Lai is a tenured historian at Seattle Central Community College. She was a founding member of the Asian Pacific Student Union and is currently active in American Federation of Teachers–Seattle 1789 and the Asian Pacific American Labor Alliance.